The Untold Andaman and Nicobar Islands

Attention Authors

Manas Publications is fighting a war to tell the world that India can win the battle not only by the bullet but also by pen. We are converting fighters into writers. There is no dearth of intellectuals in our country. However, their knowledge is confined to them only. No sincere effort has been made by any other publisher to channelise their knowledge. That is why the talent of every intellectual remains latent. An author always presents the raw material in the shape of a manuscript and it is the job of the publisher to convert it into a completely finished book. Manas has been motivating intellectuals continually and publishing their manuscripts for more than three decades and would like to publish your manuscript too. If you or your colleagues have a manuscript ready for publication or are working on it, contact us with a detailed synopsis and list of contents. Manas can also suggest you a suitable title for writing related to your area of expertise. Manas is known for its publishing quality. We take utmost care in production and give wide publicity to the book and its author through our national and international distribution network.

The Untold

Andaman and Nicobar Islands

Rabin Roychowdhury

Manas Publications
(We Convert Fighters into Writers)
New Delhi-110002 (INDIA)

MANAS PUBLICATIONS
(Publishers, Distributors, Importers & Exporters)
4402/5-A, Ansari Road (Opp. HDFC Bank)
Darya Ganj, New Delhi-110 002 (INDIA)
Off. ✆ 23260783, 23265523, Res. ✆ 23842660
Fax: 011-23272766
E-mail: manaspublications@gmail.com
manaspublications@yahoo.com
Website: www.manaspublications.in

ISBN 978-81-7049-374-7
₹ 795/-

Designed at
Manas Publications

Printed in India at
RK Offsets, Delhi
and published by Mrs Suman Lata for
Manas Publications
4402/5-A, Ansari Road,
(Opp. HDFC Bank), Darya Ganj,
New Delhi-110 002 (INDIA)

CONTENTS

FOREWORD

Andaman and Nicobar archipelago is a chain of over 500 rocky protuberances from the blue waters of Bay of Bengal. It stretches a total length of 780 kms. in the tropical sea and is divided into two groups, viz., Andaman and Nicobar. The notoriously turbulent waters of ten-degree channel, so named because it runs along the 100 North latitude, separate the two groups. Shining in the tropical sun this long archipelago of rocks and sand of various sizes, covered in tropical lush green forests reminds one of an emerald necklace. Hence these are often referred to as Emerald Islands or Emerald Isles for short.

Despite its poetic name an average Indian even today dreads the word, *Andaman*. For him it builds a picture of inhuman tortures the prisoners of Cellular Jail had to undergo. The victory of the British over what they called Sepoy Mutiny created a peculiar problem. Keeping these erstwhile rulers incarcerated in the midst of their subjects on the mainland India was not considered safe. Hence the last Emperor of India emperor Bahadur Shah Zafar was exiled to Burma as a prisoner where he breathed his last. As he was a poet, before his death in exile he composed the now famous couplet—

"*Kitna hai badnaseeb Zafar dafan ke liye,*

Do gaz zamin bhi na mili kue yar me".

(How unfortunate is Zafar that even two yards of land is not available for burial among his relatives).

A number of prisoners belonging to erstwhile ruling families were still left. The British had to build a special prison for them. Andaman about a thousand kilometers away from the mainland was an ideal location where they decided to build a special jail. From the very beginning it was so planned that all the prisoners of the First War of Independence of India had to stay isolated in cells. Hence it was called Cellular Jail. It was built with their labour to incarcerate them and later freedom fighters as well as hardened criminals. Once the British understood the advantages of the isolation of Andaman, they tried to take full benefits of it. Not only was escape practically impossible, no words could reach the mainland from Andaman.

In fact the establishment of Cellular Jail increased the interest of British administration towards its 'development'. Till then Andaman was considered of little or no consequence. As such although Archibald-Blair (a forefather of Tony Blair) established the first settlement on 25th October, 1789 by formally hoisting the Union Jack but nothing much came of it. Although it was named Port Cornwallis in 1790 after the then Governor General of India and his brother Admiral Cornwallis found the island to be a perfect spot for the establishment of a permanent naval headquarters, it was abandoned in 1794 due to inhospitable climatic condition and rampant diseases. The islands faced another 60 years of splendid isolation. In fact the isolation was so effective that the sad fate of the shipwrecked crew who were allegedly looted by the Andamanese in 1849 came to the notice only after five years in 1854.

Unfortunately for Andaman even these periods of isolation were really not idyllic. Being off the track of regular traffic these were the dens of sea pirates. These sea pirates were not satisfied by their activities in the high seas. They often raided the habitats of the tribals. These tribal people, belonging to what the anthropologists today call the Negrito stock with their typical features, were sold as fancies to the kings of the nearby kingdoms. The irony of the whole situation is that the tropical jungles of Andaman provided the pirates the timber for building the ships. Even with all these activities the prevailing condition was peaceful compared to what was to follow.

After crushing the First War of Independence of India ruthlessly, the East India Company got effective control over an area far bigger than their own country with a huge population speaking different languages and belonging to different religions in practically no time. This overnight transformation of a businessman into a ruler prompted the poet to recite:

"*Baniker mandanda dekha dilo rajdanda roopay pohale sarbari*".

(Measuring rod of the merchant metamorphosed into scepter overnight.)

Andaman and Nicobar are warm tropical islands with an annual rainfall of over 3 meters. The British being foreign to the spectrum of cultures that constitute India were liable to commit blunders at every step. Often these blunders were made more offensive to the native people when these actions appeared to be motivated not by the zeal of benefiting the common man but for the benefit of the rulers. There was always a lack of communication between the ruler and the ruled due to differences not only in language but even in terms of religion, social organization and habits and ways of life. In short the ruler and the ruled differed practically in all the aspects of culture. This huge gap in culture was soon to make its impact and disturbances were common. Many of these disturbances flared up due to unsympathetic handling of the situation by officials who were not acquainted with the culture of the people that they were trying to govern.

Having established themselves in the Andaman archipelago the British soon reached a solution that appeared to be beneficial to them. That policy was very convenient to enforce by the rulers although it was often too harsh on the ruled. Having tried this policy on a small scale when they transported the leaders of the 1857 uprising to the Andamans they started following a similar policy all over the sub-continent. Thus they transported the Moplahs from present day Kerala after crushing what the British called the Moplah uprising. Similarly a large number of Bhatus from the then United Provinces were moved to the Andamans after labelling them a criminal tribe. Today on the islands they are known as Bhatus and there is also an area near Port Blair known as Bhatu Basti. As they were extensively supported by the Jesuits, they even embraced Christianity.

In fact any individual whether he was a resident of NWFP or Bengal who was considered a threat to the British rule on the sub-continent soon found himself in chains on a prison ship bound for the Andamans. Once there he had to spend the rest of his natural life on the islands first as a prisoner and later as a 'released convict' so far as he remained on the island. In fact there was practically no way for him to cross almost 1000 kms of sea. Gradually the settlement expanded with the release of convicts who were encouraged to bring their families from mainland to settle in Andamans. The situation was similar when a particular community or a large section of it or even a group of individuals was found difficult to be controlled in their homeland. This policy helped the British in two ways. Primarily it removed the 'troublemaker' from the midst of the population. Secondarily the policy helped in populating Andaman and Nicobar with people with whom the British had more in common. Following the same principle the Karens were brought from the then Burma to clear the tropical jungles of Andaman and make it more habitable.

With Japanese occupation of the islands during the Second World War even this precarious balance that was built over a short period of 30 years was disturbed. The first targets of the Japanese occupation forces obviously were the British officers starting from Chief Commissioner who occupied a palatial residence at Ross Island downwards. Although as it usually happens people at the top were not available to endure the tortures and insults heaped by the Japanese occupation forces and their camp followers. It did not matter if the person of the Chief Commissioner was not available.

The brunt of the mob and the occupation forces was directed towards the building that was soon reduced into rubble. Today only the beautiful mosaics of the floors remain as relics. Similar was the fate of other buildings. Although Cellular Jail was no longer being used to lodge freedom fighters but only had hardened criminals even they were released to become stooges of the occupation forces. As if this devastation of the tenuous social matrix of the islands was not enough, even nature played its part when a strong earthquake hit Andaman during the Japanese occupation and toppled the central tower of the notorious Cellular Jail as if symbolizing the end of British rule. It was followed by a powerful tsunami similar to the one that hit the islands in December 2004. Although the whole world came to know of the 2004 tsunami in no time, due to wartime news censor, almost nobody knows about the earlier incident and the havoc played by it. Obviously the occupation forces took no relief measures and the residents of the islands had to fend for themselves as best as they could.

While granting Independence to the subcontinent British performed the master stroke of creating two countries on the basis of religion. Thus a large number of Hindus, who had lived for generations in the eastern parts of Bengal, overnight became alien on their own land. During the turmoil many of them had to run away with the bare minimum saving only their life. Often after moving through a number of refugee camps they were finally brought to the islands and settled there by the Indian Government giving them the bare requirements.

At the beginning of the 20th century Great Britain had an empire on which it was claimed that "the sun did not set". Most of the areas were in the tropics and yielded products ranging from tea to coal right through minerals like gold or diamond. To work at these places cheap labour was required. India provided the labour force to make these ventures profitable. This labour force was indentured from India and moved to the place of work whether it was in Malaya, Sri Lanka or South Africa. After the Second World

War when these colonies gradually became independent, resentment started growing among the local populations of these places against the Indians and even their children. Thus many Indians had to be repatriated from these places. Having left their country about hundred years ago most of these people had no place to come back. Many of the people, say, the Tamils from Ceylon and Burma thus repatriated were settled in the Andamans where they were given some avenue of earning a living. The process of settling the uprooted, unfortunately, is still not complete.

It is a fact that today when a tourist comes to the Emerald Islands on an aircraft flying from Kolkata or Chennai in about 3 hours or even by ship in about two days he fails to realize the remoteness of the islands. In conducted tours he sees only the natural beauty of the Emerald Islands. Some of them may even violate instructions and return with photographs of semi-nude tribal women. But they are unable to appreciate the nightmares suffered by the average residents during the last century or so. Unfortunately the records are so scattered and scanty that it is practically not possible for a tourist to find the details.

Shri Rabin Roychowdhury having spent almost all his professional life on the islands, as a devoted teacher under the Directorate of Education, Andaman and Nicobar Islands along with his wife is extremely competent to produce such an excellent treatise on the Japanese regime. During his long professional life on the islands he had come in contact with people who had actually suffered in those days. Since long we had been pestering him to finish it quickly and get it published so that the reading public at large can have some idea of what terrible nightmares these people or their forefathers have gone through for no fault of theirs. That day has finally dawned. The outcome of his relentless venture to epitomise the horrendous period during the Japanese rule over these islands has been purportedly depicted in his voluminous book, 'The Black Days in Andaman and Nicobar Islands'.

En passant, the present book captures the phases of migration and settlement from the prehistoric age to the neoteric period bedraggled for the unending swarm of refugees as fallout of the Partition of India.

In this excellent historical account an interested reader can trace the fact that during the last two centuries when 'civilized' man has started settling on these tropical islands, no serious attempt has been made to develop these islands. The Negrito tribes living in thousands on these islands at the beginning of the 20th century have been practically wiped out. Only about 500 Jarawas are today living in the hills and jungles of Great Andaman Island and the Sentinelese on North Sentinel Island situated on the west of Great Andaman Island. The 'civilized' man has always tried to exploit the natural resources of the tropical paradise and had been selfish enough to only exploit the advantages. The colonial British Government when decided to use the remoteness of the inland to build up the penal settlement, also followed this policy. Having taken advantage of the remoteness of the islands in keeping the leaders away from the followers after 1857, the British started sending anybody in exile to the Cellular Jail. Having once reached Andaman the convict had to depend exclusively on the British Government for his eventual return. Most of the convicts decided to spend the rest of their life on the island, partially fulfilling the objective of the government. The Japanese occupation threw a spanner in the well-oiled machinery and played havoc with the whole system. Even after Independence these islands were used for rehabilitating the refugees and repatriates. Proper systematic development, which will transform the islands from vitriolic hell to tropical paradise, is yet to take place. If this magnum opus of Shri Rabin Roychowdhury can enlighten the readers and goad the planners to accelerate the process of development of the islands and ameliorate the residents, at least as compensation for the years of neglect that they and their forefathers have endured, I feel Shri Roychowdhury will be amply rewarded.

Dr. Bhaskar Ranjan Ghosh

Former Superintending Anthropologist

Head of Office

A&N Regional Centre of ASI

Dedicated to

My most beloved granddaughter, 'Soupunya', who I believe, is the sublime incarnation of my divine mother.

ACKNOWLEDGEMENT

I have balked at the thought of conveying the acknowledgement. I feel even more hesitant to mention at least a few names. During study and preparing the manuscript, I have accumulated many intellectual and personal debts and it is unthinkable to acknowledge them in bleak words.

Indeed, I owe a deep gratitude to Dr. BR Ghosh, renowned anthropologist, who is generous in providing moral persuasion and scholarly suggestions sustaining me throughout this research. Despite his busy schedule, Dr. Ghosh has lent his valuable time to write the Foreword of this book.

I am especially grateful to Late Govinda Raju, renowned Urdu poet and Editor of 'The Light of Andaman', Port Blair, for all cheering with encouragement enquiring about the progress of my project. I am really indebted to him for providing necessary information and relevant photographs of by-gone era.

I am thankful to Dr. Rashida Iqbal, Curator, National Memorial Cellular Jail, Port Blair for spontaneous support in furnishing documents available in the Cellular Jail Library.

I am proud of my students working in different colleges and Universities who sincerely extend their active support by assisting me in many a way.

I wish to record the kind assistance and cooperation of the staffs of India Office Library, Public Record Office, National Documentation Centre of the Dhaka University Library; National Archives, New Delhi; National Library,

Kolkata; State Archives, West Bengal; State Archives, Port Blair; National Memorial Cellular Jail, Port Blair; etc. I am also indebted to *Daily Telegram, Light of Andaman, Andaman Murasu, Dweep Vani* and other Journals published from Andaman.

I heartily express my empathy to my wife, Kamala, but for her help, this massive task could not have been possible to complete. I also tender my love and affection to my nephew, Sourav Roychowdhury who is an intrinsic source of inspiration in my life to do something creative and constructive always.

Last but not the least, I must admit that due to want of proper documents and evidences, I could not justify all sections of my deliberations scripted in my book and I hope that this weakness may inspire some erudite enthusiasts to strive to retrieve the shortcomings

In fine, I have incurred many obligations, I am sorry, I cannot express adequately my depth of gratitude to each and all individually.

Rabin Roychowdhury
roycrabin@rediffmail.com

1872 – Panighat jetty where Lord Mayo was assassinated by Sher Ali, a Pathan Convict

Bazar at Ross Island – 1890

Cellular jail under construction during 1900

Chatham Island old Bhussi Ghat, convicts carrying logs jetty

Govt. Guest House, Andamans – 1895

Shompen Hut

Aberdeen bazaar during early British Days

View of Aberdeen Bazar from Y. Narayan Junction

Convicts at Dinner – Ross Island – 1890

Japanese shrine in Port Blair (Gandhi Park) in 1944

A Pathan Convict Sher Ali who killed Lord Mayo

S S Maharaja, carrying refugees of erstwhile East Pakistan

Transformed Onge

Jarawa Hut

Nicobar Tribal Dance

Nicobari Tribal Attire

1

GENESIS OF MIGRATION AND SETTLEMENT IN ANDAMAN

The phenomenon of migration has not received much attention. It is one of the most important aspects of social science. Sociologists observe that migration may be categorized as voluntary and involuntary or forced. Refugee movements start suddenly under life-threatening situation towards uncertainties. Indeed, the refugees are the victims of political morbidity so they are forced to migrate to save their life at least.

But the voluntary migrants are free to plan their move to places where their friends and relatives are settled and where their labour or skills are in demand. Usually they migrate in search of economic, educational or occupational benefits with an urge to settle to places where people of their own community and culture dominate. Hence migration is actually a complex process and is symptomatic of basic social and economic changes. Of course, the migration flows have a bearing upon several problems of the development process due to sudden boom of population explosion.

In fine, the refugees are the wretched pawns of political overture so forced to leave their homeland but the voluntary migrants are the seekers of economic opportunities. Indeed, there is no parameter to measure the extent of agonies and

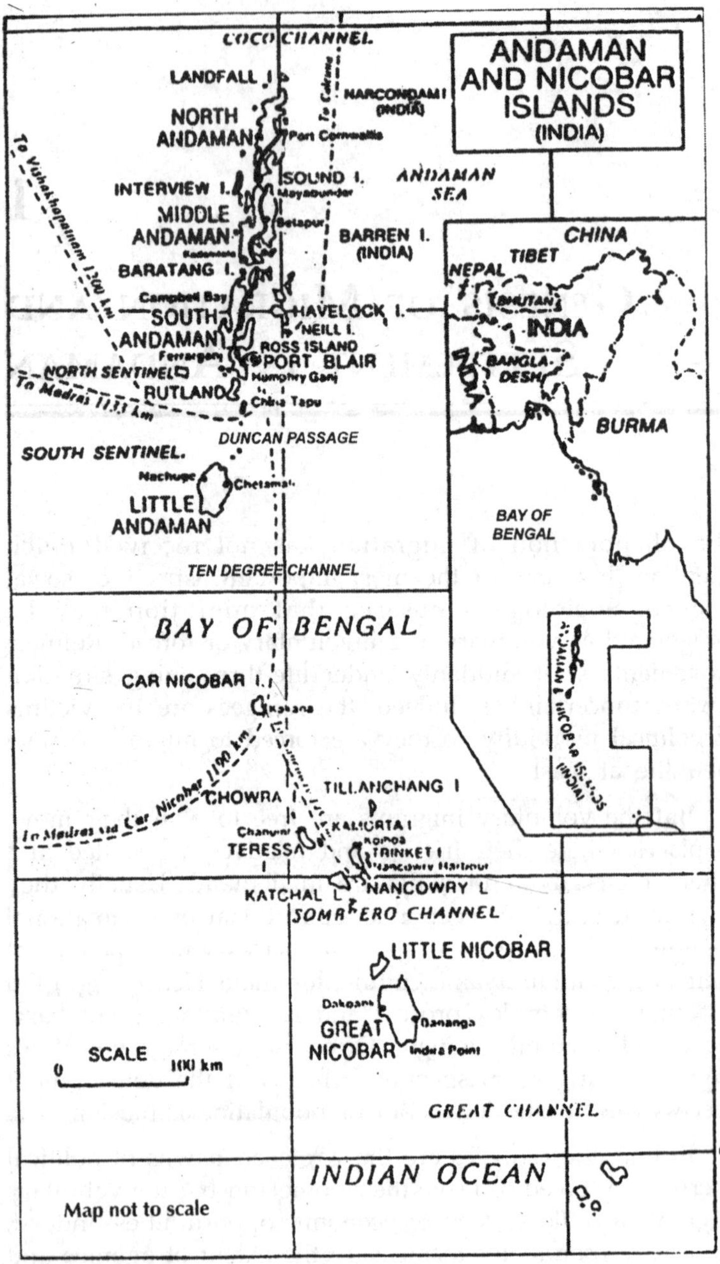

Andaman and Nicobar Islands at a glance

deprivation that throttle the refugees during the course of their forced migration.

In the case of the Andaman and Nicobar Islands, we will find both voluntary and involuntary immigration. This territory has witnessed a novel way of migration as propounded by Everett Lee in mid 1960s that there are two flows of migration—Pull and Push. 'Pull' migrants are said to be attracted by better opportunities at their destination and that happens all along in the Andamans as in the most cases adventurists or opportunists rush there to try their luck either in jobs or in business but 'push' migrants are stated to be thrust to leave their homeland in troubled conditions as occurred often during 1950s and 1960s owing to the communal disturbances in East Pakistan while the Hindu minorities were forced to abandon their hearth and home for ever. A measly portion of these wretched refugees was sent to Andaman under adverse condition to face their ineluctable fate.

After the colonial period, the process of nation building accompanied political, ethnic, and religious conflicts and created economic and environmental conditions which induced migration. The largest refugee flows occurred when Bangladesh became independent of Pakistan in 1971. Muslim dominated East Pakistan was vivisected from India on religious grounds in 1947 and again in 1971 it was separated from Punjabi-Muslim dominated West Pakistan on ethnic grounds. But the Hindus were frustrated and forced to abandon their ancestral homeland at the first instance to escape death and persecution as a consequence of the Partition in 1947 and again in 1971, these Bangladeshi Hindus rushed to West Bengal to escape perdition and execution in Islamized Bangladesh as a sequel of her independence from the claw of Punjabi dominated Pakistan. To lessen the burden of West Bengal, they were sent to Dandyakarannya or to Andaman or to some other States as economic migrants. These externally displaced people were not refugees primarily but 'mandate refugees' until and unless they were granted asylum at the receiving country where they would be treated as refugees.[1]

This thing happened in the case of East Pakistan refugees while they reached India as human flood with least botheration about their recognition.

L.W. Hotborn[2] justly defines that the refugee is an involuntary migrant. Every refugee is naturally a migrant but not every migrant is a refugee. The term refugee is encompassed by the concept of migrants. However, it is also usual to see refugees in sharp contrast with migrants. In most cases, migrants are voluntary settlers as it happened in the case of the migration of the aborigines to the Bay Islands. They came to these islands during the primordial age as wandering nomads and found the land constituting the Andaman Islands favourable so they settled there. But in due course, the land became isolated by subsidence due to terrific volcanic tremors, or due to great cataclysm submerging a greater part of the land and getting these islands totally separated. They may be classified as 'climate refugees' as they had to move from place to place in quest of favourable climate and salubrious environment.

After the advent of the British, unfortunately these primitive tribes who had settled in these islands voluntarily as climate migrants were forced to migrate to other islands leaving their own habitat. The Jarawas had to leave South Andaman under duress at the threat of the British firearms and to confine themselves on the western coast of Middle Andaman. Similarly, the Great Andamanese were banished from South Andaman to Strait Island in the name of settlement to resettle there on forced conditions.

After the Partition, the Hindus, the Sikhs, the Muslims and others suffered untold violence and massacre. Hundred of thousands of persons found themselves abruptly in the wretched position of 'refugees' and forced exodus of teeming millions continued to build up the saddest chapter of the recent history of this country.

The sequel of the vivisection of India was catastrophic leading to devastation and annihilation in the shape of murder, arson, rape, loot and persecutions. Millions and millions, victims of man-made calamities, swarmed across the border immediately after the Partition being chased by blood-thirsty ruffians, outraged by their estranged neighbours and heckled by the Pakistan officials. Under the spell of communal violence and sprouting insecurity, the Bengali Hindus and other non-Muslim families had to leave their homes and hearths as well as they were deprived of agricultural and non-agricultural sources of livelihood in East Bengal. The economic deprivation and socio-political indignance was solely responsible for wanton migration of the Hindu minority groups. Then they had no other identity but to be stigmatized in India as inglorious refugees.

Gardner Murphy[3] observes, "One (displaced person) said good bye, not just to a plot of land but to one's entire tradition, one's own home and one's language group, the shrines of one's father.....In the case of Indian refugees, there was a loss of homeland, a process catapulting one into a world of increasing miseries and no clear future whatever".

Since Independence, the massive increase in population in Indian Sub-continent due to both natural growth and immigration from outside, the neighbouring countries, has been causing numerous social, political and economic problems. Migration has several bearings upon the ethnic tension too. What had happened in Mana, Dandyakaranya, did not occur in the Andamans to that intensity. Of course, grievances and protest came to the surface when KR Ganesh of Local Born Association submitted a memorandum to the President and Prime Minister etc. requesting to forbid the settlement of Bengali refugees from East Pakistan which had started in March 1949.

Obviously it was not the fallout of the ethnic tension but the sense of insecurity of being reduced to minority as the local people indiscreetly apprehended that the State and the Central Governments had been planning to make Andaman a haven of Bengali refugees so the schemes were designed to rehabilitate these uprooted people in their islands. It was unfortunate for the East Pakistan refugees to become the victims of reluctance and rancour of the local born people of which they were not at all responsible because they did not come to the islands at their own wish, on the contrary they were resettled in these islands under various rehabilitation schemes chalked out by the Central Government itself which was, however, under legal and moral obligations to offer shelter to the distressed people who happened to be disparaged as ignominious refugees being the victims of the Partition. Instead of showing sympathy and expressing compassion, they were treated with execration and innuendo. However, it is the irony of settlement policy of the Government of India which was once strictly restricted to accommodate East Pakistan refugees as many as possible depending on the availability of lands in Andaman and later on designed to extend scope of settlement of people of all other States in the name of "quota", but taking advantage of the liberal government policy of 1950, the unrestricted influx of the mainlanders, mostly vagabonds, unskilled workers, casual jobseekers, hawkers and unemployed youths has made the situation alarming. Presently the man-land ratio of the Bay Islands is very high and per capita productivity is extremely low or stagnant. The forest area too has surpassed the norms of 80% reserve due to influx of outsiders creating a fiasco in communal harmony and racial discrimination denying basic needs of food, health, housing, education, social and economic facilities.

Recently for Andaman a Draft Master Plan has come up with numerous ambitious schemes and lofty projects which require a massive tract of land having an intricate road network. In final count of the Plan if the Master Plan is implemented, the total requirement of land may exceed an area of whopping 5,000 hectares which is practically infeasible to acquire because the revenue department has no spare land as such and the forest land being prohibited by the Supreme Court of India, is unavailable for any such gigantic project. Most of the remaining land has already been encroached as there are over 10,000 encroachments by a modest estimate.

Besides the nonce, if the necessary area of the land is acquired, it only leads to massive internal displacement of settlers branding them with ignominious cognomen, 'refugee' in their own land to be ascribed as 'domestic refugees'. Of course the Town and Country Planning Regulation, 1994 enables the administration to enforce its absolute right over the land even though allotted to the settlers and to evict them from their holdings. If the sequel speaks the saddest tale, the benefits owing to the Master Plan for the first instance go not to the 'mandate refugees' but to tourists, tour operators, businessmen, contractors, builders, etc.[4]

Moreover another burning question is to control the inflow of people into the already over-burdened territory. To review the demographic structure of this territory, the Ministry of Tribal Affairs has expressed deep concern over the alarming increase of the population of the islands which results in the reckless intrusion into the tribal reserves affecting the life and living of the autochthons so it has recommended immediate steps to be taken to restrict the influx of outsiders in the islands, otherwise the denouement will be disastrous.

Considering the stringent pecuniary condition of the islands due to over-population affecting harmony and socio-cultural integrity, it is suggested to impose Inner Permit System in pursuance of the direction of the Supreme Court of India failing which the development of the islands will be deterred and the inhabitants will suffer from financial debacle owing to severe unemployment.

ENDNOTES

1. Independent Commission on International Humanitarian Issues, 1986, p. 38.
2. "Refugees: World Problems," pub. in Encyclopedia of the Social Sciences, 1968, p. 361-373, by Crowell Collier and Macmillan.
3. Gardner Murphy, "In the Minds of Men: the Study of Human Behaviour and Social Tensions in India," New York, 1953, p. 81.
4. Source: "The Light of Andaman," published from Port Blair.

2

HISTORICAL VISTA

Shimmering in the radiant sunshine amidst the bay of Bengal, a little over 1250 kms. away from the coast of India, 193 kms. from the cape of Negrais in Myanmar and about 550 kms. from the northern extremity of Sumatra, is the archipelago of 572 emerald islands emerging from the blue spell of vibrant sea, floating like a garland of verdant pearls and throbbing with life and vivacity.

The Andaman and Nicobar territory with 38 inhabited islands stretches over an area of more than 800 kms. from north to south and 110 kms. from east to west having a population of about 4 lakhs in 2001. The sylvan glory of its virgin forest and exotic marvels of its flora and fauna, bizarre myths and quaint legends about this forbidden land and its primitive people make it a much sought after destination. What makes it unique, is its spirit of assimilation of different cultures despite diversities in languages and customs, and thereby creating a distinct human tapestry proclaiming harmony and cohesion.

The history of the islands before the 18th century is irretrievably shrouded in oblivion. How the primitive people came there, where they migrated from is still a matter of speculations. In 1789, for the first time, the British government decided to establish a settlement to control the islands in order to safeguard her vessels and to protect the

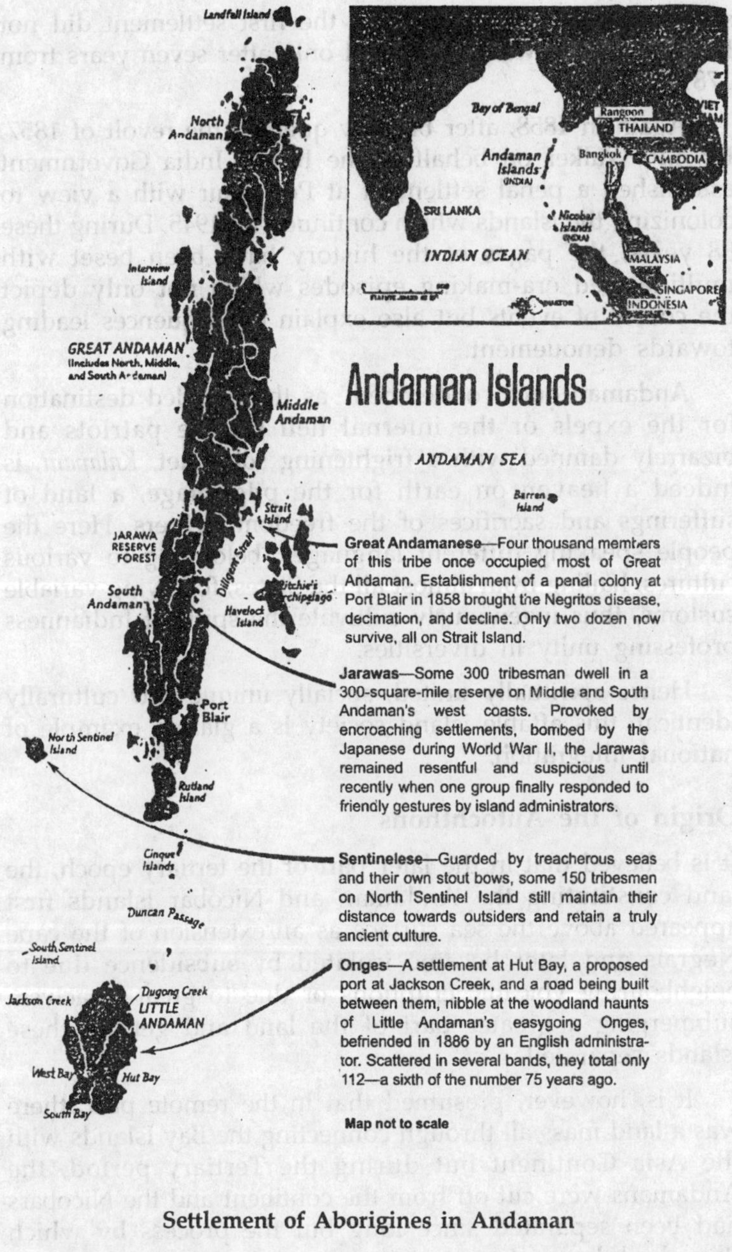

Settlement of Aborigines in Andaman

ship-wrecked crews. However, the first settlement did not last long and it was abandoned only after seven years from 1789 to 1796.

Again in 1858, after brutally quelling the revolt of 1857, Dr. J.P. Walker on behalf of the British India Government established a penal settlement at Port Blair with a view to colonizing the islands which continued till 1945. During these 88 years, the pages of the history have been beset with multi-faceted era-making episodes which not only depict the course of events but also explain the sequences leading towards denouement.

Andaman once condemned as the dreaded destination for the expels or the infernal hell for the patriots and bizarrely damned with a frightening sobriquet, *Kalapani*, is indeed a heaven on earth for the pilgrimage, a land of sufferings and sacrifices of the freedom fighters. Here the people speaking different languages, belonging to various cultures, hailing from almost all the States, following variable customs, thus ingenuously cultivate the spirit of Indianness professing unity in diversities.

Hence spiritually united, socially unique and culturally identical, this affable island society is a glaring example of national integration.

Origin of the Autochthons

It is believed that in the later part of the tertiary epoch, the land constituting the Andaman and Nicobar Islands first appeared above the sea surface as an extension of the cape Negrais and later became isolated by subsidence due to neighbouring volcanic eruptions or due to great cataclysm submerging a greater part of the land and getting these islands separated.

It is, however, presumed that in the remote past, there was a land mass all through connecting the Bay Islands with the Asia Continent but during the Tertiary period, the Andamans were cut off from the continent and the Nicobars had been separated since long but the process by which they had been disconnected among themselves, is a phenomenon of comparatively recent past.

Similarly it is a matter of great controversy to establish the origin of the aborigines of the Andamans i.e., Great Andamanese, Jarawas, Onges and Sentinelese. All these Negrito tribes are morphologically and culturally widely different from all other Negroid people of Asia and Africa continents.

Since pre-historic times, these tribes, quite short in stature with dark steel grey complexion, copper brown eyes and wooly curly hair growing in tufts, have been living there for thousands and thousands of years, antedating every historical record available which have been compiled from the fictitious tales of the sea-farers and the accounts of the traders who in the event of shipwrecks were awashed to the shore and perhaps came in contact with the tribes. Even while they had to arrive at these islands in search of food or for plunder and slave-trades, they would face violent attacks from these aborigines. Indeed their scribbles are the earliest source of historical documents.

Throughout these hoary years of history, the tribes have otherwise remained isolated and cut off from the main stream of cultures living primitively in the tropical and rain rich forests, totally unaware of the existence of any other people depending completely on the nature for their subsistence and upbringing.

According to one hypothesis, the Andamanese are some of the surviving representatives of a once flourishing Negrito race that held sway in the entire South-East Asian region inducing these outlying islands, this race was at some stage annihilated or pushed out or assimilated by more powerful racial groups migrating into this region from other regions. The other representatives of this great Negrito race are said to be two small tribal groups, the 'Semang' of Malaysia and the 'Aeta' of the Philippines with whom the Andamanese bear not only physical but also cultural resemblance. However it has not been possible to establish any linguistic affinity between these two groups. Even the four tribes of the Andamanese race speak distinctive dialects, not mutually understood among the tribes. But that does not mean that the dialects are not related, of course, the consanguinity is yet to be established.

However, the most popular theory of the origin of the Andamanese is that in the 16th century, the Portuguese ships laden with slaves from Mozambique had been wrecked on the east shore of the Andamans. Eventually those who survived, it is assumed, were the ancestors of the primitive people of these Islands and the present Andamanese are believed to be the progeny of such ship-wrecked human cargoes.

In the excerpts published in the *Calcutta Monthly Registrar*, November, 1790, it is stated, "The manner in which these islands were peopled is a matter of sheer conjecture. We are told that when the Portuguese had a settlement near Pegu, two of their ships with cargoes of slaves on board amounting in number of men and women to 300, were cast away there (Andamans) and as the inhabitants (of Andamans) are of the Coffree caste probably favours this opinion or conjecture. They are a strong, robust set of Coffrees in their appearance and mode of living resemble much what Cook describes to us of the inhabitants of South-West part of New Zealand...".

Though widely accepted, this conjecture is not beyond reproach rather it lacks authenticity and proves chronographically erroneous because the Andamanese are known to have been dwelling in these islands long before the slave trade started and it bears the documentary evidences from the accounts of the Arab traders of the 9th century which are long anterior to the navigation of those seas by the Europeans for slave trade.

Moreover, this theory of origin of the Andamanese from ship-wrecked negro slaves is also proved false after examining the kitchen middens found all over these islands. Many of them are of such dimensions and stratifications as to show that they date back to millenniums. The kitchen midden at Chouldari in South Andaman has been proved to date back to 2200 years old.[1]

Besides, as to the ethnographic study, it is contended that the Bushmen, the dwarf tribes of Congo forest and other African Negrito tribes do not belong to the same race as that of the Andamanese who are not Negros but bear Negrito consanguinity.

Under these perspectives the life and living of the Andamanese being the first settler in these islands is to be discussed.

(A) GREAT ANDAMANESE

The aborigines of Andaman consist of four Negrito tribes and the Great Andmanese are one of them, settled there as itinerant immigrants or natural inhabitants in the primordial times. In their social pattern, they were divided in ten sub-castes but collectively referred to as Great Andamanese. It is a generic term meaning the inhabitants of the Andman Islands.

In the earliest historical account of the Andamans, noted by two Arab voyagers in the 9th century, it is stated "... these islands are inhabited by Negritos". Among these Negritos, the Great Andamanese first came in contact with the Britishers since the first settlement by Archibald Blair which was abandoned later. Again with the establishment of the settlement for the second time, the first batch of the freedom fighters of the revolt of 1857 being sentenced of transportation by the British India Government, arrived at Chatham Island on March 10, 1958 and thenceforth faced frequent attacks of the Great Andamanese who resented the coming of these strangers into their own land. While the convicts were engaged to clear jungles, to construct roads or to hunt or catch fish in rivulets, there were numerous affrays between the tribal people and the new settlers. Thus the skirmishes went on between them ever since the establishment of the Penal Settlement which was constantly resisted and challenged by the Great Andamanese and ultimately the sporadic conflicts culminated into an organized attack on March 17, 1859 at Aberdeen, a small village at Port Blair, which is significantly known as the "Battle of Aberdeen".

But the British was lucky in getting an advance information from a run-away convict, Dudhnath Tewari who had been captured by the tribals and allowed to live with them on being married to a tribal girl, named Lipa whom he left eventually when she was pregnant. But he was awarded amnesty for his loyal service to the British crown.

The Battle of Aberdeen was brutally crushed by the British because it was an unmatched challenge by the Great Andamanese with their primitive weapons, viz., bows and arrows against the British armed with guns and mortars. Several of the belligerent tribals were killed and many more were wounded. They had to quit to save their life.

This was the beginning of the end of the organized resistance of the Andamanese and in due course with the changing attitude of the British, the Great Andamanese seemed to be much gratified with the gifts as to their likings and began to submit to the British policy of appeasement initiated by Haughton[2] and Tytler.[3] The gradual establishment of friendly relations accounts for the absence of violence on the part of the Andamanese who also proved useful in affording information regarding forest tracks, creeks, streams, etc., and at the same time, they helped to capture run-away convicts.[4]

Andaman Home

The British policy of appeasement towards the hostile Andamanese was pursued discreetly resulting in ostensible changes in the attitude of the aborigines. In the first half of the year 1862, the Andamanese living in the vicinity of Port Blair, ceased to attack the settlement and to murder convicts whenever they met them in the jungles. Col. Tytler being encouraged by such changing attitude sent a small party of sailors to their encampments. In such a visit on 28 January, 1863, one sailor Pratt of the party tried to rape a tribal girl and was instantly murdered by two aborigines, Snowball and Jumbo who were captured on the charge of murder. Later it was proved that the fault lay with the sailor Pratt and not with those two aborigines who acted under strong provocation.[5] They were ultimately released and sent back to forest on 12 October, 1863 with a large quantity of coconuts and bananas as gifts.

The direct result of their release and friendly gesture of the British culminated into the foundation of "Andaman Home" with a view to civilizing the Andamanese. This habitation, set up at Ross Island, was a collection of huts with an enclosure surrounded on all sides by a bamboo fence. Corbyn[6] was made Incharge of the Home where twenty eight Andamanese lived. The Government of India sanctioned an allowance of Rs. 100/- per month for its upkeep.[7] The inmates of the Home were instructed in English with the object of acquiring means of mutual understanding with them to secure lasting benefit to the settlement.

Whatsoever the intention of the Britishers towards the Andamanese was, circumstances as regards the Andaman Home were not as bright as Corbyn wanted to project, rather the condition of the Home was pitiable. The only dwelling in the Home was a small cow-shed which the tribals shared with cattle. They did not relish the food, mainly coarse rice. They resented to wear clothes and live in dingy shed. Besides, they declined to yield to the civilization processes and even would hate to learn English. Indeed, they were kept under strict surveillance at the Home and their movements were restricted. In the sequel, the Great Andamanese became acrimonious and rancourous.

Consequently to defy the confinement and for an urge of freedom, on the night of 1 March, 1864, a band of forty Andamanese inmates of the Home including women and children left Ross Island and crossing the channel fled to the jungle of South Andaman.[8]

Major Ford who succeeded Tytler as Superintendent of the Penal Settlement remarked about the semi-captivity of the Andamanese "... It was impolitic to restrain them on Ross Island, they must be free to go and come amongst us".[9]

The Government of British India also realized that the forcible detention of the Andamanese in the Home would not yield any good result. But what was the most catastrophic sequel of confinement is referred to the close contra community interaction that resulted in addiction to opium, tobacco and liquor in the one hand and sexual exploitation and concomitant admission of venereal disease on the other hand. As a result, epidemics like pneumonia (1868), syphilis, measles, influenza broke out that decimated the Great Andamanese and their population came down harrowingly to 19 in 1961 from 624 enumerated in 1901 census. Though there has been a slight increase from 19 in 1961 to 43 in 2001 during the last 40 years, the overall sex ratio has been 60 females per 100 males which has become alarmingly deterrent to the further growth of their population. Fortunately one of the women in the tribe, Licho by name who was pregnant during the Tsunami of Dec. 26, 2004, gave birth to one of the two girls, born during the post Tsunami period.

Causes of Resettlement

From the time immemorial, the Great Andamanese had developed their own ethnic culture enriched with age-old experiences, sufficient to endure the vagaries of nature, which aptly helped them to survive for thousand and thousand of years. Unfortunately, they had to surrender to the gloats of civilization. Though they could survive in the ecological niche, the recent Tsunami of 26 December 2004 yet it is sadder that the same endemic ethnic culture failed to protect them from the aggression of the outsiders shadowing their vitality and leaving them with an aberrated morale. Thus their social and cultural life became completely disarrayed, their customs and traditions, their feasts and festivals, their animistic rituals, their social and communal cohesion— all have been lost to oblivion generating sequacious mentality. They now live on the mercy of the outsiders.

Consequently the Andamanese males have lost their vitality and their females their fertility. They are perhaps today the weakest ethnic community awaiting total extinction in the days to come.

Strait Island

Hence, considering their dwindling condition, a scheme for their rehabilitation was drawn up by the Andaman and Nicobar Administration which led to their ultimate settlement at a small island off the eastern coast of Middle Andaman in 1970, about 126 kms. north-east of Port Blair. In 'Strait Island' they have been relocated in barrack type huts with some facilities of medical treatment to acquaint them with the knowledge of health and hygiene and of elementary education to develop language skill.

Government Facilities

According to the administrative report, Strait Island being a tribal reserve has been shutout to the outsiders. The settlement is a neat little village with fruit and vegetable orchards attached to each hut duly fenced, proper roads and footpaths with the arrangement for drainage. A dispensary with an all-time compounder, an all-time social worker of the Adimjati Sevak Sangh, a piggery centre and schemes for goat rearing, canoe making and fishing to obtain bigger catches in addition to their traditional turtle fishing are now a part of their life. Proper protected water supply and last but not the least, a community centre which is also used for running a school and a balwadi, has also been constructed.

De-addiction treatment has been started for 13 opium addicts in a phased manner. Four addicts are completely free, eight are responding to the treatment, only one person is a little resistant and has been hospitalized for treatment.

Moreover, Strait Island has been provided with electricity. This is the second island populated by the primitive tribes supplied with electricity and the first being Dugong Creek is in Little Andaman where the Onges live.

Considering the imbalance of their sex life, reproduction has been frustrated so on behalf of the Administration, attempts have been made to explore how adjustments could be made in sexual relationship among those still capable. There has been active thinking also whether it would be possible to contact the Onge tribe in Little Andaman Island to explore possibility of inter-marrying with them. In that case the lost brethren of the tribe would have a happy reunion after many years of circumstantial separation. All these flights of imagination are symptomatic of their will to live and to continue not as a 'dying tribe' rather to survive to regenerate their race through inter-marrying with any of the Negrito tribes of Andaman i.e., Great Andamanese, Onges, Jarawas and Sentinelese. Thus their demographic profile may improve with time and sustained efforts but their cultural debacle remains obtrusive years by years.

It's really painful to observe that the present progeny of the Great Andamanese is averse to lucubrate their own ethnic culture and even to learn their own language or carry out their age old tradition, rather they now feel quite at home with Hindi and Hindi culture attiring modern dresses. Obviously all these have an adverse effect on their health and mind and thereby degenerating them as a hybrid offshoot.

Now-a-days, they look enlightened too. Setting aside their centuries old tradition, they have significantly chosen a queen instead of a King. For want of suitable male, they have selected 55 years old Surmai, wife of their last king to become the queen of the Great Andamanese whose numbers had fallen from 10,000 in the 1760s to 43 in 2001. They have never had a female ruler so the idea of choosing a queen sparked a heated debate among the Great Andamanese who were elated of a fine tradition of good kings like Loka and Jirake.

The social and religious life of this present generation is totally unorganized. The salient characteristics of their way of living; communal huts, communal feasts, festival, dances, folklores, traditions and ancient customs etc., have been gradually ignored and antiquated. There is practically no social cohesion among them.

During the British period, the effects of Andaman Home on the Andamanese were disastrous and their numbers except the Onges and the Jarawas started to decline alarmingly. Von Eickstedt, a German Anthropologist who visited the Andamans at the beginning of the twentieth century rightly observed: "The Andaman Home was the door of death to the Andaman race."[10]

Notwithstanding, certain changes were made in their traditional way of life and some of the inmates were guided to do cultivation of which they were quite ignorant. This may be considered as a turning point towards being civilized.

After the Independence, the government became anxious of their dwindling condition and attempts were made to bring them to such a level of civilization in which they could enjoy the minimum comforts of civilized life. But to bring them to human level, sufficient care should have been taken to see that these efforts may not lead to further deterioration in their numbers already reduced to 43. For the last one hundred and fifty years, the Great Andamanese had to bear with all sorts of physical and cultural domination which ultimately led them towards gradual extinction. During the course of transition, though they have been exposed to all sorts of evils of neoteric society like addiction to drugs and inducement to veneral diseases, etc., and have developed a pander to low tastes, yet they become conscious of their importance to the intellectuals and officials being the only surviving tribe of the paleolithic age so the government is to shoulder all the responsibilities to supply food and provisions and is to be held responsible for any decadence caused to them.

This attitude may lead them either to disaster or to a right direction to adjust with the changing situations so that they can overcome all odds and survive in a better way as the Nicobarese do.

(B) ONGES OF LITTLE ANDAMAN

Among the four Negrito tribes of the Andaman Islands, the Great Andamanese and the Onges are friendly whereas the Sentinelese of North Sentinel Island are still hostile and Jarawas too in the recent past were ferocious towards the outsiders.

The Onge settlements of Little Andaman are about 100 kms south of Port Blair. The nomenclature 'Onge' being a generic term might have been derived from "en-iregale" which means perfect human beings in their dialect. According to the Onge folklore, their progenitor 'Engigegi' and his wife came down to Little Andaman from the sky and started living there. After some days while returning from hunting, they saw one pair of Onges in each branch of their 'Tukwegetako' tree and these couples reproduced hundreds of Onges. Indeed, in 1901 Census, they were 672 but after close interactions with the outsiders, their population decimated to only 112 in 1971 and shriveled further to 96 in 2001. There are many a reasons for their dwindling condition.

Unlike the Jarawas whom the jungle and terrains of Andaman have protected, the Onges had no such natural allies as Little Andaman is a small flat island. Like the Great Andamanese, the Onges had no immunity nor any resistance to most of the diseases of the civilized men. Thus their number has been reducing threateningly due to contact with outsiders.

The Britishers immediately after their arrivals in the Andamans with a view to establishing a penal colony, ventured to know about other tribals in different islands including the Onges who always resisted any sort of invasions of the outsiders. But the island of substantial size and of vast vegetation located only about 100 kms away from Port Blair naturally attracted the Britishers to extend their suzerainty. Initially the Onges rebuffed aggressively the advancement of the invaders but retreated after a demonstration of firearms leaving about 70 Onges dead. In another encounter reported by Dr. Douglas nearly 30 Onges were shot dead but the Onges continued their hostility towards the outsiders. Meanwhile the British tried to cultivate friendship with the Onges but all in vain.

Portman[11] renewed the efforts to establish friendly relations with the Onges in 1880 by offering liberal gifts. Though there were stray attacks or skirmishes, Portman became successful to win over their faith and the Onges also laid down their primitive arms and embraced the friendship by the end of the nineteenth century.

Pattern of Settlement

Unlike the Great Andamanese the Onges are semi-nomadic and live in semi-permanent huts made of leaves, creepers, and wild bushes. Till some years back, they were food gathering and fish catching community. Among them, there are about three main groups residing in three different places; South Bay, Jackson creek and Dugong creek and these groups are called 'Girimeka Gobeula', 'Girera Gobeula' and 'Engaquale' respectively. They are not permitted to marry in the same group. Monogamy is strictly followed among them and widow marriage is prohibited.

In the Onge society, the primary unit is a family comprising of husband, wife and children. Men go for hunting, fishing, turtle hounding, etc., and women along with children collect water, wild roots, eatable tubers, fruits, firewood etc. They also make baskets, weave nets and prepare mats.

They like to decorate their faces with a clay paste mixed with turtle fat, saliva and proportionately water. They also crop their hair very neatly. Though the males go stark naked, the females wear a bunching tassel to cover their private parts.

They eat pig's meat, fish, crabs, turtle, honey, boiled mangrove fruits, etc. The introduction of dogs in the island has enhanced their hunting prowess and sometimes dogs become the carriers of several diseases.

They collect honey in a very innovative way. To get honey and to avoid stings, they chew 'tonjoghe' leaves, supposedly narcotic and blow their moist breath over the hives and thereby drug the bees. For further protection, they would smear their bodies with a paste made of the chewed leaves. Thus they save themselves from the attacks of the bees and collect honey safely.

By nature they were self-contented and led a peaceful life in isolation. But after the British occupation, contact with the civilized men proved disastrous as the British in order to civilize them tried to bring sudden changes in a radical manner in their way of life and thereby blighted their old habits, practices, ideas and beliefs. Besides, to appease them, the British made them fetish of gifts and crazy of tobacco and opium which ultimately threatened their existence.

Though they were not infected with venereal diseases, they became easy victims of malaria, dysentery and pulmonary diseases as they did not have any immunity against all these hazards. Hence the rate of decline in their population has been alarming. From an estimated 700 in 1858, they were reduced to barely 96 in 2001, presently they are less than that.

Government Facilities

Plagued with infertility and high child mortality, the Onges are declining in numbers. Being less nomadic in habits makes them increasingly dependent to the government supply and dainty public help or at the mercy of traders. The government has realised their problems, arranged free supply of rice, atta, etc., as a gesture of goodwill. Some Onges have learnt the use of oil and spices for the preparation of 'sabji' vegetable curry. Coconut water and tea are common but they don't like milk.

To ameliorate their condition, various welfare measures have been taken. The Administration has made pile houses at Dugong Creek for the Onges, making the floor higher than possible reach of the sea but they do not feel at home so they use to leave and spend a considerable period of the year in jungles. These brick-made huts with asbestos roofs have intensified their health problems because they are not used to living in such houses.

Earlier, the Onges would live stark naked and feel easy and comfortable in the jungle under the sky. But under compulsion, they are persuaded to wear clothes. However, in the rain-rich forest, washing the clothes is a great problem causing health hazards.

Dr. Cipriani,[12] the noted Italian Anthropologist who lived with the Onges from February to May 1953, observed that the "smooth naked skin" of the Onge does not harbour fleas but their reeking semi-damp clothes give shelter to harmful fungi and bacteria thus causing skin and other diseases.

Besides dress, electricity has been provided in the Onge hutments at Dugong creek in the midst of jungle. Even Balwadi for Onge children has been set up. A social worker has been posted there and several health centres have been opened to look after them. Thus the Onges have become so allured to the comforts of civilized life that they have been slowly driven away from nature.

Prof. L. P. Vidyarthi[13] of the Ranchi University warned that the Onges may experience a culture-shock and may be reduced to become substratum of the new society.

Indeed, the resettlement colonies of the Onges soon became exhibition sites for the VIPs visiting the islands. These visits have disastrous consequence on the Onge's life. This paradoxical attitude brings about only deterioration in the life style of the Onges. The dilemma over them is the sequel of changes, brought into poignant focus by the colossal cultural disparity between the state of the tribal society and that of the rest of the country. The dilemma before the Parliament arose as the members accused the government of killing the Onge's distinctive identity through too many modern amenities; providing brick-made huts, electricity, metalled road, cooked meals, dresses, tobacco, opium, etc.

The Government of India led by Indira Gandhi deplored the perception of human groups as 'museum pieces' and insisted that basic services, especially health, agriculture and emergency relief have to be extended to this endangered community. There is little doubt that given the choice between risking human lives and risking cultural survival, a government has to opt for the latter. Hence in the name of civilization, bearing the 'Brown men's burden, to dress up such primitive tribals who usually wear no clothes, in fine feathers to parade before visiting VIPs is not only of bad taste but also shows a lack of understanding on the part of persons entrusted with the servicing of a tribal community.

However, the moot question was whether they should be persuaded to embrace civilization. Among the protagonists, one group wanted to retain these tribes as 'museum piece' while the other group was for going all out to incorporate them in the national mainstream, even if it meant the oblivion of their culture and society. But nothing can come out of this dilemma and all the sensible people are totally against these experiments.

The then Prime Minister Indira Gandhi announced discreetly in the Parliament, "Our basic objective is to help them (Onges) develop without losing their identity, way of life and culture".

Earlier Jawaharlal Nehru had explained the government's policy of protection in simple words, "There is no point in trying to make them a second rate copy of ourselves. ...they are a people who sing and dance and try to enjoy life... not a people who sit in stock exchange, shout out at each other and think themselves civilized.

"...we do not mean to interfere with their way of life but want to help them live it... according to their own genius and tradition". This should be our objective in dealing with them.

But in reality, the picture is different. Felling trees in the forests for timber as well as to make room for settlement of the migrant people and of the Nicobarese have an adverse effect on them and their pastoral areas are being shrunken so the Onges are now confined only to Dugong creek and South Bay. They are virtually exiled in their own land. Indeed, they are now mute witnesses to their ultimate end and apathetically seeing their domain being shrunken in the face of accelerated settlement leaving their culture, a fable of the past.

Of course, they enjoy civic facilities provided by the Administration, i.e., electricity, tap water, medical treatment, food and provisions, living in brick-made rooms in exchange of no labour which has made them indolent.

Presently Tambolai and Nabikuti have become leaders of Dugong creek group and South Bay Group respectively. Tambolai, well experienced and adept in all traditional practices has been inducted as a member of the Pradesh Council, a non-legislative body, as the representative of the Onges. After the formation of Panchayati Raj, they have got a greater access to self-government.

(C) JARAWAS

The other group of Negrito stock belonging to the Andamans is the Jarawas who were widely known for their uncompromising hostility and savagery. Of course, virile and lively as they are, unfortunately their love for freedom and for their habitat, has been mistaken for hostility which has never been pathological but only environmental. Even today among the outsiders, the very utterance of the word, 'Jarawas' evokes a melange of awe, wonder, curiosity and mystery. Because of their isolation and hostility for centuries together, innumerable myths and folklores have loomed large but remain unnoticed so far.

'Jarawa' is not a generic term and it means 'stranger' or 'other people', as addressed by the Great Andamanese in their Aka-bea dialect. The Jarawas refer themselves as 'Ang', a word meaning human beings.

POPULATION OF THE ANDAMAN & NICOBAR ISLANDS

Year	Total	Andaman Islands	Nicobar Islands	Population of the Tribal Communities			
				Andamanese	Onge	Jarawa	Nicobarese
1901	24,649			625	672	468	5,962
1911	26,469			455	631	114	7,991
1921	27,086			209	346	114	8,248
1931	29,463			90	250	70	9,589
1941	33,769						
1951	30,971			23	150	50	11,902
1961	63,548	48,985	14563	19	129	500	13,903
1971	1,15,133	93,468	21665	24	112	275	17,874
1981	1,88,741	1,58,287	30454	27	100	200	21,172
1991	2,80,661	2,41,453	39208	28	101	250	
2001	3,56,265				100	250	

Figures for Jarawas are estimates.

The Jarawas settled in the Andamans in the same process as the Andamanese had settled in the primordial times. Radcliffe-Brown[14] remarked in his book: "They are the descendants of emigrants who some time in the past made their way down from Little Andaman and thrust themselves upon the inhabitants of Rutland Island and South Andamans maintaining their footing in the new country by force of arms".

E. H. Man[15] was the first to make a systematic study of the Andamanese. As to his classification, the Jarawas were divided into 3 tribes inhabiting South Andaman, Rutland and North Sentinel Islands. In the Census Report of 1921 at page no. 11, the Onges and the Jarawas have been classified as southern section group.

In 1788, when the islands were first surveyed and the first settlement was established by the British under the stewardship of Archbald Blair, the Jarawas came in contact with the outsiders and strangely enough, they were more disposed to friendly relations with the Britishers than with the Aka-Bea(da) tribe of the Great Andamanese who were their natural enemy. Unfortunately, owing to their friendly relation with the outsiders, they were exposed to diseases introduced by Blair's men.

Causes of Hostility

During the establishment of the second settlement in 1858, the Great Andamanese became more intimate with the settlers and the Jarawas were ousted from the vicinity of Port Blair by the Aka-Bea(da) with the support of the British which made Jarawas annoyed and provoked to become hostile towards the outsiders. To them, the area from where they were driven out, was the land of their ancestors and the forest to them was sacred not only for shelter but also for hunting and food gathering so the destruction of forest and forceful occupancy of their homeland made them revengeful. This was the beginning of a long bizarre era of enmity and hostility.

There was pressure on the Jarawas to submit and follow suit but they refused to succumb and for more than a century, they remained isolated and hostile. In 1872, they reportedly attacked the establishment first and subsequently up to 1930, punitive action was taken to cow them down by the British Administration. Thus the Jarawas faced attacks from both the sides, the Great Andamanese and the British. Thus fighting a defensive battle on two fronts, the Jarawas were forced to move to other parts of South Andaman.[16]

Even during the World War-II, the Japanese Occupation forces in these islands also followed the oppressive measures to quell Jarawas and often strafed their camps which made them more aggressive. Besides innumerable attacks during the British rule, seventy six encounters took place between

1946 and 1961 in which fifteen lives were lost on the side of the settlement and many Jarawas were killed.[17]

After 1947, the pressure on the Jarawa community further increased with the settlement of Bengali refugees from East Pakistan and other migrants around the Jarawa Reserves. With the expansion of settlement areas, their hunting ground has shrunken further, their access to water resources has been endangered and intrusions by unauthorized hunters and fishermen have affected their natural resources of food supply.

Destruction of forest to facilitate settlements and construction of the Andaman Trunk Road cutting through the 30 sq. miles Jarawa Reserves forest, made it convenient for reckless settlement and wilful encroachment. Din and bustle of the labour force and high cracking sound of the movements of bulldozers and caterpillars have shattered the peace and tranquility of the forest. All these hindrances posed a continuous threat to the Jarawas.

Hence out of hostility and in search of food, they used to raid the houses of the settlers of the fringe villages who to the contrary sneaked into the Jarawa reserves for hunting, collecting honey and rasin, fishing and even for stealing the Jarawas artefacts.

Peace Mission

Thus to prevent the incursions of the Jarawas into the inhabited areas of the settlement villages as well as to protect the Jarawas from encroachment of the poachers, a string of fourteen Bush Police posts with a strength of 140 men, was set up all along the Jarawa reserves.

After the Independence, the Andaman and Nicobar Administration has been following Portman's policy of sending friendly expeditions and treating kindly the captured Jarawas in order to win them over. The Administration resorted to gifts dropping mission in the Jarawa areas to express goodwill. Initially the Jarawas were reluctant but in due course they relented a little and expressed friendly gesture in February 1974 which was a great breakthrough.

In 1996, a young Jarawa boy named Ennui who had fractured his leg, was brought to the hospital at Port Blair and treated successfully. After full recovery, he was sent back to his jungle area with plenty of food items and other gifts. He carried the message of friendship. It was a major milestone in the history of friendly contact. This paved the way for friendly contacts with a major group of the Jarawas.

Considerable care was taken not to harm them in any way and gifts were being dropped in their area every month on the full moon night for their apprehension. Thus the Administration was successful to win them over. Ultimately in 1997, the Jarawas shed their age-old hostility and yielded to the policy of conciliation and started friendly interaction with outsiders.

Unfortunately such interaction of the Jarawas with the non-tribals has brought a lot of changes in their way of living. Other than traditional bows and arrows, digging sticks, woven baskets, etc., they now have cooking pots, dah, plates etc. They are now more and more dependent on the government supply, i.e., cooked food, dress and other provisions. They have fallen a prey to drugs especially the chewing varieties, viz., pan, zarda and tobacco. Without provocation or persuasion, they themselves come out from jungles to seek alms from the non-tribals or tourists. The hand-outs are mostly fast foods which are totally unhygienic affecting their health badly.

At the time of the establishment of the Penal Settlement, they were roughly estimated around 600 and by now they are reduced to about 200. Though the Andaman and Nicobar Administration has taken several actions for the protection and well-being of the Jarawas, the High Court of Calcutta in response to a Public Interest Litigation, issued some directives to the Central Government and the A&N Administration.

In pursuance of the directives, the A&N Administration has taken the following measures.

i) Prevention of unauthorised contact of the non-tribals with the Jarawas *ii)* Demarcation of Jarawa tribal reserves

iii) Providing health cover in the Jarawa territory itself as far as possible

iv) Control of traffic on A.T.R. near the Jarawa reserves, (territory) through a convoy system to prevent interaction of a traveller with the Jarawas

v) Withdrawal of non-tribal officials as far as practicable from the Jarawa reserves area

vi) Administration has associated itself in the study of the Jarawas through an expert committee notified by the Ministry of Home Affairs as per the directions of the High Court and organissed seminars/open discussion with the experts of National and International repute/NGOs and others

vii) The Central Government and the Andaman and Nicobar Administration are formulating the policy and programmes for the welfare of the Jarawas on the basis of the inputs received from the seminars and the report of the expert committee for submission to the High Court for further orders within the time specified by the court

Sadder is the fact that so long they were hostile, they could protect their identity and their way of living remained unspoilt and their culture grew undeterred but with their surrender to the aggressive civilization and submission to the allurement of gifts and to the threat of firearms, they have not only given up their hostility but also lost their values and culture as they are to survive at the mercy of the outsiders and become dependent on the Administration for sustenance.

The A.N. Administration and the Andaman Nicobar Adim Janajati Vikas Samity are aware of all these hazards and actions are being taken to promote the welfare of the Jarawas but the efforts to civilize the Jarawas to the human level are in a quandary. Even the villagers of Triur, Manpur, Collinpur, Templemyo, Kadamtala, Kalsi, etc., around the Jarawa reserves are aggrieved of the government's one-sided policy to preserve the Jarawas at the cost of life and property of the non-tribals.

R. Raja Ram, Up-Adhyaksh, Zilla Parishad states emphatically: "The police and the administration follow the axiom: Jarawas can do nothing wrong and act accordingly. If the villagers oppose the stealing spree of the Jarawas and in a tussel, if a Jarawa is injured, the villager will end up in jail".

Beer Bahadur, Sarpanch remarks that Andaman Adim Janjati Vikas Samity used to supply coconut and banana to the Jarawas and now stopped the practice so the Jarawas started to collecting them stealthily from the plantations of the villagers. They also pick-up anything and everything as they find in the yards of the villagers such as areca nut, drum, utensils, rice, sugar, tools, etc.

Mahadev Majhi, Pradhan of Tusnabad Panchayat observes that before the famous Bakhtawar Singh's contact with the Jarawas, they never entered the village. "We were better off during that period of hostility".

Indeed the Jarawas are very much conscious of the provisions of Protection of Aboriginal Tribes Regulation and cunningly draw maximum benefits from it. If the things go against their wishes, they lodge complaints against the villagers. Often the police react to appease them and villagers suffer.

Govind Raju,[18] alias Raz Andamani has rightly remarked, "They (Jarawas) are going through a difficult period of churning. They want to switch from their traditional to modern way of life....They like the comfortable bed, timely food without hard labour, the TV programmes, the clothes, etc. To them it comes as a rude shock when they are pushed back to jungle after the pampering."

Beer Bahadur states: "They take cooked food, they use modern gadgets like flashlight, match boxes. They demand that their children be taught in school, they know trading, stealing and lying, attributes of modern civilization".

Indeed, the Jarawas crave for a new life and the villagers want to lead a peaceful life. The Jarawas have learnt how to frighten the villagers with their arms or by lodging a silly complaint of harassment against them. The villagers live in mortal fear of the Jarawas and are scared of police excesses. The Andaman and Nicobar Administration is in a dilemma to keep Jarawas at ease and villagers at bay.

Both the Administration and the A.N.A.J.V.S. should plan in such a way so that the Jarawa must emerge not as a begger or burglar but as producer to yield one's own food. They must learn the value of one's honest labour. Moreover, efforts should be made to develop cordial relations between the Jarawas and the villagers keeping in mind the opinion of Govinda Raju that intellectual discourses, academic discussion and media hype might benefit, but certainly not the Jarawas who are at the end of the precipice.[19]

(D) SENTINELESE

Another Negrito community inhabiting the North Sentinel Island about 47 kms. situated south west of Port Blair, is referred to as the Sentinelese, an offshoot of the Onge-Jarawa tribe who have developed a distinct character due to their total isolation and inhabitance in a separate island ushering hostility towards outsiders whoever dare approach the island.

The Sentinelese are dark skinned, well-built with bark strips around their biceps and amazingly long arrows tucked in their bark belts. Apparently with bark belts they resemble the Jarawas wearing bark belts around their chest with only difference that the Jarawas use to tuck knives made of shells in their bark belts instead of arrows as the Sentinelese do.

Even now the Sentinelese are so hostile that they receive outsiders by shooting arrows, hurling stones and driftwoods. Their arrows are made of a six-foot cane shaft tipped with a scrap of iron fastoned to a point lashed with bark.

Apart from ship-wrecked sailors, no one has ever set foot on the island of the Sentinelese so knowledge about them is scanty or fabricated. Owing to their isolation and hostility, they still have not suffered the trauma of intimate contact with civilized men. As they could not be made victims of the civilized men, the Sentinelese are probably the world's only palaeolithic people belonging to the pure race and surviving today without any knowledge about the outside world.

During March, 1867 Homfray[20] who succeeded Rev. Corbyn[21] in 1864 ventured to land on the North Sentinel Island in search of runaway convicts but refrained from landing as his accompanying Andamanese were terrified on seeing the belligerent Sentinelese on the shore with bows and arrows. In successive visits, Portman also came across a few of them on the seashore. This sort of pursuits went on but no attempts were successful to win over their friendship. Even after the Independence while the Jarawas had surrendered and yielded to the policy of conciliation, the Sentinelese remain hostile till recently.

However, it has been decided to leave the Sentinelese undisturbed in their small island and vigilance has been kept around their territory to ensure against corrupting contacts from outside. Though occasional dropping of gifts to augment their resources and to infuse goodwill is all that is being done at present, no serious attempts to conciliate them have been made so far on account of the distance of the island from Port Blair and for the same reason, the Sentinelese unlike the Jarawas do not interfere in the activities of the settlers.

In 1950, a policy of protection was adopted towards all the tribal peoples of India. However, in their zeal to improve economic, social and educational conditions of the tribals, welfare organizations have pushed assimilation more than protection. They often ignore the prediction of Jawaharlal Nehru, "There is no point in trying to make them a second rate copy of ourselves. We do not mean to interfere with their way of life but want to help them live according to their own genius and tradition.

Although the aboriginal tribes of the Andaman Islands are declared as a scheduled tribe under section 243(2) of the Constitution of India, in May, 1959 by the President of India proper steps have been taken so that it would not lead to further deterioration in their numbers. And to ensure the rights delegated to them as scheduled tribes, keeping in mind what Rajiv Gandhi said in an interview with UNI on 27.9.1985: "...the adivasis have been so deprived to be done to provide them facilities and opportunities on an equal footing. Our basic objective is to help them develop without losing their identity, particular way of life and culture".

The Andaman and Nicobar Administration makes periodical ventures to drop goodwill gifts like a tethered pig, utensils, coconuts, bananas, colourful baskets and lengths of red cloth which these aborigines like most. While the gift dropping party retires offshore, the Sentinelese arrive. An Onge accompanying the party shouts in his dialects, "We come in peace but the message falls to deaf ears". Though all the Negritos speak dialects with the same linguistic base, differences in vocabulary prevent communication still the goodwill mission is going on.

The Andaman Nicobar Adim Janajati Vikas Samity (ANAJVS), an autonomous body was created in 1976 under the auspices of the Chief Commissioner with the aim to look after the welfare of the primitive tribes of these islands and to implement approved schemes and programmes for the benefit of the Sentinelese and other tribal people. Certain restrictions have been imposed to stop all nefarious and unequal trading with the aborigines, particularly with the Onges and the Great Andamanese, to ban the sightseeing trips in the vicinity of tribal habitats and to turn down the requests for studies in behavioural sciences, etc., in order to give respite to the tribal people from constant disturbances and exploitation. Similarly free mixing with the population has been discouraged as far as possible till the desired stage is reached for free social intercourse.

On 28th December 1985, first contact was successfully made with the Sentinelese under the stewardship of the Chief Commissioner, P.S. Oberoi. For the first time, the Sentinelese came to the contact party along with some of their ladies carrying children and without arms. They were greeted with gifts such as bananas, coconuts, iron scythes, large knives and other domestic items which they accepted gladly. This was really a breakthrough in the age old rivalry and hostility of the Sentinelese. It is expected that sooner or later, they will shed their hostility and embrace friendship with the outsiders and at the same, from the government, all out efforts should be made to wipe out negative factors responsible for depopulation and demeaning of tribal culture in order to save the Jarawas and the Sentinelese from the same misfortune that befell on the Great Andamanese and the Onges. They are in all respects considered the weakest in our neoteric society and their survival poses a challenge to our ancient heritage of tolerance and coexistence following the spirit of 'let them live' with honour and identity.

The government is anxious to bring them to such a level of civilization in which they can enjoy the minimum comforts of civilized life. It is the prime duty of the government to bring them to human level but enough care should be taken so that it would not lead to further deterioration in their numbers which is hardly 240, according to the Census of 2001.

(E) NICOBARESE

The Nicobars constitute a group of 22 islands which are situated 80 miles south of the Andamans and 110 miles west from Sumatra. The major islands are Car Nicobar, Tilanchong, Chowra, Teressa, Bampoka, Kamorta, Nancowrie, Kachal, Little Nicobar, Great Nicobar, Trinkat, Kondul and Pulo Millo. The Nicobar group has been declared as a district on 1st August 1974. Out of 22 islands, only 13 islands are inhabited by the Nicobarese. The total Nicobar district except seven villages on the east coast of Great Nicobar, has been declared as the Scheduled Tribe Reserve Area by the Nicobar Islands Regulation Act 1956. In these seven villages, 330 Ex-serviceman families have been rehabilitated during 1969-72. As to the Regulation Act, no outsider is allowed to visit the Nicobar district without tribal pass.

All the tribal villages of the Nicobar district are controlled traditionally by their own captains, say 'pradhan' but the seven villages of Ex-servicemen are under two panchayats and counted as revenue villages. Total population of the Nicobar district is 42,026, according to the Census of 2001.

Ethnological Origin

The aboriginal inhabitants of the Nicobars have been living on the present site at Nicobar since ten thousand years and it is believed that in the remote past while there were waves of migration from Indo-China during fifth to thirteenth centuries, such migration took place from Malay Peninsula to these islands, for the Nicobars and the East Indies were natural destinations. Earlier perhaps, the Negritos would inhabit these Islands[22]. Globe-Traveller G. Hamilton[23] described that the natives of Car Nicobar were of sematic feature and dress, short in stature but very well-built, active and strong. They cut hair short but the women completely shaved their heads. The men wore only a narrow strip of loin-cloth between their thighs but the women wore a dry grass lingerie dangling around the loin.

A study of the customs of the Nicobarese also leads us to believe that some of them are of Malay origin. Similarities in environments and cultures reveal a possible connection between the Nicobarese and the Malayees. The Nicobar language contains a marked Malay element. Even the people of Teressa believe that the inhabitants of Nancowry are the descendants of Malayees who used to visit the island on a fishing spree and settled there in the remote past.

The new study by the scientists[24] at the centre of Cellular and Molecular Biology (C.C.M.B.) in Hyderabad has shown that the Nicobarese share a genetic mutation commonly found among the populations in China and South East Asia. The mutation known as the "9bp deletion/insertion" is probably rooted in China and expanded via Cambodia and Thailand to the Nicobar Islands.

The Mongolian features of the Nicobarese have earlier prompted scholars to suggest that their ancestors must have come from South East Asia. The new study by the above C.C.M.B. provides solid genetic evidence for that hypothesis.

Religion

Primarily the Nicobarese are animistic and their traditional religion centres round beliefs in various spirits of nature as well as the spirits of dead ancestors.

Earlier, the Nicobarese had no conception of Supreme Being and the concept of God has perhaps been acquired quite recently from the Christian Missionaries. Down the years attempts were made to preach the gospel and provoke them to embrace Christianity. The Jesuists were the first to preach Christianity some time in 17th century but in their absence, the Nicobarese fell back to paganism. The conversion works were revived by Danish, Spanish and English missionaries. These contacts with the Europeans, no doubt, paved the way for conversion to various ecclesiastical orders.

A majority of the Nicobarese during the past three decades since the Independence, has been converted to Christianity. Now 98 percent of them are Christians and 2% are Muslims. But the Nicobarese of Chowra Island still believe in their traditional rites. They are also under the influence of "Shamans" witch doctors, that they cannot escape because they are higly superstitious. The art of witch craft with its multiplicity of charms, medicine, demon-scaring, totems etc., is practised extensively.

Firstly a group of youngsters, mainly of Mus village became the torch bearers of the Christian faith. Amongst them, John Richardson[25] for his dedication and devotion during the last thirty years as a catechist and priest was appointed the Reverend Bishop for the Nicobars in 1950. Besides his social and missionary servicecs, he translated the Bible into Nicobari dialect through Roman script. He is regarded as the father of the Nicobari community. In 1952 he was nominated as the first Member of Parliament from this Union Territory.

Trade and Economy

Since the advent of the maritime powers of Europe in India and South East Asia for trading and colonization, the Nicobar archipelago was used as a trading post and for replenishing food and fuel. Over the years, the Nicobar offered great attraction for maritime and commercial powers as stated by Captain Man[26] in his empirical books.

By 1900 A.D., Car Nicobar along with the other islands was brought under direct control of the British administration with its headquarters at Port Blair. By 1948, at the instance and guidance of the local administration, small cooperatives were formed in every village with the contributions from the householders.

The village cooperatives, called "Penam Henang" means 'all the villages together' and as a rule, every householder must sell 'copra' and 'betel nuts' to one's village cooperative.

Ellon Hinengo Ltd. is the main cooperative organ at Car Nicobar, running a shipping line also. At Nancowry, Manula-Mathai Ltd. is another cooperative society to collect betel nuts and copra by paying a fair price to the people.

The bulk of the traders, except some Burmese were mostly Muslims from southern India, Gujarat, Maldiv, Lakshadweep etc. The influence of the Muslim traders increased and resulted into matrimonial ties with the Nicobarese. Ibrahim was the first Nicobari Muslim who helped spread Islam.

Now-a-days most of the Nicobarese are non-animistic and they are either Christians or Muslims but the undercurrent of animism that was quite prevalent even 100 years ago is discernible even today in almost all the traditional activities including the 'Ossuary'[27] rites, the rites connected with the collection and consecration of bones. When the captains of 15 villages meet to participate in the rites, the occasion is called 'Kana Haum'. On that occasion, the ceremonial killing of pigs is regarded as the most humane.

The Nicobarese have developed an irresistible avidity for rice which was perhaps introduced by Burmese traders. Otherwise, their main sources of food are the gardens of Yams (sweet potatoes), bananas, taro and coconuts. They don't drink milk so they do not rear cattle and cattle are incompatible with their food habit. But canoe (Ap), a small lanky boat, holds an important place in their economy and social life.

During the Japanese occupation, the Nicobarese suffered a lot. Their food supply was totally at the mercy of the Japanese authorities. Although hard hit by the disorganization of trade, destruction of coco-palms, killing of pigs and cattle, etc., the Nicobarese were forced to work and were paid in paper currency, issued by Japan only for the use of the islanders but hardly there was anything to procure. In 1944, to combat the attacks of the allied Task Force, the Japanese tortured the innocent tribals to divulge the facts regarding espionage activities and more than hundred Nicobarese, mostly English knowing Christians were killed until the reoccupation made by the British Force in September, 1945.

Government Facilities

The Nicobarese, a hardy sea-faring people with a highly developed sense of community feeling, conduct most of their affairs with prior consultations with their respective captains. The Nicobarese have all along been on a higher level of receptivity as far as development and progressive measures go.

Apart from the sacerdotal activities of the local Nicobarese missionaries, their efforts for spreading education have been remarkable. During the fifties, five out of the six school houses were constructed by the villagers themselves. Presently there are 33 Primary Schools, 10 Middle Schools, 20 Secondary Schools and 20 Higher Secondary Schools. Compared to almost zero literacy rate, in 1971, it was 18 per cent and has been increasing continually to 39.91 per cent in 1981 and 72.49 per cent in 2001.

For the welfare of the Nicobarese, the A&N Administration pays special emphasis on expansion and development of education in the tribal areas by formulating schemes envisaging construction of schools, upgradation in their status and by providing the tribal children incentives such as free text books, travel concessions, merit scholarships and mid-day meals. With the extension of educational facilities, the enrolment of tribal students in the tribal areas at the end of the Sixth Plan (1980-85) increased considerably at the Primary, Middle, Secondary and Higher Secondary stages – 3400, 1193, 425 and 47 respectively. Adult literary Centers were also opened at various places in the tribal areas for the benefit of aged Nicobarese.

Under District Rural Development Agency (D.R.D.A.) a number of rural development programmes have been implemented. Indira Awas Yojana benefits the Nicobarese by constructing 50 twin houses and under TRYSEM, the Nicobarese are being trained in different trades for self employment. Rural electrification also finds an edge in tribal villages and non-conventional source of energy is being organized.

The Car Nicobar Island with its modern ambitions and tribal heritage with traditional dress, culture and social institutions remains a haunting memory for whoever goes there. The traditional sports like, 'boat race', 'pig-fight', etc., are unique. Their festivals also project a combination of their old tribal taboos and modern faiths – Christianity and Islamism and even animism have been wedded in Nicobarese life. For their adoptability and acumen to adjust with the changing situation, the Nicobarese are one of the most prosperous tribal communities in our country today.

The Nicobarese are no more mere predators, they have entered the stage of productive economy. They cultivate coconut gardens, pandanus, areca nut, jam, banana, lime, jackfruits, etc., and also a few vegetables. They keep large herds of domestic pigs. They also exploit the food resources of the sea and have developed a variety of harpoons, nets, hooks, dahs, etc., for fishing in the sea.

Entire Nicobar including the Great Nicobar has been declared reserved for forest and environmental protection. Campbell and Galatia, these two sites have been protected as National Udyan. Besides, these islands of the Nicobar group have been declared as wild life sanctuary. Of them, Batimilad Island and Megapod Island are famous for Nicobari pigeons and Megapod birds respectively.

Car Nicobar Island is having the largest population and Tilong Chang of Nancowry tahsil is recently declared as wild life sanctuary. Now-a-days the Nicobarese are more conscious of facilities of modern living than any other tribals. Some of them have already entered into the government services as qualified doctors, lecturers, teachers, government officials. Twelve percent of the total outlay of the Seventh Plan has been earmarked for tribal welfare and the Nicobars being the largest chunk of total tribal population in the A&N Islands, have the greatest share of this allocation. Out of 32000 population in Nicobar district, around 28000 are the Nicobarese including about 210 Shampens of Great Nicobar, are enjoying the benefits of Poverty Alleviation Programme. (Source: *The Daily Telegram*, pub. from Port Blair, 29.8.87)

The Nicobarese inhabiting 13 islands have more or less normal population distribution and are growing at a reasonable normal rate with the rest of the population of India. They have not only withstood contacts with modern civilization, but also continued to flourish after a century of close association. Of course, during this period of transition, some of their traditional beliefs and customs have lost their force and been forgotten at some places. But on the whole, the basic Nicobarese culture and rituals remain more or less intact in spite of the new ideas and the close contact with the people from the mainland. Justin[27] has rightly remarked, "Today Nicobarese youths are absorbing the values of an outside (exotic) culture at a rate which outstrips any deep thinking or careful selectivity about the kind of influence they are accepting".

(F) SHOMPENS

The Shompens, a smaller tribal group of Mongoloid race, live in the Great Nicobar Islands under the Nicobar district with an area of about 404 sq. miles. The interior tribe of the Shompens inhabit in their jungle abode close to river valleys and gorges, and another group lives close to the seashore and both the groups still live in a pre-agricultural age. They are a primitive, semi-nomadic group who have been forced back into the forest with the expansion of settlement. Notwithstanding, they still preserve their ancient cultural characteristics bearing consanguinities with the Mongoloid people living in Indonesia. C. Boden Kloss[28] visited Great Nicobar in 1901 and mentioned in his book that in 1900, the coastal Shompens numbered only 87 while the interior Shompens were estimated to be about three to four hundreds. By 1998, the Shompen population has been taken to be 214 but in 2001 their population grew to 398.

Origin

About the origin of the Shompens, different authorities have propagated different theories. Anthropologist Dr. Lidio Cipriani comments in his book, 'The Andaman Islands' that the Shompens sustain resemblances with the Mongoloid people living off the west coast of Sumatra.

Sir Richard Temple[29] observes that the origin of the Nicobarese though emerges from the Indo-Chinese race does not explain the strong Malay influence which is prominent among the Shompens of Great Nicobar and as a result of their isolated life in different places, nominal differences have developed over the years in their looks, customs and habits due to regional variations and racial dissimilarity.

According to C. Boden Kloss, these islands were originally inhabited by a race of Malay who was gradually driven towards the south by the immigration of the Indo-Chinese settlers from the coast of Burma but that in this process, there was a certain fusion of races which would account for the Malay elements in the Nicobarese today.

Boden Kloss believed that the Shompens were the last remnant of the Malay race because they have been able to maintain a separate existence in the dense forests situated in the interior of Great Nicobar.

As for the dark skin and curly hair of the Shompens, Kloss opined that there might have been a mix with Dravidian mariners who might have migrated to Great Nicobar during the reign of the Chola king, Rajendra the Second, in the beginning of eleventh century when he conquered Car Nicobar and Great Nicobar which were marked in the pages of Indian history as 'Kardipa' and 'Nagadipa' respectively.[30]

Life Pattern

Though the Shompens are semi-nomadic, wandering from place to place for food, they build temporary huts on poles of a height of 10 to 12 feet from the ground level with flat platform and roof of palm leaves. They sleep on these platforms without any bedspread. After coming into contacts with the government officials and being assured of food and medical treatment, now-a-days they have started to live at their convenience in permanent huts built by the Administration. After much inducement, they have taken up horticultural operations by utilizing seeds and saplings of different varieties being supplied to them and thereby developed some sort of attachment for their own garden.

Like the Nicobari women, the Shompen women wear a petticoat made of pounded bark of trees and men use only a strip of such bark like a loin cloth with a tail behind. After friendly interactions, the Shompens wear ordinary clothes and necklace made of beads which they got from the Nicobarese by barter.

The staple food for the Shompens is pandanus and they build their huts where the pandanus is grown aplenty. They eat the bread of pandanus pulp with fish, pork, turtle, etc. Pigs and tortoise are just boiled and eaten. Oyster is also liked by them as delicacy. Throughout the day, they chew betelnut leaves with betelnuts or tobacco leaves and lime. After chewing, they spit around.

Like the Nicobarese, the Shompens have some faith in supernatural powers and evil spirits. They also believe in priesthood or witchcraft. Polygamy and remarriage of widows are permitted in their society. Dead bodies are buried, but exhumation of the dead body by the Nicobarese is not followed by the Shompens.

The economy of the Shompens of Great Nicobar may be said to be somewhere between that of the Andamanese and the Nicobarese. Like the Great Andamanese, they go out for hunting wild pigs and collecting honey, areca nut, lemon and other plant products from the jungle. At the same lime, they also rear pigs and cultivate small gardens of coconuts and yams. Their economy remains mainly acquisitive and they barter their collections with the coastal Nicobarese of the west coast and with the Nicobarese of Kondul Island in exchange of tobacco leaves, bidi, cloth, dah, etc. But after contact with outsiders, they have started bringing their goods to Campbell Bay and they being ignorant of the value of their collections, are easily exploited by the traders. Now the Administration has taken steps to control the unscrupulous traders and the Adim Janajati Vikas Samity in consultation with the government, is on the move to implement welfare programmes for the Shompens. Hence care has been taken to see that during the heavy rains when the Shompens are unable to collect honey as the bees are not able to produce sufficient honey for lack of seasonal flowers, the exchange rate should be enough to enable the Shompens to survive considering their actual requirements adequately irrespective of whatever be the scale of issue.

According to 1971 Census, their numbers were more than 92 distributed in 13 nomadic villages, spread over a wide range of north eastern, northern and western coastal areas of Great Nicobar. They were estimated to be around 348 in 1901 but by the last Census of 2001, it is about 400. They belong to mainly four isolated groups and each of them consists of a number of families scattered over a particular area and these groups remain unknown to each other.

Although by nature, the Shompens are meek, shy and tender, only one of these four groups living somewhere in the interior forest at the mount Tuliar, sill remains hostile towards the other Shompens living in the north eastern coast and the outsiders.

Due to epidemics of influenza and polimyelitis, which raged in 1918 and 1947 respectively, their population has been reduced considerably and the reduction in population over the past years must have been a positive factor for giving up hostility. Besides the welfare policy of the Administration wisely meted out to the Shompens, may have conciliating effect on them and ultimately win their confidence.

While opening Great Nicobar Island for settlement of Ex-servicemen's families in 1964, constant care was taken to prohibit the free mixing between the Shompens and the outsiders otherwise their diseases from which they have been suffering for centuries might have been exchanged with the communicable diseases of the civilized world. Moreover, with the spread of modern civilization into the darkness of the virgin forests of Great Nicobar, it is quite likely that the ecological balance in nature enjoyed by the Shompens for centuries together may get disturbed and cause agonies in their mind.

Indeed, the Shompens need our assistance to a great extent with respect to their health and nutritional problems. In 1953, a health survey was conducted in Great Nicobar by the Government Medical Unit and also investigations on behalf of the Anthropological Survey of India were carried on among the Shompens in 1966 and again in 1974. The Adim Janajati Vikas Samity of Andaman & Nicobare Islands has taken up more detailed and systematic welfare schemes for the benefits of the Shompens and they, too come out voluntarily from the deep forest habitats for food and medical treatment of any ailment. Ultimately they have shunned their shyness and hostility and become more friendly to get the benefits of the welfare schemes. This is a great breakthrough and marks the beginning of a new era in the life of this primitive people. Meanwhile the Administration has provided educational facility to the children of the Shompens to develop their language skills and help them learn about health and hygiene.

ENDNOTES

1. "On the Origin of the Andamanese," by Dr. Lidio Cipriani.
2. Captain Haughton, Supdt. of Port Blair from October 1859 to May 1862.
3. Colonel R.C. Tytler, Supdt. of Port Blair, May 1862–Feb. 1864.
4. Administration Report, 1865-66, Chapter on Aborigines.
5. N.A.I., Home Deptt. Public Branch, O.C. No.16, 24 June, 1863.
6. Corbyn. Rev. H., the Christian Priest at Port Blair.
7. N.A.I., Home Deptt. Public Branch, O.C. No.17-20, 31 July, 1863.
8. N.A.I. Home Deptt. Public Branch, O.C. 24, 28 July, 1864.
9. Ibid.
10. Census Report 1951, Appendix A, p. xlvi
11. Portman M.V., Officer Incharge of the aborigines from 1879 to 1900, the author of 'A History of Relations with the Andamanese', vol I and II, London 1899.
12. Dr. L. Cipriani: Author of 'The Andaman Islanders', London, 1966 p. 55.
13. L.P. Vidyarthi: renowned anthropologist, visited Andaman several times to study on the tribals of the islands. His observation published in the report of ANAJVS, 1977-1991.
14. A. Radcliff Brown, Author "Andaman Islands: A Social Study", Illionois 1922.
15. Man E.H., Author, "Andaman Islanders", The Head of Penal Settlement (Officiating) March, 1968. His other book, "The Nicobar Islands", London.
16. Census Report, 1921, p 5.
17. Census Repot, 1961, part IV-V, p. 104
18. Govinda Raju: Editor, "The Light of Andaman", published from Port Blair, an erudite writer and renowned Urdu poet, member of Sahitya Academy.
19. Source : Cover Story : "Jarawas : Why this Hypocrisy", written by Govinda Raju, published in "The Light of Andaman", dt. 7 Aug., 2009.
20. Homfray, Assistant of Rev. Corbyn, revived Corbyn's policy of visiting the tribal settlements and succeeded in establishing friendly relation with them, so that they could give up their jungle life and settle down to cultivation and a life of industry. He established an

orphanage for Andamanese children.

21. Rev. H. Corbyn, Christian priest at Port Blair, was given the charge of Andaman Home. He made expeditions to the tribal camps from June 1863 to February 1864 for opening friendly communications with different tribes. Corbyn's mission was to civilize the Andamanese and make them successful in the long run.
22. Observations made by S.H. Roberts in his book, "Population Problems of the Pacific".
23. "The Travel Accounts" by Hamilton, pub. in Asiatic Researches in 1799, p.p. 337-344.
24. Scientists of C.C.M.B, Lali Singh, K. Thangraj and others. Their views published in Human Genetics.
25. John Richardson Hachevka, disciple of Rev. V. Soloman who established the first Anglican church in Car Nicobar. The spread of Christianity and education in the Nicobars is attributed to Richardson. He translated the Bible into Nicobari dialect through Roman scripts.
26. Captain Man, Executive Engineer and Superintendent of convicts at Moulemein in 1858. From March 1868 to March 1871 worked as Supdt, the Penal Settlement at Port Blair. Author of "Nicobar Pottery", "Andaman Islands", "Nicobar Islands", etc.
27. Ossuary: a feast of the dead called the Ossuary feast is held in every village of Car Nicobar every second or third year by rotation, a very laborious and costly festival.
28. Anstice Justin, himself a Nicobari, an anthropologist by professing, In-charge of A.S.I., Port Blair Branch, wrote many articles on the Nicobarese. His famous book is 'The Nicobarese'.
29. C. Boden Kloss visited the Andamans in January, 1901. Travelled on a cruise in the schooner and wrote, "Andamans and Nicobars" explaining the natural history and ethnological materials collected by him.
30. Richard Temple, Chief Commissioner, A.N.I, 1894-1904, Author, 'Andaman Language', Editor "Indian Antiquary".
31. Source: Tanjor Inscription of 1050 AD.

3

Beginning of Settlement

India has got almost 1200 islands and of these, about half, constitute the territory of the Andaman and Nicobar Islands. The total area of the islands is 8246 sq. kms. Over 80 per cent of this area is covered with dense evergreen tropical forests. The original natives who are the earliest migrants, consist of both Negritos and Mongoloids, living in these islands in their respective areas since time immemorial and in total isolation till recently.

Though the Arab and European traders mentioned about these islands sporadically in their accounts, yet no treatise on their origin is available nor any systematic study has been made to explain the course of their settlement. Hence the modern period of settlement in 1789 when the British India Government first attempted to establish a colony there to develop a safe harbour for the Royal Navy and to provide shelter to the distressed ships to escape the fury of monsoons were forced to anchor in search of fresh water and fuel.

Of course, a little earlier, the government took some interest to take possession of the islands with a view to exercising hegemony in the Deccan Plateau and monopolizing the trade route through the Bay of Bengal. When attempts to establish a harbour in the islands of Negrais in 1752 failed, attention of the British was diverted to the Andamans.

John Ritchie being assigned to conduct a survey of the islands of the Bay of Bengal visited the islands in 1777 and was the first man to emphasise on the importance of the islands. He submitted a report to the Governor General, Warren Hastings, explaining the great utility of the islands[1].

Capt. Thomas Forrest was the first person who felt the necessity to establish friendly contact with the aborigines of the Andamans as most of them were not hostile to outsiders[2] but he was not paid any heed to.

In 1788, Captain Buchannan after visiting the coasts of the Andamans explained the importance of the islands to the East India Company[3].

Apart from all these reports, what made the East India Company worried was the regular information of increasing numbers of Malay piracies and gruesome experiences of the shipwrecked sailors to encounter the hostile aborigines.

It was only during the rule of Lord Cornwallis, the authorities took up the matter seriously and decided to send a survey team to Andaman under Lt. Archibald Blair of the Indian Navy. In the survey team, Lt. Robert Hyde Colebrooke was also included to accompany Blair.

In a letter dated 19 December 1788, Blair was clearly instructed about the purpose of the research, "The material object of the survey is to ascertain in which part of the island, there are good harbours and which it would be most suitable for the Company's advantage to project one".[4]

He was further instructed to ascertain about natural and vegetable production, reigning winds and currents, rise and set of tides, variation in atmosphere, changes in climate due to stormy weather, availability of fish, wood, water, clay, lime and stone. Commercial possibilities of timber and sea-shells available in large quantities in the Andamans was also to be determined.

As regards the aborigines, Blair was advised to follow a conciliatory policy to win their confidence by means of "persuasion, presents and other allurements but not by force or deceit".[5]

With the assignment to do survey in and around the coast of the Andamans, Lt. Blair left Calcutta on 20 December, 1788 and reached Interview Island on 29 December. While surveying the coast towards the south, Blair visited a small island where he first met a few aborigines but no untoward incident happened. Later he examined the shores of South Andaman, Baratang and Barren Island which he found erupting violently. After spending several months in the Andamans to complete the survey works, Blair returned to Calcutta in the first week of June and submitted his report to Lord Cornwallis on 9 June, 1789.

Lord Cornwallis was very much impressed for the clarity of the report containing valuable information about the land, vegetation, flora and fauna, winds, tides, climate, etc. supported by charts and maps whenever necessary.

About the hostility of the aborigines, Blair opined very prudently, "...it would not be difficult to establish a friendly entrance with them and that with proper attention and management they might be made useful to settlers."[6]

On 12 June, 1789 in the meeting of the Governor General in Council, it was decided to take possession of the islands in order to establish a safe harbour for the British fleet in the event of war and to provide shelter to the vessels of the East India Company to escape the fury of monsoons. Besides, to prevent the predatory activities of Malay and Chinese pirates and to exercise the hegemony of the British Government, it was felt necessary to establish a colony, not a penal colony in the islands.[7]

But Dr. Mouat believed that Blair was entrusted to establish the first convict colony in Andaman.[8]

The new task was assigned to Lt. Blair who sailed for Andaman on 17 September, 1789 with some artificers, labourers and a few soldiers and reached on 28 September Chatham Island where he built a wharf and cut a path through jungles from Phoenix Bay to Navy Bay. Thus the first ever attempt to establish a settlement in the Andamans was made in October, 1789 and named Port Cornwallis, now called Port Blair.

This was the beginning of the ingress of the non-aboriginals into the tribal territory and for the first time convicts from British India were deported there "...to help in its development precisely as they were sent to Bencoolen and afterwards to Penang, Malacca, Singapore, Moulmein and Tenessarin province."[9]

Within a few days, with the help of the convict labourers, Blair was able to clear some area and make a redoubt on which the Union Jack, the British colours were hoisted to proclaim the official possession of the island by the British.[10]

By August, 1790, the settlers numbering one hundred and nineteen had cleared the greater portion of the site in Chatham Island and planted vegetables and fruit trees on it.[11] Meanwhile the settlers who had paid visits to Calcutta in batches for their private affairs, were allowed to take their families to the new colony.[12]

Earlier on 13 April, 1790, Blair had reported that north east harbour in North Andaman (now at Diglipure) was deserving the attention of the Governor General for its advantageous position to start settlement work. Consequently in November, 1790, Commodore Cornwallis after visiting the site informed his brother, Lord Cornwallis, "I think north east harbour vastly superior for a fleet of Man-of-War to Port Cornwallis..", and recommended to shift the colony from its present site in the southern harbour to the new harbour in the north east islands.[13]

On 16 October, 1792, the final order was issued for the shifting of the settlement to the new harbour and the object for the settlement was to develop a naval arsenal base there.

On 5 November, 1792, the Governor General engaged Captain Alexander Kyd of the Bengal Engineers to be the Superintendent of the new settlement and advised Lt. Blair to effect the shifting of the colony.[14]

After the abandonment of the old settlement at Port Cornwallis, Blair came to the new site in North Andaman with 360 settlers on 30 December, 1792 while Kyd took over the charge on 5 March, 1793.[15]

Captain Kyd was very optimistic to the bright future of th new settlement and started with all enthusiasm to make a success. For the welfare of the settlement, turtles from Diamond Island, now Diamond Harbour in West Bengal, rice and livestock from Achin, a harbour on the northern extremity of Sumatra and coconuts from Car Nicobar— all were brought to the new settlement for culture and cultivation. Even fruit trees were imported from Sumatra for further plantation.

But with the passage of time, the condition of the new settlement deteriorated because of insalubrious weather and incessant growth of mortality. Towards the close of 1793, the first year after the transfer of the colony, sickness prevailed to an alarming extent among the settlers. The Surgeon incharge of the Settlement reported that one-fourth of the number were quite unfit for any kind of duty, suffering chiefly from intermittent fever, ague and enlargement of the spleen, etc.[16]

Moreover, complete dependence on the government supply made the Settlement a constant burden. Extensive work for the Settlement was also too expensive as labourers were to be brought from India and other places only on higher pay.

Meanwhile the devastating rainfall in 1795 severely acted upon the health of the settlers. Many of them, even the Surgeon himself and other officers became victims of malaria and other diseases resulting into a loss of 50 lives.

According to the report of Colonel Syme who went on a mission to Ava in 1795 and visited the Settlement, there was a population of 700 including a company of sepoys.[17]

On 4 February, 1796, Kyd reported to the Secretary to the Governor General about the continued unhealth of the Settlement and proposed to abandon it.

On 8 February, 1796, the Governor General in Council decided to withdraw the Settlement "considering the great sickness and mortality... and the great expense and embarrassment to Government in maintaining it".[18]

It was further decided that the withdrawal was to be completed before the outbreak of the monsoon. Finally in May 1796, the first settlement in the Andamans was abandoned by bringing back 550 free Bengali settlers, men, women and children, the European artillery and Sepoy guards to Bengal but provisions and 270 convicts were sent to Penang.[19]

Thus the first recorded attempt to establish a non-tribal settlement in the Andaman proved futile and was abandoned after a tenure of six and a half years leaving it unoccupied till 1856.

According to Portman[20], "Port Cornwallis was perhaps the most unhealthy spot in the whole of island". He further observed that the immediate cause for this disastrous end primarily owed to the hasty decision of Commodore Cornwallis who considered the strategic importance only but not the impact of the tempestuous climate and unhealthiness of the malaria-prone area. Hence the shifting of site of settlement from South Andaman to North Andaman proved a failure.

(A) SECOND SETTLEMENT

After the abandonment of the first settlement, the Andaman Nicobar Islands remained unoccupied for almost sixty years till 1856. During this period of isolation, there were only stray references and hasty mentions in the scribbles of sailors and in the accounts of European voyagers while crossing the Bay Islands. As the islands remained untenanted for several years, the Malay pirates resumed their slave trading from the islands.

The isolation of the islands was broken only in 1824 when Sir Archibald Campbell as a Commander of the British fleet carrying army to Rangoon to take part in the First Burmese War, was directed to visit Port Cornwallis.

Lt. James Edward Alexander[21] during his tour to England from India visited Little Andaman Island in November 1825.

Sir John Malcolm[22] touched the shores of the Andamans on 12 February, 1836 and reported his experiences to the British authorities.

The murder of Dr. Helfer[23], a Russian scientist engaged by the British Government to hunt for gold and other precious minerals in the Andamans was committed by the aborigines.

Many more events occurred during this period but what made the British Government extremely worried, were the horrendous experiences of ship-wrecked crews of the troop ships of 'Briton' and 'Runnymede' being drifted and crashed by a terrible cyclone on 11 November, 1844. In all six hundred and twenty heads including a few women and children had to bear with indescribable sufferings being deprived of provision, pestered and tortured by the aborigines for fifty four days[24]. This incident created tremendous commotion and made the British Government think of taking measures to protect the crews.

Again in 1849, two ships "Emily" and "Flying Fish" were wrecked and plundered by the aborigines. Even an officer of "Emily" was killed in a skirmish. All these incidents forced the East India Company to reoccupy the islands for salvaging distressed ships and crews.

On 29 August, 1855 in the dispatch to the Government of India, the Court of Directors commented on the outrages and in reply on 28 November, 1855, the Government of India directed the Government of Bengal to chalk out a plan to establish a colony and to stop the savagery of the aborigines. Coincidentally only after two years, on brutally quelling and crushing the Great Indian Revolt of 1857, the British India Government was compelled to take immediate actions to establish a penal settlement in the Andamans. Thus steps for the pacification of the aborigines might be undertaken and an abode of punishment for mutineers and other dangerous criminals whose offences had not merited the death penalty, could be built up.

However, Lord Canning, the then Governor General, expressed his opinion against the occupation of the Andaman

Islands[25]. According to him, there were only two inducements in favour of setting up a penal colony:

(a) the establishment of a penal settlement, and

(b) the obligations to make the islands safe for ship wrecked crews.

As regards the first object, while there was a number of penal settlements in Singapore, Arakan and Tenessarin, it was useless to set up a new one in the Bay Islands ignoring extremely tempestuous climate, and highly epidemic-prone area incurring fabulous expenditure of life and money.

Considering the second inducement, it was absurd to ascertain safety and security of the sailors thrown ashore being ship-wrecked and to civilize the aborigines which might take generations to achieve the goal.

Interestingly Lord Canning did not give much value to the strategical importance of the islands because he might have thought that no foreign powers would dare challenge the susperior naval strength of the British to occupy the islands.

However, enough time had been spent on discussions and correspondences between the Court of Directors and the Governor General in Council over the decision to establish a penal settlement in the Andamans. But after the outbreak of the Great Indian Revolt of 1857, there was a sudden thrust for taking an early action as to deport several thousands of rebels there after suppressing the revolt.[26]

For immediate solution of the imminent problem, "Andaman Committee" was formed on 20 November, 1857 under the Presidentship of F.J. Mouat[27] to examine the shores of the Andaman group of islands and select the best site which may be found there for the establishment of a penal settlement".[28]

The committee submitted the practical report in January 1858 recommending the old harbour site where the first settlement had been established by Archibald Blair to be the suitable place to set up a penal settlement and suggested the name of the place to be 'Port Blair' in memory of his distinguished service in discovering the site about eighty years ago.

On recommendations of the "Andaman Committee", the Governor General in Council resolved on 15 January, 1858 to establish a penal settlement in the Andaman Islands for the reception of convicts for the crimes of mutiny and other criminals convicted under sentence of transportation.

The genesis of the policy of sending Indian convicts to Andaman was supported by the cogent argument as to keep such dangerous mutineers in Indian Jail might imbibe a spirit of hatred against the British Government among the ordinary prisoners and other inmates.

Captain Henry Man, an experienced superintendent of settlement of Moulmein was sent to Port Blair to reoccupy the islands formally. In the letter of C. Beadon, Secretary to Government of India, Captain Man was instructed: "It may be assumed that the class of rebels and mutineers who are sentenced by the Civil and Military Tribunals to the secondary punishment of transportation or to imprisonment, will not include any of the worst offenders, and therefore, that the convicts with whom you will have to deal in the first instance will, for the most part, be men who have been led to the commission of crimes against the State by the example of others and not men of a desperate or unmanageable character[29]. He was vested with full judicial and executive authority over the whole of the Andamans.

Though Captain Man proceeded to annex the Bay Islands and to make preliminary arrangements, the responsibility of the new settlement was actually assigned to Dr. J.P. Walker who was appointed the first superintendent of the settlement in the Bay Islands. Lt. Man left Andaman after two months.

On 4 March, 1858, Walker left Calcutta with 200 convicts of the revolt of 1857 and Lalla Mathoora Doss, a native overseer, two native doctors, and a guard of 50 men of the old Naval Brigade. He arrived at Port Blair on 10 March, 1858 with the human cargo comprising the great heroes of the first war of Independence. Hence the date 10th March is very significant in the history of the Andaman-Nicobar

Islands. So it is celebrated to mark the beginning of settlement in the islands[30].

Of course, very little is known about the earliest convicts (political) transported to Andaman being convicted for their involvement in the great revolt of 1858.[31] But the least we know is amazing and wondrous. Among the first batch of prisoners, there were some very famous personalities, litterateurs of Urdu language, viz., Allma Fadl-e-Haqq Khairabadi[32], Moulana Liaquat Ali, Mufti-Inayat, Musai Singh, Khushi Ram Shajahanpuri (author of 'Tarikh-e-Jazirah-ye Andaman, 1861), Moulvi Ahmedullah, Yahiya Ali, Muhammed Jafar Thaneswari[33] (author of Kalapani ma'ruf beh Tawarikh' Ajiba, 1879) Qadiri (author of Jang-e-Azadi, 1859), Syed Allahabadi, Ahmed Kakaurvi, etc.

However, the residents of the penal settlement were broadly divided into two categories, the convicts and the free population. The latter consisted of the guards, the supervising, clerical and departmental staffs with their families and a limited number of trading settlers with their families besides some ex-convicts. The administration of the settlement has been discussed in the following pages.

Administrative System

During the initial period of penal settlement in Andaman, there was no rule and regulation followed by the administrators and Dr. Walker, the Superintendent of the settlement, armed with enormous powers, exercised whatever suited his whims and fancies.

In the settlement, the convicts had to live under thatched roof, to work in the scorching sun or tempestuous rain in dense forest infested with centipedes, leeches, mosquitoes, snakes, and under the constant threat of being killed by the hostile aborigines. The notorious criminals were kept under fetters even when they were put to physical labour like earth cutting, felling trees, husk pounding, brick making, grinding mustard seeds or copra in the oil mills, thrashing coir to make rope, etc. At night the truculent 'chain-gang' criminals were chained together as to bind their legs via coupling of irons while they were asleep. Flogging on slightest pretext was very common. Every inmate capable to escape was locked into an iron cellar to prevent them from fleeing.

In the letter, dated 7 May, 1858, the Secretary, Government of India, Home Department advised Dr. Walker, "The President in Council desires me particularly to caution you against being lulled in a false sense of security by the absence of any apparent intent or desire on the part of the convicts to defy our authority. The firearms of the guards should always be loaded and it should be impossible for any number of convicts by a rush or otherwise, to get them into their hands for a moment and the guard should always be ready to fire at once on the shortest notice".

Thus being supported by the Government, Dr. Walker resorted to the means of cruelty and inflicted brutality as and when he desired. As a result the brutal treatment and inhuman torture forced the convicts to bear with severe punishment. They were given a meager daily allowance of one anna, and nine pies, equivalent to one rupee for their food, clothing and other needs. Despite lack of balanced diet and absence of proper medical care, the convicts had to work hard throughout the day and soon became victims of various diseases like malaria, dysentery, pneumonia. So the number of escapees increased day by day.

As to Walker's report in June 1858, out of a total number of 773 convicts in the settlement, 65 died in the hospital, 140 fled away. During March and April, 1858 as many as 258 had escaped of which 88 were recaptured. Though two of them were forgiven, 86 were hanged in one day.[34] This was the nature of torture and outrageous oppression meted out by Walker. For this sort of cruel treatment, he was under constant threat to his life. On 1 April, 1859, nearly 200 Punjabi convicts conspired to murder him and he had to run away to save his life. To tackle the problem Walker not only adopted more savage measures but also sought certain steps to keep himself and other officers safe even by alluring the convicts to be dependent on the mercy of the British.[35]

Meanwhile, on 3 October, 1859 Captain Haughton succeeded Dr. Walker. Haughton followed a reformative policy rather than a repressive policy pursued by Walker. Fadl-e-Haqq Khairabadi narrated the plight of the convicts incarcerated in Andaman during the tenure of Walker, that for the mutineers, better say, freedom fighters of the revolt of 1857, transported to Andaman, the life was horrible under terrible conditions inimical to the living souls as inflicted insidiously by the British.

During the rule of Haughton, the system of convict management in the settlement began to develop. Upto his time, the settlement was directly under the Government of India but in 1861, it was ordered to be transferred to the Chief Commissionership of Burma which was delayed till 1 April, 1864. In 1862, Col. R.C. Tytler succeeded Haughton and continued his mild policy.

The Andaman penal system in sui generis, grew up on its own lines and considering the requirements of a penal settlement, out of an area of 473 sq. miles, officially 327 sq. miles were occupied containing grazing and arable lands, swamps, dense forests, harbours and inlets of the sea, hills upto 1500 ft. and small villages of the tickets-of-leave, known as self-supporters, convicts, ex-convicts and free persons, convict stations, work-shops and jails.

Indeed, the administrative system of the penal settlement in Andaman had always been independent and was never at any time totally based on the Indian prison system. Hence this had been continuously under development for almost a hundred year upto the time of its abolition in 1945.

However, in later years, the administration of the settlement was taking shape on the line of that of the Straits settlement. Captain Henry Man was instructed to exercise powers under the Mutineers Act, XIV and XV to develop the settlement. These Acts were followed by the Port Blair and Andaman Act, XXVII of 1861 since annulment and by modification of the rules by successive Superintendents and by Lord Napier[36] of Magdala as the result of an official inspection of the settlement in 1863.

Up to that time, 8000 convicts had been sent down altogether and the settlement consisted of Ross, Chatham,

Viper Island and small clearings at Aberdeen, Haddo, Mithakhari, Hope Town and Mount Harriet. Col. B. Ford took over charge of the settlement in May, 1864 and wrote the first Annual Report of the Settlement, 1864-65. He commenced the building of Viper Jail and brought 149 acres of land under cultivation.

Before him in 1863 General Man became the Superintendent and at his sincere persuasion, the Andaman and Nicobar Regulations of 1874-76 were passed by the Governor General in Council. Then bye-laws formed the core of Penal System of the Andaman and fundamental principles remained the same till 1921 when the rules were again modified to ameliorate conditions of convicts as noticed in the Andamans Administrative Circulars upto 1938.

In March, 1868 during the tenure of Man, it was decided that the penal settlement was not a prison but a place for the detention of a certain class of prisoners only, viz., transported convicts. The Andaman system for the management of Indian convicts was practically worked on rules contained in Andaman and Nicobar Manual consisting of two parts as follows:

(a) Rules and Orders issued under legal authority.
(b) Administrative and Executive Orders.

The system always rested on the Indian Prisoners Act and the Andaman and Nicobar Regulations. The rules and orders having legal authority in the Andaman and Nicobar Manual as they now stand, are:

1. Rules of the Governor General in Council for the management of transported convicts under Section 34 of Act V of 1871 (Prisoners) bearing date 29th July, 1874 and since modified by many orders of the Government of India.
2. Subsidiary Rules of the Chief Commissioner with the sanction of the Governor General in Council under section 18 of A&N Regulation of 1874, dated 4th December, 1874 and continued under section 33, A&N Regulation, 111 of 1876.

3. The Governor General in Council's Rules for licenses to reside under section 26 of A&N Regulation, dated 30 December, 1881.
4. Bye-laws of the Superintendent, section 32 (4), A&N Regulation 111 of 1876 and Rule VI of the Governor General in Council's Rules for transported convicts, 1874.

These bye-laws are known as Settlement Standing Orders and are included in the Manual and issued whenever necessary. The Prisoner's Act, 1874 had been repealed by the Prisoners Act (III) of 1900 and though no rule-making power is conferred by the new Act in this connection, the present rules of the Governor General in Council and the bye-laws referred to therein were still in force under the General Clauses Act X of 1897, Section 24.

In 1868, General Man took up the administration as the Chief Commissioner and formally introduced the discipline and system of the Strait's Settlements[37] which were followed with modification in the penal settlement in Andaman till its abolition in 1945.

In 1869, the settlement was removed from the control of the Chief Commissioner of Burma and placed again under the direct orders of the Government of India and in 1870, it was brought under the jurisdiction of the High Court of Calcutta.

On 16 April, 1869, the islands of the Nicobar Group were formally occupied and placed under the control of the Superintendent, Port Blair.

A penal settlement was also established at Nancowry harbour and it continued till 1888.

In 1872, the Chief Commissionership of the Andaman and Nicobar Islands was created and General Steward became the first Chief Commissioner of the islands.

In 1975, General• C.A. Barwell succeeded General Steward. Barwell received the Andaman and Nicobar Regulations, Section 111 of 1876 which consequently superseded the previous one and was followed by various special rules and orders which with the Superintendent's own bye-laws (Settlement Standing Order) were consolidated into the Andaman and Nicobar Handbook drafted by Captain Protheroe, Deputy Superintendent of the settlement.

In 1879, Col. T. Cadell[38] succeeded Gen. Barwell and his administration and the settlement for thirteen years until 1892 is memorable in many a way. He took steps for agricultural and forest development. Due to his efforts, the Forest Department was established under A&N Administration.

Henceforth penal settlement in the Bay Islands was administered by the Chief Commissioner, one Superintendent with a Deputy and a staff of Asst. Superintendents and Overseers - almost all of them were Europeans and all of the wardens were natives of India. All the petty supervising staffs themselves were convicts. There were special departments—Police, Medical, Commissariat, Forests, Marine and so on. All civil officers were invested with special powers over convicts who were treated with strict orders and punitive measures.

Pattern of Settlement

During the early period of settlement, the convicts were mostly engaged in clearing jungles, reclamation and constructing buildings and roads. Mutineers were virtually freedom fighters and not habituated in hard labour. Some of the works imposed upon them such as cutting massive trees and woods in dense tropical forest, preparing bricks and lime in the kiln, extracting logs in the scorching sun or torrential rain under the constant threat of attacks from the aborigines—all these were often really so difficult and toilsome that every convict would try to run away in fright and many committed suicide when they were not able to get back home.

To incite a terror-phobia among the convicts, on 8 October, 1858, a small island named Viper Island in front of Port Blair was developed as the first open air prison where mainly hardcore criminals called 'Chain-gang' were kept for punishment and rigorous labour. The first gallows was built there on a hilltop so that it could be seen from far off places to infuse terror.

The Provincial Government in consultation with the penal settlement authorities and considering the seriousness of the offence, decided to send convicts from almost all parts of India being sentenced for transportation to Andaman. Thus the dreaded sobriquet 'Kalapani' was in common parley among the convicts to feel shivering down their spine on listening the name itself. Then transportation meant nothing less than banishment keeping convicts in total isolation from their homes and relations, from their known environment to abysmal destinations.

On arrival from the mainland, the convicts were first confined in the jail for six months where the discipline was severe but the work was not very hard and they were not paid any allowance for labour.

For the next three years, the life-convicts would live in barracks at convict-stations and go out to do hard works under strict supervision during day time but remain locked up at night.

For the next five years he was considered as labouring convict on a pay-roll of very small amount.

After completion of ten years in imprisonment without any adverse report, the convict was entitled to receive a ticket-of leave being termed as 'self-supporter' and thereby eligible to live in a village. He could marry a female convict or send for his family. He could do farming, keep cattle and earn in his own way but was not free and could not leave the village at his own will or enjoy the civil rights.

After completion of his sentence for twenty or twenty five years with approved character, he was released finally. At the beginning, he was assisted with house, food and tools and was not required to pay any tax or cess but after three to four years, he was charged with every public payment.

But the term 'convict' was to follow all the rules of the jail and released on the merit of good conduct after the expiry of their sentences.

Classification of Convicts

While in the settlement, the convicts were divided up in several ways. The main economic division consisted of labouring convicts and self-supporters. The former group was to do all the labour of the place, skilled or unskilled, but the latter one was to be engaged in agriculture and food supplies.

The Commissariat division was divided into rationed and non-rationed groups. All the labouring convicts belonged to the rationed group and the non-rationed group comprised the self-supporters along with some of the labouring convicts.

The financial division meant for the classes indicated those with and those without allowance consisting of numerous divisions.

For supervision, obedient convicts were engaged as Jamadar, Tindal, Peon, etc., having monthly allowances of different slabs. For the invalids there were allowances according to classes.

For convicts without allowances, there were sub-divisions like 3rd class, chain-gang, domestic servants and self-supporters. Among them, self-supporters would enjoy monthly pay while engaged as compounders or in other government jobs.

Female convicts were dealt with less rigorously and engaged in supervision as Jamadarni, Tindalani, Daffadarni or put to labouring classes or considered for ticket-of leave or self-supporter. They were allowed to marry male convicts of the same category.

There were also disciplinary gangs on account of bad character on arrival or while in the settlement. They were marked 'D' for doubtful ticket-holder and also known as Cellular Jail prisoners.

All the convicts were pressed to learn Urdu, the lingua franca of the settlement. It was also the vernacular of the local born people whatever their descent. With the help of the common language, the convicts could mix up or discuss among themselves whether in barracks, boats or on work place. Every care was taken to split up communities except on matter of daily common concern, the convicts would be unable to converse confidentially. The 'D' ticket holders came about in this way.

Prisoners in the 3rd class were obliged to wear wooden neck-ticket on which the convict number, the section of I.P.C. for his conviction, the date of his sentence, the date for release—all these were mentioned. If the convict was of doubtful character, it had a 'D', if one of a gang of criminals it had a star, if a life-convict it had 'L' the presence or absence of 'A' showed the class of ration.

Free and Convict Districts

To make the less arrogant and obedient convicts unctuous, Walker had planned to set up thirty two villages in the first phase between Port Blair and Port Mouat to accommodate 421 free-settlers. The Government of India also encouraged these convicts to bring their families from the mainland so that they would be busy among themselves and dare not violate rules of the settlement so that peace would be maintained.

But very few families were prepared to cross the sea for fear of losing their caste. Notwithstanding, the settlement grew with the few arrival of families and with the marriages held between the desirous male and female free-settlers.

"There is a sharply marked division of the settlement in what is known as the 'free' and 'convict' portions by which the free-settlers living in villages are separated from the villages of the ticket-of-leave (self-supporter) convicts. Every effort is made to prevent unauthorized communication between these two divisions. No adult person can enter the settlement without permission or reside there without an annual license, and certain other necessary restrictions are imposed on him as to his movements among, and his dealing with the convicts etc., on pain of being expelled from the settlement or punished under its laws".[39]

The free subdivisions were located at Ross, Haddo, Aberdeen and Garacherama but the convict sub-divisions were at Viper and Wimberleygunj.

The penal settlement was divided into two districts and four sub-divisions which remained constant but their distribution between the districts varied from time to time. Two districts were Eastern district with Aberdeen being the headquarters, consisted of the sub-divisions—Ross, Haddo and Garacherama, and other one was Western district with Viper island being the headquarters and Wimberleygunj being its sub-division. Within the sub-division, there were stations, places where labouring convicts were kept and villages where either free-settlers or self-supporters would live.

In the following Table[40], districts-wise sub-divisions, convicts stations and villages in details have been stated.

EASTERN DISTRICT

Ross Subdivision

	Stations	
Ross	North Corbyn's Cove	Middle Point
North Bay		Rutland Island
Mount Harriett	Madhuban	
	Villages	
South Point		Aberdeen
	Haddo Subdivision	
	Stations	
Phoenix Bay	Rangachang	Minnie Bay
Haddo	Garacherama	Pahargaon
Tea Garden		
Navy Bay		
	Villages	
Chatham	Bumlitan	Austinabad
Phoenix Bay	Taylerabad	Pahargaon
Janglighat	School Line	Lamba Line

contd...

Niagaon	Garacherama	Dudh Line
Birch Ganj	Protheroepore	
	WESTERN DISTRICT	
	Viper Subdivision	
	Station	
Viper Island	Port Mouat	Namunaghar
Dundas Point	Elephant Point	
	Villages	
Mitha Khari	Port Mouat	Maglutan
Namunaghar	Dhani Khari	Baghelsinghpura
Ograbaraj	Homfray Ganj	Nawashahr
Chauldari		
	Wimberley Ganj Subdivision	
	Stations	
Shore Point	Kalatang	Bajajagda
Goplakabang (including Middle Straits)	Jatang	Bindraban
	Villages	
Bamboo Flat	Bindraban	Tusonabad
Stewart Ganj	Anikhet	Manpur
Wimberleyganj	Cadell Ganj	Temple Ganj
Kadakachang	Hobdaypur	Alipur
Mathura		

Construction of Cellular Jail

In 1885, the Government of India deputed Sir Charles James Lyall and Surgeon-Major Sir Alfred Lethlridge, Inspector General of Jails of Bengal to investigate the penal system in the Andamans. They visited Port Blair in January, 1890 and submitted their report on 26 April, 1890.[41] They suggested a good many changes chiefly in the direction of increased penalty and discipline. They felt that the existing penal system in Andaman had no deterrent effect on the criminals so the convicts in India preferred transportation to the Andaman Islands than their imprisonment in an Indian jail. They were in favour of segregating female convicts and encouraging released convicts to settle in Andaman.

The Government of India agreed to their suggestions and decided to convert the settlement from an almost purely agricultural institution into a largely industrial one, in order to construct the building required mainly from local resources to accommodate the convicts in the first instance in one complex and to increase the rigour of punishment.

On the basis of the report of Lyall and Lathebridge, the construction of the Cellular Jail commenced in October, 1896 and was completed in 1906 when Sir Richard Temple was the Chief Commissioner. The main idea behind the construction of the Cellular Jail was to keep largest number of revolutionaries as well as hardened criminals condemned to long term imprisonment at a minimum cost and to run only by a few personnels with maximum efficiency. Only one sentry vigilant at the central tower could keep watch on all seven wings of the Cellular Jail housing 663 cells, all separate and isolated in order to minimize the chances of dialogue among the convicts. The jail was so constructed that the front portion of one wing was to face the back side of the other wing. Hence the degree of segregation had become terribly unbearable[42].

Though the revolt of 1857 was brutally quelled, the unquenchable thirst for freedom and indomitable urge for achieving martyrdom could not be subdued. The brave heroes of Wahabi movement, Moplah revolt, Manyam rebellion (Rumpa revolt), Manipuri and Tharawardy uprisings, etc., fought against the British tyranny and many of them were transported to Andaman on the charge of treason or sedition.

Indeed, the penal settlement in Andaman grew with the arrival of the freedom fighters along with thousands of dreaded criminals. Initially, attempts were made to accommodate all these people in different convict stations at Viper Island, Navy Bay, Phoenix Bay, Brichgunj, Dundus Point, etc., but the Andaman authorities faced innumerable problems to enforce discipline and ascertain safe custody of the convicts. Hence it was urgently felt to have a large jail complex not only to accommodate all the convicts inside the common periphery but also to provide spaces to grow up industrial centers to engage the convicts. The policy of the Government of India was then directed towards the conversion of the penal settlement into a self-supporting settler's colony, comprising ex-convicts and their families who had decided to settle in Andaman.[43]

ENDNOTES

1. National Archives of India, New Delhi, Home Deptt., Public Branch, Misc. vol. no. 77, p. 41.
2. Ibid, Public Branch, O.C. No. 43-44, 28 April, 1783.
3. NAI, Home Deptt., Public Branch, O.C. No. 30, 10 March, 1788.
4. N.A.I. Secret Deptt, Proceedings Vol, 22, Dec. 1788.
5. N.A.I. Secret Deptt, Proceeding Vol. 22. Dec. 1788, p 47-88.
6. N.A.I. New Delhi, Secret Deptt. O.C. No. 6 to 29, 30 Dec. 1789.
7. N.A.I. Secret Deptt. Progs. Vol. 12 June 1789.
8. Adventures & Researches among Andaman Islands, p 18.
9. Census Report p 258, 1901.
10. N.A.I. Home Deptt. Public Branch, O.C. No. 3, 3 Feb. 1790.
11. N.A.I. Home Deptt. Public Branch, O.C. No. 3, 3 Feb. 1790.
12. N.A.I. Home Deptt. Public Branch, O.C. No. 3, 18 April. 1792.
13. Ibid. O.C. No. 4-4A, 13.7.1791.
14. N.A.I. Home Deptt. Public Branch, O.C. No. 1, 5 November. 1792.
15. N.A.I. Home Deptt. Public Branch, O.C. No. 4, 1 February, 1793.
16. N.A.I. Home Deptt. Public Branch, O.C. No. 7-15, 7 Oct. 1793.
17. A Mission to Ava, by Col. Syme.
18. N.A.I. Home Dept, No. 5, 8 Feb. 1796.
19. Ibid, O.C. No. 30. 23 May, 1796.
20. M.V. Portman, Incharge of Andaman Home from 10 July, 1879-1900, Author, 'A history of our relations with the Andamanese', London 1897, 'Exploration and Survey of Little Andaman, 1888.

21. Lt. J.E. Alexander: Served His Majesty's 13th Light Dragons and attache to the Suit of Col. MacDonald Kinnier, Envoy Extraordinary to the court of Tehran in 1825. He wrote an interesting account of Little Andaman.
22. Sir J. Malcolm: Joined the service of East India Company in 1782, wrote 'Political History of India' in 1811, 'History of Persia' in 1815, appointed Governor of Bombay in 1827.
23. Helfer, Dr. Johann Wilhelm, a geologist by profession, a naturalist having profound knowledge of plants and animals, visited Andaman in a schooner, named Catherine along with his wife in search of gold but the aborigines killed Dr. Helfer in 1989.
24. The account of the above wreck published in 'Englishman' from Calcutta in 1845 – reproduced in 'A History of our relations with the Andamanese' in vol, 1, p 156 by Portman.
25. National Archives of India, New Delhi, Home Deptt. Public. Branch, O.C. No. 79, 6 Aug. 1858.
26. N.A.I. Dispatch No. 37 of 1856, dated 1 October, 1856.
27. Monat, Fredrick John (1816-97), F.R.C.S., 1844: Served in India as Dy. Inspector General, Bengal Army, deputed to survey Andaman in 1858, author of Adventures and Researches among Andaman Islands, 1864, p. 301.
28. N.A.I., Home Deptt. Judicial Branch, O.C. No. 14-27, 15 January, 1858.
29. N.A.I, Govt. Communique, Home Judicial Deptt. O.C. No. 21. dated. 15.01.1858.
30. "Black Days in Andaman & Nicobar Islands," 2004, p.54 by Rabin Roychowdhury, the author of the present book.
31. No reliable record is available. R.C. Majumdar remarked in his book, "Penal Settlement in Andamans", p 233, "An ex-Political Prisoner of the Cellular Jail estimates the number (of the mutineers) to be about three thousands. The number 3000 seems to be a highly exaggerated figure."
32. Fadl-e-Haqq Khairabadi (1797-1861), a renowned scholar of Islamic studies, a literary personage, especially in Arabic literature, issued a fatwa-e-jihad against the British, drafted the first constitution of India, deported to Andaman on the charges of treason for his role in the revolt of 1857, while in confinement in Andaman, wrote two of his famous political treatises, i.e., "Alsuratui India" and 'Alfitnatui India" on cloth pieces and papers with soft charcoal and pencil, secretly sent to his son at Khairabad through another prisoner, Mufti-Inayat Ahmed-Kakurvi, the books reflected his life and the appalling condition in Andaman jail, died on 12

February, 1861 at Port Blair and buried near seashore on way to Corbyn's cove, now a well known sacred place regarded as Mazar.

33. Thaneswari, Mohd. Jafar : A well known Wahabi leader, arrested and sentenced to death, later reviewed and commuted to transportation to Andaman, reached there on 11 January, 1866, incarcerated in Ross Island, due to his sobriety and intelligence elevated and served as Mir Munshi at the office of the Chief Commissioner, married a female convict, spent 18 years of penal servitude, released on 9 November, 1883 and returned to Ambala, wrote a famous book, "Kalapani Ma'ruf beh Tawarikh Ajiba" describing his horrible experiences in Andaman.
34. N.A.I. Home Deptt. Judicial Branch, A. Progs. No. 66. July 1858.
35. Ibid. O.C. No. 32, 29 July, 1859.
36. Napier, Lord Robert: Joined the Bengal Engineers in 1828 at Calcutta, took part in Sikh war, 1848, Chief of Staff to Outram, 1861, Brigadier General in 1858, suppressed mutiny in Central India, Major General in 1861, Viceroy in 1863, Field Marshal in 1883.
37. N.A.I. Home Deptt. Public Branch, O.C. No. 58, 26 September, 1861.
38. Cadell Thomas: Educated at Sunderland, served during Mutiny in Delhi and Oudh, served in Central India and Rajasthan, Chief Commissioner, A.&N. Islands, 27 February, 1878, 12 December 1879, 27 November 1883, 28 April, 1889.
39. Gazetteer, 1908, p. 126 as quoted in 'Penal Settlement in Andamans' by R.C. Majumdar.
40. Ibid, p 126.
41. Ibid, p 60.
42. N.A.I. Home Deptt. Port Blair Branch, A Progs, No. 74, June 1890.
43. "Black Days in A&N Islands", p. 56 by R. Roychowdhury.

4

PENAL SETTLEMENT

After the revolt of 1857 having been crushed, hundreds of the great heroes of the first war of independence were either hanged or transported to Andaman being sentenced to life imprisonment. Most of the heroes incarcerated in the islands, went back to their native places in the mainland after the term was over but the rest of them either passed away unsung on the way while being transported or died in despair on the soil of Andaman. Though a large number of mutineers as the Britishers viewed them, had been transported to Andaman, their total number is still not known and no reliable record of the individual prisoner is available.

However, as to the information jotted in "Unsung heroes of freedom struggle in Andamans—Who's Who[1]," by Rashida Iqbal, and from other sources, it is learnt that on records, there are only 302 names of the heroes available from the sources. Out of them, 20 persons breathed their last on the soil of Andaman, 5 were hanged/killed, 4 were murdered by the aborigines and at least one committed suicide. The rest of them on being released went back to their native villages. And those who settled there, of course a few, lived infra dig and died unsung. Among them, the most prominent one was Fadl-e-Haqq Khairabadi[2] and the other one was Musai Singh[3] of Mirzapar who lived with his wife Mussammat Roop Kunwar and sons Drigpal Singh and Bhagwan Singh, and his grandson Ram Singh at Dollyganj village of South Andaman. After spending 47 years in penal servitude, he was released in 1907 at the age of 82 on 50th anniversary of the revolt of 1857.

Again in the last quarter of the 19th century, a large number of the Wahabi revolutionaries who started anti-British movement against its ruthless exploitation on the plea of collecting land revenue, was transported to Andaman as convicts but it's very difficult to discern how many of them had really settled in Andaman. In the above said book, some references of 16 Wahabis have been mentioned. Among them, the most eminent was Mohd Jafar Thaneswari who after marrying a Brahmin female convict lived in Andaman for 18 years. Abdul Rahim Sadiqpuri after 9 years of imprisonment was sanctioned ticket of leave and spent his days by running a shop at Ross Island. Ahmedullah died at Viper Island[4] at the age of 80. The rest of them, it is presumed, left the islands on being released after the expiry of their terms.

In the last decade of the 19th century, there was the outbreak of Manipuri revolt against the British tyranny in 1891 and the British officers were executed publicly. Unfortunately, the revolt was brutally crushed and the rebels were either killed mercilessly or transported to Andaman being sentenced to rigorous punishment. Indeed, no information is available to establish the number of rebels sent to Andaman or to suffice any proof in support of settlement of any one of them. It seems that all of them probably had returned to Manipur on being released. In the "Who's Who" of Andamans, some references are available about only four heroes of the Manipuri uprising and they are Angou Sana (Prince of Manipur), Aya Purel, Kula Chandra Singh and Luwang Ning Thou.

During the British period, Burmese convicts were brought to engage in the forest department or to accompany the British officials in their survey works in dense forests. On being granted self-supporter status, many of the Burmese convicts settled in Andaman.

Again after the suppression of the Tharawardy rebellion in 1935, a large number of Burmese was transported to

Andaman as convicts and most probably, some of them settled there but due to lack of documents, it's very difficult to trace their whereabouts.

The Karens from Burma were also brought to Andaman as labour force to work in jungles. In due course, they were settled and concentrated in Webi village under Mayabunder Tahsil in North Andaman.

Meanwhile other revolutionaries involved in Mopillah or Mopla revolt, Rumpa movements, etc., were also transported to Andaman and many of them were granted lands and other facilities to settle there after the expiry of their specific terms.

Similarly with the onset of the 20th century, began the second phase of transportation of political prisoners to Andaman, being convicted on the charges for their involvements in the Alipur conspiracy case in 1908, in Mandalay conspiracy case of 1916, Gadar Movement, Kasoor supplementary riot case. Nangla Conspiracy case of 1910, Barisal conspiracy case, 1912, Lahore conspiracy case, 1915, Shibpur Action case, Dacca Arms Case, 1914 etc., started and the Cellular jail had been turned into a breeding ground of patriotism. Hence with the outbreak of the First World War, the Government of India under the British decided to abandon the penal settlement. Though the transportation of political prisoners to these islands was resumed in 1932, finally all the political prisoners left Andaman and were repatriated to their respective States by January, 1938. Ultimately no one of them settled in these islands.

However, since the inception of the penal settlement, several hundreds notorious criminals on being charged with heinous crimes, i.e., murder, dacoity or arson, etc., were transported to Andaman and after spending specific period of penal servitude and on satisfactory completion of terms of rigorous punishments, they were granted the ticket-of-leave or self-supporter status. Then many of them got married to female convicts or brought back their families from the mainland and settled in the villages around Port Blair on being allotted lands by the government.

In "Penal Settlement in Andamans",[5] R.C. Majumdar observed that "although the self-supporter convict was entitled to send for his wife from India, he very seldom did so and his wife would also not, as a general rule, choose to join her convict husband across the sea, even apart from the fact that the Hindu wife would thereby lose her caste.

So the "local born"—nearly all of them—were the issues of convict marriages".

In the Provincial Gazetteer, 1909,[6] it was remarked, "A large proportion of the free settlers are 'local born', i.e., descendants of convicts born in the settlement and permanently residents there (Andaman)".

Indeed, these 'local born' people irrespective of their caste, creed, colours or culture have formed the foundation of a unique society and their progeny are true champions of nonpareil culture contributing to the emergence of a Mini-India and comprise every kind of personal character.

Since Independence, attempts have been made for the all-round regional development of the islands by throwing opportunities of settlement mainly to the East Bengal refugees and migrants from south India.

The great variety of the settlers can be classified into two broad groups—colonial settlers and latter settlers. The former one includes the Andaman Indians, better say old settlers or 'Local-borns' Moplas, Bhantu, Rumpa peasants, Karens, Burmans, etc., and the latter one, say new settlers, comprises of the refugees from East Pakistan, migrants from other States, mainly from South India, and people from the mainland on the government services or in search of jobs and to try their luck in business.

However, the details of the background of their settlement as well as their socio-cultural fruitions have been discussed in the following chapters.

(A) THE BURMESE

In the human tapestry of the island population, the Burmese in general ornated the mosaic to carve out a niche for themselves. The Burmese commonly called as 'Burmans' were brought from Burma by the British as convicts and engaged to clear jungles and to act as forest guards during 1907 and 1923.

Though the British wilfully brought the Burmese convicts to meet their requirements of labour, yet these islands were not unknown to the Burmese. Since time immemorial, the sea-faring Burmese used to come to Andaman to pirate the forest and marine products. While Tennesarim, Aracan, Moulemein ceded to the British in 1826 at the consent of the Burmese ruler, access to these islands was made easy for the Burmese and they were engaged to accompany the British to venture into the tribe-infested dense forests.

In 1905, a Bush Police Force was formed in Andaman with a Burmese Jamadar along with selected friendly Andamanese to hunt the Jarawas and to capture run away convicts.[7] In April 1873, the murder of five Burmese crews by the Onges attracted the British expedition to Little Andaman Island.

Though evidences are very scanty to prove Burmese contacts with Andaman since the remote past while they used to venture in these islands for piracy, still the Nicobarese believe that they are the descendants of the Burmese who were forced to flee from Tenessarim and seek asylum in the Nicobars[8]. In the Nicobari Folktales[9] anecdotes are there to speak well for the Burmese connection.

In 1873, to colonize the settlement areas in Nancowry[10], small plots were leased free to the Burmese convicts who were deployed there as labourers under P.W.D.[11] While the colonization scheme in Noncowry was abandoned after a few years, the Burmese convicts were brought back either to Port Blair or to Penang. In and around Port Blair, a number of villages, i.e., Phoenix Bay, Maimyo, Monglutan, Herbertabad etc., where the Burmese had settled, grew up.

Tharawardy Rebellion

During the peasant rebellion in Burma under the leadership of Dr. Saya Sen who cherished a bitter hatred for the British and was determined to drive away the tyrannical British from the land of Burma, in order to establish a free and peaceful society with the help of a rebellious peasant army raised by him and to lead them, he organized a secret association and set up its secret headquarters in the dense forest of Tharawardy in Burma. Thus this peasant movement is called Tharawardy rebellion.

Under the able leadership of Dr. Saya Sen, the fire of rebellion spread all over Burma like a wild one but emotion is helpless against ammunition. The British government resorted to the most ruthless barbaric means to crush down the rebellion which lasted for four years.

According to an official report mentioned by K.C. Ghosh in his book 'Roll of Honour', at page no. 458, it is described as follows: "In connection with the Tharawardy Rebellion in Burma, the Home Member, Burma government stated on February 24, 1933 that 274 persons were sentenced to death of whom fifty one had already been executed and the number of persons undergoing transportation for having taken part in the rebellion was 535". Thus the rebellion was brutally crushed and a large number of Burmese involved in the Tharawardy revolt was transported to Andaman.

Notwithstanding its tremendous significance in the history of Burma, it has got little impact on the Burmese settled in Andaman with only effect that the Burmese population was swelled up due to the transportation of the rebels. Baratang, Jirkatang, Thoraktang, etc., all these names hail from the Burmese origin and bear the testimony of their inhabitance in those areas. The presence of spring water, streams, nullahs, rivulets, serene atmosphere, little fear of aborigines, and plenty of arable lands attracted them to develop their own settlements in Andaman.

Social Pattern

The Burmese are strictly endogamous. They generally marry within their own community but while their population grows considerably, sometimes they do not get suitable match among themselves so they find marriage partners from the neighbouring people and inter-community marriages are not rare.

In general, the Burmese are very fond of liquor and bootlegging and often involved in smuggling and bloody scuffles. They are prone to criminal activities. But in Andaman, their life style is somehow peaceful and hospitable to other communities such as Ranchis, Bengalee, Tamil, Telegu, etc. They interact with these people sincerely in all respects, socially and economically, to maintain healthy relations among themselves.

Among the Burmese, both nuclear and extended families exist. The oldest male member of a family is regarded as the head and his advice is followed in case of marriage, death, birth and in all social or religious affairs.

Burmese women play important roles in social functions and religious festivals. Normally they don't go to work outside but remain busy in household activities.

In Andaman, the Burmese are progressive to embrace modern education, and conscious of health, hygiene and sanitation. Though the children are taught mother tongue at home, they learn Hindi and English in schools. They share public utilities such as schools, hospitals, roads, wells, electricity, transport services, tap water, ration shops, banks, etc.

In the past, the Burmese had their own village council or association of the elders elected by the villagers. It was entrusted to do welfare of the community by settling disputes, protecting the villagers during any crisis, maintaining law and order, etc. But after forming statutory 'Gram Panchayats' in 1961 in A&N Islands, the traditional village council became defunct. Now-a-days the Burmese form their own Gram Panchayat through election.

They were brought to Andaman first in the year 1907-08 and in large batches in 1923. In 1931 in Andaman, there were as many as 2953 persons of Burmese origin. After the Independence, many Burmese repatriated to their homeland and only a few families stayed back who were mostly Buddhists and their number was 421 according to 2001 census.

Occupation

The Burmese are primarily agriculturists and rice is their staple food. They also eat cereals like pulses, grams, vegetables like potatoes, onion, brinjal, jack fruit, etc. They like country liquor, aiza and delicacy like 'nappi' and many other hard drinks. They like vegetarian and non-vegetarian foods including beef, pork, venison, mutton, chicken, wild birds and various kinds of fish. They are accustomed to forest life in order to collect many of their needs, i.e., the timber as building material, edible roots, wild animals, etc. Because of their daring nature, they find jobs in the forest department and Bush Police Force. They are also fond of seafishing and marine exploitation. They are also engaged in a variety of occupations, business, private jobs, etc.

Religion

Most of the Burmese are the followers of Buddhism. They have their own temple known as Phongyi Kyanng to perform all the religious activities. One of the temples is situated at Phoenix Bay at Port Blair which houses a big statue of Lord Buddha. The priest of the temple, 'fungi' visits home to conduct special prayers and also to teach the Burmese language to the children. They treat the sick in the traditional ways by exercising spiritual power.

The Burmese bury the dead and the fungi lead the funeral procession. The dead body is laid to rest with its head lying towards the east.

The wedding ceremony is held at the bride's house during the day time and the rituals are quite similar to those of the

Hindus but the priest has no role in the wedding process which is conducted by the elders.

The Burmese celebrate many occasions such as the birth day of Goutama Buddha, Phoyamoine, Tejao, Thajamboonclo and Tadenju.

The Burmese, once posed terror to the general people passing through torrid times, have got a lot of changes in their nature. Due to close contact with the neighbouring people of different communities, they have developed good qualities, brotherly affection and fellow feelings. They now belong to the island society, keeping their own identity and traditions unaffected. As they were brought before 1942, they enjoy pre-1942 status and are eligible to get the government services and other preferential facilities provided by the government to the 'local' people.

However, the few Burmese residing in the islands have been carrying on with residential permits being renewed from year to year but still they have never evinced any desire to return to the Burmese mainland, Myanmar. Indeed, they are now an essential part of the island society.

According to the Census, 1951: "Their (Burmese) contributions both past and present towards the development of these islands and the economic life of the community are remarkable. They find it difficult, however, to adopt Indian citizenship and only a few have taken out Naturalization certificates. Non-violence is not their strong point[12]."

(B) THE KARENS

"Karen" a name adopted from Burmese, "Kayin" is a small and migrant ethnic race of Burma where they being nomads once lived on as food gatherers and hunters. They are adventurous in nature and move in the jungle like wild beasts.

They were brought from Rangoon to Andaman by one Bashir Ahmed in 1923, an agent of the British government, to work in the forest around Mayabunder to facilitate the settlement of the free holders, ex-convicts. Since March, 1925, a few hundred Karens were brought by the Christian missionaries to meet the scarcity of labourers to be engaged to clear jungles and to handle elephants of the Forest Department. Tucked away several hundred miles from their homeland in Burma, this Christian Karen community of 384 heads has been developing on its own means and labour[13].

Settlement Pattern

Initially 45 Karen labourers, all Christians, were brought to Andaman at the aegis of Rev. Lugiji and Thra San Ba from Burma in March, 1925. During 1926-27, regular settlers numbering around 250 started coming to the islands. Though they had been brought to work in the Forest Department, later they were granted land for their own settlements. For utilization of land, they had to undertake an agreement with the British government that each family in addition to some other facilities would be provided with ten acres of land including house site. Their rights over the land were to be granted by the government under the provisions of Andaman and Nicobar Land Regulation Act, 1926.

In 1928, they were granted land for their settlements in a village, named Stewartgunj by the side of a freshwater stream. As the area seemed to the Karens safe and the land fertiled so they named the village "Webi" meaning 'harbour' in their language. Webi is now under Mayabunder Tahsil in the third district, Madhyottor Andaman.

After their arrival, free ration at proportion to the strength of the family was sanctioned for one year. Meanwhile they would start paddy cultivation. In their spare time, they used to do a lold of fishing and hunting. They build their houses in a traditional pattern common in South East Asia having roofs sloping on four sides. The houses are built on piles, mostly 5 to 6 feet raised above the ground level and thus the houses look like double storied. They keep the ground area clean for thrashing, cleaning, storing of foodgrains and firewood, etc.

The village, Webi has been developed wholly with the efforts and labour of the Karens settled there along both the sides of a river. With the growth of population, they moved to Deopur, Latao, Lukno, Burmadera, Panighat and in later successive phases spread to Karmatang-9 and Karmatang-10, Chipo, Burong Island and even to Landfall Island.

In the note of the Inspector General of Forests, Government of India, it is stated, "One very successful forest village at Webi, Port Bonnington already exists and it is not anticipated that there will be any difficulty in attracting villagers. They must, however, be selected from communities which are known to take to forest working. They should be given a small area for cultivation, not more than 2-3 acres per family, as their main source of livelihood will be forest labour"[14].

According to requirements, only the Karens were settled at Webi to fulfill the need of forest labour and with the growth of population, expansion was allowed and new villages were established.

In 1937, though a sizable numbers of the Karens had gone back to Burma due to slowdown of forest activities in the islands, yet their migration to Andaman from Burma continued. Their numbers from 236 in 1931 had gone upto 384 in 1954. Again in 1967, some of them went back due to repatriation opportunity and those left behind inhabit the sprawling villages of Webi, Lataw, Lukno, Deopur, etc. According to 1981 Census, their population was 920 and by the Census of 2001, the strength has grown considerably to 1400.

Origin

Considering blood groups, dermatoglyphic patterns and anthropological backgrounds, it is presumed that they belong to a Tibetan race. Of course, others speak of their lineage with the Chinese but the usually agreed upon fact is that they are the primitive nomads of Burma and migrated to Andaman on being converted to Christianity. Now-a-days, most of them are the followers of Christianity.

The word 'Karen' sounds as the Burmese word, 'Kay in'. The Burmese call them 'Karen' because they are wild and rustic. The word, 'Karen' bears two significances—aborigines and wild. As to the Buddhist tradition, 'Karen' is adopted from Pali meaning 'dirty' or 'inferiors'. With the passage of time, they have undergone a lot of changes and their nature has become amicable and peaceful.

The All India Anthropometric Survey, 1990 of male Karens of the Andamans reveal that they are below medium stature with broad head, long and moderately broad noses without much of a bridge, and they have Mongoloid epicanthic fold in the eyes.

Religion

Originally the Karens are monogamous and practise a form of native worship. As it happened with almost all the Mongoloid races, the Karens too embraced Buddhism and later, coming in contact with the Christian missionaries, they were converted to Christianity. So Baptism is one of the most important events in Karens' life. They believe in the forgiveness of sin and also 'eternal life' as they have been preached through Baptism which also marks an occasion for naming the child. They are Protestants and belong to the Baptist Mission. The Bible is also available in Karen language. They observe Christmas, Good Friday and Easter. Previously the Church was managed only by the Karens but in recent years, at the organizational level, non-Karens are also members of the Church that maintains social control for communal harmony and community development.

Education

The Karens were earlier taught and preached by the European missionaries and some of the schools in their villages are maintained by the missionaries. Now the children are going to government schools also.

They speak their own dialect, Karen, which is an offshoot of Tai branch of Sino-Tibetan language. Their language is monosyllabic and their syllables are open, yet there is no final consonant. It has no written form and they use the Burmese script. In Andaman they study in Hindi medium schools. In Webi, there is a private English medium school run by the Christian missionaries where the students are taught Karen language along with English and Hindi. Of course, cases of dropouts are alarming because their parents are not aware of education and most of them want their children to earn money instead of going to school. In their villages there are schools starting from Balwadi to Senior Secondary level.

However, the literacy distribution of the Karens reveals 62.57 per cent literate of which 32.91 per cent are males and 29.66 per cent females and the literacy rate is little higher than that of the Union Territory i.e., 60.95 per cent.

Food Habits

Their staple diet is 'nappi', some sort of pickled fish paste and rice, although the range of their diet includes ravens, ospreys, snakes, wild cats, crocodiles, in addition to what is generally available, i.e., deer, geese, ducks, chickens and various kinds of fish. Vegetables are generally eaten raw. Tea is their staple drink but they drink water rarely. Though the use of liquor is a religious taboo, yet some of them brew illicit liquor and drink on the quiet. Both men and women smoke Indian 'beedis', and a few of them smoke homemade Burmese cigars also. The use of betel nut is prevalent among the women folk while men prefer pan and tobacco chewing.

Social Pattern

In the Andamans, there are two groups of Karens—the Sgaw and the Pwo. Though their dialects differ, they belong to the same community. The Karens are generally endogamous, though owing to their free mixing with other communities, some Karens are married to local Burmese and other neighbouring people like Bengalee, Tamil, Malayalese, Ranchi and Muslim. Thus inter-community or inter-religious marriages are on the rise, too. The Karens being receptive to development schemes, involve themselves to take advantage to improve their living conditions.

The nuclear family is the norm among the Karens but joint families are quite common. The senior most male member of the family is regarded as the head to maintain peace and command discipline.

Despite the existence of the Church Committee, in 1961, the statutory Gram Panchayat was introduced consisting of 15 members elected through adult franchise by the villagers. Among the members, there are two reserved seats for women who are now aware of their rights and duties.

Occupation

The Karens are predominantly agriculturists but some of them prefer other jobs to earn daily wages as labourers. They are fond of fishing and hunting. Almost all families keep poultry. Some rear cows to sell milk. They also sell their surplus agricultural produce in the market. But the young generations are not interested in agriculture and prefer jobs either in the government establishments or private enterprises.

The following table shows the occupation distribution of the Karen population.

TABLE

Male Students	***-12.53%***	***Female Students***	***- 12.78%***
Male Cultivators	- 16.46%	Female cultivators	- 22.14%
Males in Fishing	- 2.09%	Females in Fishing	- nil
Males in Service	- 3.92%	Females in Service	- 1.51%
Males in Business	- 0.58%	Females in Business	- 0.08%
Male Labourers	- 1.59%	Female Labourers	- nil
Male Others	- 0.42%	Female Others	- nil
Total Males engaged	**- 37.59%**	**Total Females engaged**	**- 36.51%**

By nature, they are adept in handicrafts, preparing basketry articles of bamboo and cane, wooden articles for household use and implements for agriculture, fishing (nets), hunting (bows and arrows), etc. The common implements made by them are plough, yoke, leveller with wooden teeth, knife, dao, axes, etc.

Due to their education and technical training, they know utilities of electricity to light bulbs and to run husking and sewing machines, etc. A few of them who are engaged in government jobs, use scooter or motorcycle. They have now started using power tiller, tractors, pump sets and insecticides. They are benefited under various schemes of the National Rural Employment Programmes. With the upliftment of their community, they have learnt to make use of modern facilities in their day-to-day life.

Indeed, they are a prolific lot and have multiplied fast. The sense of community is deeply embedded in them as they attend and participate in all functions of their locality and in the neighbouring households. They appear to be contended and aspire to stand on their own.

"Recently they have all naturalized themselves as Indian citizens and as such been recorded as Andaman Indians in their Census. An integrated population is to be very much preferred to a mosaic of little communities".[15]

The Karens enjoy the 'Local' status given to them by the Andaman and Nicobar Administration so that they can be benefited with the specific quota in government jobs and in reserved seats for technical and higher studies.

(C) MOPILLAH OR MOPLAS

W.R.H. Merk, the Superintendent of the penal settlement of Andaman and Nicobar Islands from 1904 submitted a note explaining the exigencies of abolition of the penal settlement because it was extravagant to Andaman which had lost its reformative value[16].

Besides, the existence of immorality among the convicts to a large extent and the abnormal sickness and mortality rate were also to be considered against the continuation of the penal settlement. But the opinion of the State governments went against it: "They were opposed to the total abolition of penal settlement as a place for reception of criminals[17]. Moreover, they were worried for the shortage of space in the jails of different provinces for accommodating a large number of prisoners in case the transportation to Andaman ceased altogether[18].

Under the circumstances the Government of India formed a Jail Commission to investigate the whole system of jail administration and to have a first hand knowledge about the prospect of the penal settlement. The Commission submitted its report to the Government of India in 1920 with the suggestion to abolish the settlement in Andaman.

The Government of India on principle, inclined to restrict the transportation of convicts by retaining long term prisoners in Indian jails. Further all the unmarried female convicts were sent back from Andaman to the mainland and no more male convicts were transported to Andaman.

But the Provincial governments expressed their inability to provide accommodation for the increased number of prisoners in the existing jails[19] so the Government of India delved to renew the transportation of convicts to Andaman except female convicts and political prisoners. Subsequently the government decided to chalk out a scheme towards the conversion of the penal settlement into a self-supporting community.[20] Ex-convicts were also encouraged to settle into the islands along with their families. Transportation was also open to such prisoners from the Indian jails who were willing to settle there.

However, closing the transportation of prisoners to Andaman resulted in serious overcrowding in the jails of nearly all the provinces, especially in Madras due to influx of prisoners sentenced for their involvement in the Mopillah rebellion. Hence the Government of Madras was allowed to send their prisoners immediately to Andaman. As a special measure, the transportation of Mopla prisoners[21] was sanctioned to relieve congestion in the jails of Madras province.

Mopillah in common parlance, Mopla rebellion of Kerala was virtually the outbreak of animosity and anguishment of poverty-stricken Mopla peasants towards the government officials as well as against the Hindu landlords, mainly Nambudiris and Nairs. It is presumed that the impact of Khilafat movement gave rise to the Mopla rebellion which convinced the Hindus that an organized minority could terrorise a disorganized majority.

The Moplas are all Muslims and their rebellion was basically agrarian in character and deep rooted discontentment prevailed in the exploitative tenancy system, giving vent to the outbreak of the Mopla rebellion. Though some downtrodden among the Hindus too joined hands with the Moplas, the Britishers often lent a communal colour to it in order to belittle its zeal and to create disharmony among the people. "To crush it, the British government let loose a reign of terror. Some ten thousand Moplas were killed and several thousands were deported to Botany Bay in Australia and the Andamans.[22]

The District Gazetteer of Kozhikode 1972 remarks: "The Rebellion of 1921 was a gigantic popular upheaval...It was unprecedented in its magnitude and extent. At its height, the Rebellion covered more than 220 Amsoms, that is sub-district and large masses of people were involved in it ...The action of the police enlisting the support of Hindu landlords and their men in their search for the rebel leaders, made certain sections of the Mopillah community turn against the Hindus. Some of the fanatics among the Mopillah took advantage of the situation to resort to forcible conversion and looting of the Hindus, the Government took full advantage to give currency to highly exaggerated versions of anti-Hindu excesses committed by the Mopillah rebels".

However, certain sporadic incidents by a fanatic Muslim gang cannot take away the glory of the rebellion as it was undoubtedly directed against the British oppression, oppressive moneylenders and unscrupulous landlords, impelled by the grinding poverty and age-long exploitation faced by the commoners.

In 1852, T.L. Strange Commission could not go into the real cause of the outbreak but in 1881, William Logan Commission appointed by the Madras government to probe into the land tenure system in Malabar observed: "Moplah peasants wanted to end British rule in India and make their country free". Logan believed that the problem was rooted in the feudal elements represented by the landowning Jenmis incidentally Hindus who were largely responsible for the miseries and impoverishment of the peasants, both Hindus, and Muslims so he commented that essentially the Moplah revolution was agrarian in nature.

Origin

According to Arabic language, the word 'Mopillah' is derived from the word, 'ma fella' meaning non-cultivators. As to the famous linguist, Lewis Moore, Mapillah in common parlance means a bride-groom or son-in-law. He states that it is the name given to the Mohammadan, Christian or Jewish colonists in Malabar who had inter-married with the natives of the place but in due course, the name Mapillah came to be confined to the Mohammadans only.

Moplas in Andaman

After beastial suppression of the revolt, about 1400 Moplas out of several thousands taken prisoners, were transported to Andaman from the Madras jail as special measure during the tenure of Col. H.C. Beadon as the Chief Commissioner of Andaman and Nicobar Islands from 1920-1923.

In Andaman, the Moplas proved difficult prisoners and there were constant riots. After one such riot, they were chained hand and foot for a period extending to three months. A peculiar invention of the Cellular Jail was the long, stout iron bar to which the prisoner was chained which prevented him from bending or making any movement. The rigour of punishment only brought forth a further desperation among the Moplas.

However at the suggestion of K. Nair, Dy. Collector of Malabar, the system of granting ticket-of-leave to the prisoners was extended to the Moplas also who were allowed to bring over their wives and children from the mainland.

Thus a general amnesty was granted to the Mopla prisoners in 1932 and some 500 women with their children joined their folk in the Andamans.

Despite the vehement protest of All India Khilafat Conference against the settlement of the Moplas in the islands as if it was a banishment from their homeland, the transportation went on and by 1926, out of 1133 Mopla convicts, 258 were given the status of 'self-supporters' in Andaman after six months imprisonment in the Cellular Jail. They were settled on the land allotted by the government where they built their habitation, in the area west of the Mount Harriet ranges.

In 1925, there was considerable agitation in the press in India against the ill-treatment towards the Moplas incarcerated in Andaman. The Government of India sent a deputation of four non-officials including three Muslims and one European to Andaman to report on the situation, and they held the view that the grievances of the Mopla were somehow genuine. According to them, the elements of ordinary village life were absent in the Mopla villages in Andaman. They were ill-fed as the rations given to them were neither good nor sufficient. The Government of India refuted all the allegations but decided to allow them to return to the jails in the mainland if they so desired[23].

Uptil December, 1925, when cash allowances were substantiated, rations including fish and meat were granted on a liberal scale, not only to the convicts but to their dependents. The Government of India decided that the Moplas colonization scheme should continue on its present line but on a voluntary basis.[24]

The Government of India encouraged the transportation of women convicts to increase the female population so as to provide wives to the convicts and also deportation of male convicts in order to reinforce the dwindling ranks of labouring convicts.

Interestingly enough, in spite of grievances and the refutation of the government, in 1926 more Mopla prisoners opted to settle in Andaman and they numbered as many as 1885 in 1931. Thus they had become the largest homogenous group in the islands as they refrained themselves from mixing with the local people keeping their own identity unblemished. By 1989, their population grew to more than six thousands and as their mother tongue is Malayalam, the numbers of Malayalam speaking people became 26075 according to 1991 population Census.

Social Pattern

In these islands, the Moplas are the remnants of the deported rebels of Malabar in Kerala and their progeny with considerable volunteer settlers thrown in. Malayalam is their mother tongue but they can speak some of the south Indian languages. Younger Moplas study in Hindi and English medium schools but surprisingly no one wants to study in Malayalam medium so in the Andaman and Nicobar Islands not a single school imparts education in Malayalam medium, not even at primary level!

The Moplas on being deported to Andaman from the Madras Jails, were given the status of 'self supporters' or employed as labourers in the Forest Department. They came either accompanied by their families or later appealed to send for them from the mainland.

The old settlers of the Mopla origin were settled at Bambooflat and with the growth of population, they spread to new places and new localities grew up viz., Calicut, Ograbraj, Panighat, Womberlygunj, Mannarghat, Wright Mayo, Govindapuram, Mallapuram, Nayapuram, etc., and interesting enough, these names are quite similar to those of Malabar in Kerala where these Moplas belonged to.

The staple food of the Moplas is rice and most of them are non-vegetarian. They do cultivation, plantation, fishing, rearing cattles, and poultry or ply petty trades. But the young generation prefers white collar jobs to farming. They constitute a substantial segment of Malayalam speaking population. The traditional pattern of their life over the years has not changed much and they have retained their own identity observing their own customs and rituals.

As to their old traditions, in Andaman, they are divided into three religious groups—Sunni, Wahabi and Qadiani and each one follows their own rituals concerning birth, marriage and death. Now-a-days inter-caste and inter-community marriages are in vogue and they happen to prefer partners from Bengali, Tamil, Ranchi or local born people.

To settle their disputes, each village has its own village council consisting of four elders which sometimes advises their mosque committee but in 1961 with the setting up of

Panchayat Raj, the village council lost its importance. Gram Panchayat consists of fifteen elected members and two of them are women members and its tenure is for a period of five years. In 1985, the Andaman and Nicobar Islands Pradesh Council was formed, Abdullah Kutty who himself belongs to the Mopla community became the counsellor, elected from Ferrargunj Tahsil, according to the A& N Islands (Adm.) Rules, 1981.

The Moplas by nature are industrious and intelligent. Though they maintain their own identity, they are hospitable to other communities so they have become part and parcel of the island society. As they were settled in Andaman before 1942, they are regarded as pre-settlers and awarded 'local' status by the Andaman and Nicobar Administration so that they can enjoy all benefits and privileges meant for the local born people.

In Kerala, especially on the Malabar coast, the Mopla Rebellion still evokes a high exaltation among the people. The Government of Kerala, to pay a glowing tribute to the great heroes of the rebellion, has declared the survivors of the Rebellion as freedom fighters and granted them pensions as freedom fighters. Their properties though the British failed to confiscate, are now maintained with great honour by trusts formed by the community.

Their descendants in Andaman are aware of all these developments and loath to go back there but prefer to remain in these islands and nurture an appetence to win the recognition as freedom fighters for their forefathers who had participated in the Mopla revolt in the mainland and were transported to Andaman as convicts in 1922 onwards.

Through the local political leaders they placed their demands to the Central Government by citing the case that in Kerala, the participants of the Mopla rebellion of 1921 have already been granted pension as freedom fighters, so the compatriots of the same rebellion residing in Andaman since the outbreak of the rebellion should be granted similar recognition and pension as freedom fighters.

After prolonged persuasion, the then Prime Minister Indira Gandhi, however, agreed to consider the question of granting pension to the serving participants of the Mopla Rebellion who were settled in Andaman during the British regime.

Unfortunately, the ramification still awaits justice.

(D) BHANTUS

In the Bay Islands, there are some outlandish communities who had migrated there and instead of merging themselves with the local inhabitants, maintained their separate identity all along. Among them mention may be made of Bhantus, Moplas, Karens, Bengalee, Tamils, etc.

The Bhantus, commonly called 'Bhatu' were brought to Andaman from the United Provinces, now Uttar Pradesh as convicts in 1922 onwards on terms and conditions similar to those of the Moplas,[25] enjoying the facilities of free-settlers as granted by the British authorities.

The Bhantus clan, a wandering tribe of the United Provinces with their habits of loot, theft and dacoity was notified as a criminal tribe under the Criminal Tribes Act (III) of 1911. The government took severe actions against the Bhantus to control them. Besides the repressive measures, certain reformatory steps were sorted out to bring about idyllic changes in their nature. Through settlement in Andaman, they were given scope to lead a peaceful agricultural life. Even among the Bhantus, those who were transported for life to Andaman, were permitted to bring their families with them to settle there. Thus their descendants have built up a separate society and they now reside in Caddlegunj, Aniket, and other villages in South Andaman. These villages are commonly called 'Bhatu-Bastis'.

Origin

Regarding the origin of the Bhantus, Bonnington[26] mentions that they have descended from the Chauhan Thakur clan of Chittorgarh Rajputs. Crooke[27] and Bhargava[28] believe that the Bhantus are probably of Dravidian origin.

According to their own tradition, the Bhantus being the progeny of the Rajput soldiers of Rana Pratap Singh of Chittorgarh ran away to the jungle after the defeat of Rana in the battle of Haldighati in 1576 and many of them were killed by the Mughals. Those who survived, led a nomadic life with firm determination not to settle until and unless their cradle land, Chittor, was freed. Hence to survive and for mere sustenance, they resorted to looting, robbery and dacoity. Thus these valiant people have turned out to be a wandering tribe and were condemned as a criminal tribe under the Criminal Tribes Act (III) of 1941.[29]

However, to quell and control them, the British government took drastic steps. Most of the Bhantus were rounded up and confined in the Salvation Army Settlements at Kanth, Moradabad, Aryanagri, Lucknow and Kalyanpur of Kanpore. For the slightest infringement of disciplines or for minor offences, they were treated harshly and the same applied even if they stepped out of the settlements.

Settlement in Andaman

Since long the Bhantus had terrorized the people in the mainland by looting, killing and thereby affecting peace and security. The British Administration was also disturbed for the odious activities of this unruly Bhantu tribe so the government resolved to deport many of them, particularly those sentenced to over 15-year imprisonment to Andaman. Between 1926 and 1928, nearly 300 Bhantus along with their families were transported there from different jails and Salvation Army Settlements. In the following years, others came voluntarily to live with their relations who had come to Andaman, earlier as convicts. In 1931, their number was 285. The government assured them of free movement in the islands and offered the status of free-settlers to settle there at government's expenses.

Initially for six months, they were confined in the Cellular Jail. After satisfactory completion of the term, they were shifted to Bambooflat barracks for 3 to 4 months. On good record of one's conduct, they were allowed to settle down as free settlers or free-ticket holders and granted some agriculture land for cultivation as well as homestead land for habitation. Moreover, they were given some cash advances for initial expenses for cultivation and for maintenance of their families.

During the first year of settlement, each family was sanctioned an amount of money as to the proportion of Rs. 4/- per month per adult male, Rs. 2/- per adult female and Re./1 per month per child to meet household expenditure. This facility was accorded only for the first year as an ex-gratia grant. Thenceforth, they were to give normal yearly revenue.

As to the system, the Bhantus had to clear a part of the jungle and the government would issue the deed of right on the land to the concerned family considering its strength. The occupancy right of agriculture land was accorded on the basis of number of family members as such one member was entitled for 6 bigha, two members for 8 bighas, 3 members for 12 bighas and 5 to 8 members for 15 bighas.

Apart from allotment of land, two he-buffaloes for tilling the land, and two she-buffaloes for milching were given to each family on loan to be repaid in instalments as Takavi loan.

When the Bhantus were brought to Andaman, they were all disorganized and reluctant to adjust with the new environment. There they found a new ethnic situation where their own tradition and religious beliefs were baffled and became feeble. In course of time they came into close contact with the neighbouring Hindu communities and slowly became accommodating and sociable renouncing their obstinacy.

In the early stage of their settlement, the Bhantus were asked to settle down at Mathura village under Ferrargunj Tahsil in South Andaman but being frightened of the Jarawas[30] attacks, they were shifted to Caddlegunj and Aniket villages.

Religious Beliefs

Most of Bhantus are Hindus and only a few were converted to Christianty when they had been confined in the Salvation

Army Centers under Christian supervision. They claim that they are the descendants of the Rajput clans so they are Kshatriyas and place themselves in between the Brahmins and Vaishyas in the local social hierarchy.

The Christian Bhantus observe all the ritual practices under their church. Both Hindu and Christian Bhantus participate in social celebrations of their own. The Hindu Bhantus worship only ancestral deities like Lakshmi, Satya Narayana, Rama, Shiva and participate in the community worship of Durga, Saraswati, Kali, etc. There is usually a Shiva temple built at one end of the village where all family members are supposed to be present during worship.

The Hindu Bhantus celebrate all the Hindu festivals i.e., Ram Navami, Diwali, Janmastami, Shivaratri, Rakshabandhan, Holi, etc. The Bhantu Christians celebrate Sunday prayer, Good Friday, Easter Saturday, Christmas Day, etc.

After coming in contact with their neigbouring Hindus, renouncing some of their traditional beliefs and practices, they have started to embrace the religious traits from the local Hindus. Thus they have become more liberal.

Social System

As the Bhantu society is patrilineal, women have a subordinate status in social and religious matters. They are not allowed to worship in temples and participate in social functions.

Bonnington mentions that the Bhantus are divided in thirty six 'gotras' and only 22 of them are now considered for all socio-religious purposes.

As to the practice, no one is allowed to marry in the same 'gotra' and usually they follow the rites, even coming over to Andaman.

In 1961, the statutory Gram Panchayat was introduced in the Andaman and Nicobar Islands and their traditional caste panchayat became defunct. Hence the minor disputes and offences are settled on the basis of evidence and not orally as it happened in the old system of Panchayat.

Due to impact of the Hindu Succession Act, Bhantu women are now entitled to inherit proportional share of paternal property with the male survivors.

Once endogamous, the Bhantus now accept inter-community marriages. Putative kinship or ritual based friendships are allowed within their own community, as they are in practice among the Bengalees, the Moplahs and the locals. Among the Bhantus there are many sub-castes viz., Beria, Ahria, Sainsi, Dom, Kanjur, Kanwal and casteism still prevails in their society.

The Bhantus are interested in modern education for their children. In their villages and nearby areas, there are schools right from the Primary to the Higher Secondary levels. Bhantu children study mostly in Hindi medium and a few go to English medium schools. The following table shows that the Bhantus are very conscious about the education of their children.

TABLE

Sex-wise Literacy

In Total Population					
				Male	Female
Illiterate	82	19.29%	-	26 (11.71%)	56 (27.59%)
Literate	343	80.71%	-	196 (88.29%)	147 (72.41%)
Total	**425**	**19.29%(illit)**	**80.71%(lit)**	**222 male**	**203 female**

According to Bonnington, the dialect of the Bhantus is TAPI that is related to Hindustani. Besides their own dialect, they can speak Hindi and a little English and almost all of them are quite aware of government facilities, conscious of modern education and careful of health and sanitation.

The Bhantus are primarily agriculturists. Some are now engaged in other manual works usually on daily wages. They also rear cattles and keep poultry. Others who are not interested in agriculture, opt for different government jobs, e.g., labourer at Chatham Sawmill, Marine Department or

Forest Department. Now-a-days educated Bhantus seek white collar jobs.

Population: In 1928, a large number of the Bhantus came to settle in Andaman voluntarily. In 1931, they were 285 but in 1936, their population grew up to 700. During the Japanese regime in these islands, many of them perished due to Japanese torture or starvation, or mal-nourishment. In 1945, the British reoccupied the islands and the penal settlement was abolished. All pre-evacuation convicts were allowed to return to their native places. Along with free-ticket holder convicts, many Bhantus took the opportunities and went back to the mainland but failed to struggle there afresh for livelihood and faced a lot of troubles, viz., the insalubrious climate, no land for cultivation, no source of income and even no place for their living.

Therefore, within 8 months, they again applied to the Chief Commissioner, Andaman and Nicobar Islands on 21 November, 1947 expressing willingness of their return to the islands as follows:

"...We, therefore, repent on our hastiness and beg that all our faults may kindly be excused and hope that your honour will kindly issue your order to call us[31]".

Signed by

Kathi – s/o. Ganga Ram – 14 members
Jakir Singh – s/o. Ganga Ram – 4 members
Sukh Singh – s/o. Kanhaiya – 9 members
Roop Singh – s/o. Meghai – 7 members
Kanhaiya – s/o. Durga – 6 members
Bigaija – s/o. Bahadur – 5 members
Raja Dass – s/o. Ram Sarup – 6 members
Lakhan Singh – s/o. Ram Sarup – 4 members
Farida – d/o. Binda – 4 members
Hari Singh – s/o. Bhme – 8 members

Ariju – s/o. Mendab – 5 members
Pillin – s/o. Sittaali – 9 members
Bulla – s/o. Biharro – 6 members

Even Lt. Col. A.T. Huges, Salvation Army, wrote to the Chief Commissioner on 13 January, 1948 to consider their request favourably:

From

The Salvation Army,
35, Queen's Road, Lahore.

To

The Chief Commissioner,
Andaman Nicobar Islands.

Sir,

Our leader, Commissioner H.S. Hodgson has just returned from an extensive tour in the United Provines and some returned settlers now located at Kanth Criminal Tribes, Settlement, U.P. again begged to be sent back to the Andamans.

These people have already approached you through the usual U.P. government channels in the hope of being allowed to return tc Ferrargunj, Annekate and Caddlegunj. From our side, we would like to say that these settlers are the best and most successful... and we would be able to pay the cheapest deck passage for them from Calcutta to Port Blair or Madras to Port Blair. The colonists say, they had much better condition in the Andamans and have not settled in India[32].

Yours sincerely
Sd/ (A.T. Hughes)
Lt. Col. (S.A.)

Meanwhile, the homesteads and the agriculture fields of the gone-back Bhantus were occupied by the people of other ethnic groups so it was difficult for them to regain their old settlements at Mathura village under Ferrargunj Tahsil. They however, applied for the return to their habitat following their previous occupancy rights which could not be fulfilled.

When the government decided to allow them to come back and resettle, the returnees were allowed to rehabilitate at some other places.

It is learnt from the report of the Tahsildar, (South Andaman), "For settling up here I (Tahsildar) would suggest the following two courses :

1. That the original colony viz., Ferrargunj be restored to them.
2. The Chouldari valley where only 6 cultivators may be vacated and Bhantus may be settled there. If number increases, they can be settled at Mongluton. Hence I hope to bring about 100 cultivators[33].

Sd/Tahsildar

However, all these Bhantus came back to Andaman. Many of them were settled in Caddlegunj and Aniket villages. Among them, Janune Bai as Head cooley and Bijaiya, Rama, Rupa, Ilaicha, Raj Kumari, Panna, Ramkali, etc., as cooley—all were engaged in the Forest Department[34].

From the official report by the Dy. Commission to the Chief commissioner, memo. no. 116, dated 8 January, 1948, the status of some Bhantus who worked in different capacities, is stated below:[35]

Name	Status	Residence
Jagan Singh	Working as Clerk at Dy. Commissioner's office	Aberdeen Village
Ganga Singh	Working as Compounder, Medical Deptt.	Aberdeen Village
Sunder Singh	Working as Compounder, Medical Deptt.	Aberdeen Village
Bhagawan Das	Working as Orderly, C.P.W.D.	Aberdeen Village

Nihal Singh	Working as Driver, C.P.W.D	Bombooflat
Basant Lall	Working as Driver, C.P.W.D	Bombooflat
Ram Prasad	Working as Compounder, Medical Deptt.	Bombooflat
Hironja, w/o Monohar	–	Tushonabad
Shehzadi, w/o. Raja	–	Tushonabad

Moreover, many Bhantus were engaged in Central Public Works Department (C.P.W.D.) as labourers, working at Port Mout, Ograbraj and in other places.

With the passing of time, the Bhantus have adjusted with new environment and undergone a lot of changes in their innate habits. They lead a peaceful life as they have co-mingled with other communities. Like the Moplas, they are also granted pre-1942 'Local' status to enjoy all sorts of privileges accorded by the government to all local people.

(E) THE RUMPA PEASANTS

In the history of peasants' movement in India against the British atrocities, the Rumpa Revolt of 1922-24 is regarded as a glorious epoch to establish their rights over their lands and to cherish a bitter hatred for the British who massacred the peasants by a systematic and persistent process of exploitation and plundered everything the peasants possessed, with the help of their stooges and lackeys. No doubt, the Rumpa Revolt was an anti-British and anti-imperialist movement but to the British, it was nothing but 'Fituri' or rebellion so it was crushed brutally.

Manyam or Rampa Chidavaram Agency, close to the then Northern Circars, was under the control of a British Commissioner. The area, not far from Bastar of Madhya Pradesh, is full of virgin forests and inhabited by jungle tribes e.g., Koyas, Bhil, etc., under the British hegemony. For administrative purpose, the area was within the Godavari and Visakhapatnam districts of the then Madras Presidency, presently in the Andhra Pradesh. Taking advantages of the naivety and simplicity of innocent tribes, corrupt British officials and their lackeys exploited them. They had to work hard throughout the day without any wage and on refusal they were treated harshly in inhuman brutality, and even the women were not spared, rather molested publicly. The worst sufferers were the peasants as they did not have any rights over their lands. Often being evicted from their lands and homesteads, they were reduced to paupers and destitutes. They had to live at the mercy and threat of the sycophants of the British officers.

Under this fissiparous and rigmarole situation, heaping sorrows upon sorrows, in 1860, the people of the South India, particularly of Andhra Pradesh faced a devastating famine pushing them on the verge of starvation under untold miseries and penury.

To put fuel to fire, land tax was also raised by fifty percent and the preventive laws against the use of the forest products were enacted to impose heavy taxes on the collection of timbers. Collecting firewood in the jungle was also banned.

The ulterior motive behind all these reactionary measures was to raise extra fund to support the Afghan war without bothering that these persecutionary steps only hit the main source of living of the Rumpa peasants pushing them on the verge of starvation so they became resolute to avenge for all these oppressive measures. The agitated peasants took up arms, whatever available with them and attacked the police stations and other establishments under the leadership of Chandria Sardar. Though the British force could not repulse the initial attack, and was routed out, quickly it reinforced its strength and reacted offensively to quell the mob violence. Privation and misery reigned in the village ravaging its peaceful atmosphere.

This was the first Rumpa revolt of 1878, though short lived yet it had great impact on the minds of the suffering people and made the spade work for future upheavals.

After an interval of forty four years, the Rumpa revolt broke out again in the year of 1922 under the able leadership of Sree Alluri Sitarama Raju of Godavari, widely regarded as 'Sadhu' who had dedicated himself for the moral upliftment of the people. He used to lodge complaints against the injustice or torture of the local authorities but all in vain, the British paid no heed to his reproachful appeals, on the contrary, made heinous tricks to put Raju behind the bars.

Being disheartened, he mobilised the wretched people and organized the peasants to take up arms against the British atrocities. Gradually he raised a band of 1200 defiant and valiant followers, mostly the tribals who were deprived of their age old rights over the swidden type or jhum type of shift cultivation, the only method they knew. So the fuming discontentment and resentment were fanned by the stirring speeches and personal contacts of Raju. Thus the peasants movement became anti-British as Raju could impress upon them that the British and their lackeys were solely responsible for their miseries and sufferings. In no time, he being an ascetic by nature happened to be the apostle of the revolution to uphoid the interest of indigent people aiming at the termination of the British rule so that the prolonged humiliation inflicted upon them by the British and their henchmen could be stopped.

With a retinue of only 300 peasants armed with outmoded weapons, Raju began his offensive first on 22 June, 1922 and became successful in raiding Chintapally Police Station and looting the armoury. The mobility of his peasants, army and its lightening attacks made the British administration of the locality totally collapsed.

Raju would often change his strategies and plunge into sudden attacks of different government positions at far off places. Raju's successive victories and his revolutionary activities terrified the administration of the Rampa Chidamvaram Agency area. It was a matter of grave concern for the British government which then decided to tackle the situation on war footing in order to put an end to the peasant's insurgency. It enforced more ruthless measures to squeeze information about every detail related to Raju and his men. It let loose a reign of terror and to make people panick, loot, plunder, arson, etc., went along.

To the contrary, Raju's success spread euphoria and hundreds of tribal youths joined the warring forces of Raju who needed arms and ammunitions, and food for his army. So snatching arms, looting treasury and ransacking government's grain storages started.

On 22 October, 1922, the peasant's army of Raju fought a glorious battle against the British platoon under the command of Happel who had to leave the battlefield to save his life.

Unfortunately, with the passage of time, Raju's army was short of arms and tired of uncertainties. The people of the area were also terrified of inhuman torture and could not bear with the tension so they submitted and yielded to pass information about Raju.

On 6 December, 1923, Raju was attacked suddenly by a large Malabar contingent at Padagadda under the command of I.G.P. John and was defeated miserably. Many of his followers were either dead or arrested along with their arms. But Raju could escape unhurt.

On 7 May, 1924, Raju was trapped but he desperately tried to break into the cordon to escape, but he failed. He was arrested and brought before Majŏr Sergeant Goodall, Commandant of the Assam Rifles who shot him instantly dead.

Thus the idol of the Rumpa peasants' movement, a symbol of courage, self-sacrifice and a luminary among the freedom fighters died a hero's death. In fine the Rumpa rebellion was crushed. Many of the peasants' army were dead in the war, many more were killed in inhuman torture or hanged, and some more were sentenced to transportation for life to Andaman.

Rumpa Rebels in Andaman

Shortly after the brutal suppression of the Rumpa peasants' revolt, the barbaric activities of the British did not stop. The farmers of the area became victims of vengeance of the British authorities and their financial condition became miserable as they were made the beasts of burden. Though condemned as rebels by the British, in the national history they are regarded as patriots.

Many Rumpa rebels were sentenced to long terms of imprisonment and many of them were transported for life to 'Kalapani,' Andaman. But for want of documents, it's very difficult to know the details of those who were brought to Andaman. From "Who's Who of Andaman", there we get only seven names and from other sources, we have references of a few more heroes. Whatever information about them is available, is mentioned below:

- Gam Mallanna Dora, popularly known as Mallu, spent thirteen and a half years in the Cellular Jail and on being released, went back to his native village in Andhra Pradesh.
- Taggi Veerayiah Dora, resident of Vishakhapatnam, Andhra Pradesh joined the Rumpa peasant revolt during 1922-24. On suppression of the revolt, he was transported to Andaman and incarcerated in the Cellular Jail for several years. Later he was granted the status of free-settlers and settled possibly at Brichgunj in South Andaman.
- Aggi Raju, resident of Vishakhapatnam joined the Rumpa army under Alluri Sitarama Raju. After defeat, he was sentenced to transportation and confined in the Cellular Jail for many years. On the basis of good conduct he was allowed to settle in Andaman. After a couple of years, he died there.
- Kuncheti Sanyashi, resident of Vishakhapatnam, joined the Rumpa movement against the British but after the defeat on 7 May, 1924 he was arrested and deported to Andaman to serve the life imprisonment. Later on being released, he settled at Brichgunj in South Andaman.
- Golivilli Saniage Saiah, resident of Vishakhapatnam, a valiant warrior of the Rumpa revolt was sentenced on the charges of treason to transportation to Andaman. On being released from the Cellular Jail after the expiry of penal servitude, he settled in Andaman.
- Korabu Pettaiah, resident of Vishakhapatnam, took part in the Rumpa movement under the leadership of

Sitarama Raju. After suppression of the revolt, he was sentenced to transportation for life to Andaman. On satisfactory completion of his term of punishment, he was released and settled in Andaman.

- Korabu Kotaiha, resident of Vishakhapatnam, joined the Rumpa rebellion which was beastially crushed down. He was sentenced to transportation for life in Andaman. Later he was granted the status of free settlers and settled in Andaman on being released for good conduct during the period of imprisonment.
- Bonangi Pandu Padal was born in Gondipakala in 1890. He took part in the Rumpa revolt and fought defiantly against the British, shoulder to shoulder with Sitarama Raju, the apostle of revolutionaries, in every encounter. The British government declared a heavy reward for his arrest. On being captured he was sentenced to death and later it was commuted to life imprisonment. He was deported to Andaman in 1926 and incarcerated in the Cellular Jail during 1922-32. His jail record number was 48907. During the period of penal servitude, his jail mates were Korabu Kotaiha and Taggi Veerayiah Dora of the Rumpa force.

While the tenure of confinement in the Cellular Jail was over, Padal was allowed to send for his wife who refused to settle in 'Kalapani'-Andaman as it was sacrilegious so Bonangi married a female convict, Parvati and settled at Brichgunj in South Andaman. After spending almost fifty years in Andaman, he breathed his last in 1974 on the soil of Andaman and is survived by five sons and two daughters.

In due course, the descendants of the heroes of the Rumpa peasants' revolt mingle with the local people and contribute their might to the development of a unique island society. They have been granted the pre-1942 status and enjoy all the facilities meant for the local born people.

(F) THE WAHABIS

After the brutal suppression of the revolt of 1857, in order to quell the spirit of freedom movement and to infuse spine-chilling menace in the minds of the revolutionaries, the great heroes of 1857 were transported to far distant islands on the charge of treason to bear with extreme hardships and to share with many hardened criminals in Andaman.

Following the footsteps of the great heroes of the revolt of 1857, there were many anti-British uprisings such as the movement of the Wahabis, the Rumpa revolt, the Mopillah rebellion, the Tharawardy and Manipuri insurgencies, etc., and the rebels of these movements were either executed or convicted on the charges of sedition and transported to Andaman.

Initially in the first half of the 19th century, the Wahabis launched one of the earliest and the most remarkable anti-British movements which had a great impact on other freedom struggles in the later half of the 19th century. The main reason for the outbreak of the Wahabi revolt was the forceful seizure of the farmers' land on the pretext of non-payment of land revenue. As a result, the villagers were not only deprived of the produce of their toils but also pushed to the brink of starvation which ultimately fomented a pique among the people against the tyrannical rule of the British. The incessant discontent aggravated the situation that found expression in the armed uprising of the Wahabis.

Though the movement was started at the aegis of some Muslim stalwarts led by Abdul Wahab Neijidi of Saudi Arabia, the word, 'Wahabi' is a misnomer and is generally regarded by a vast majority of Muslims as un-Islamic. Thus the word, 'Wahabi' is owed to Abdul Wahab but this terminology was ascribed by the British to suit their ulterior motive.

The real name of Indian Wahabis who were on the move to reestablish the 'path of Mohammed' and 'Farz', i.e., command of Allah in order to liberate their land, 'Dar-ul-Harb' from the claws of the British and to convert it into 'Dar-ul-Islam', the land of peace, was Tariqa Mohamedia or Mohammed ka Tariqa. Its founder was a Fakir of Raibereilly named Syed Ahmed Brelhvi.

While in the north, Syed Ahmed was propagating the spirit of 'Jehad' or holy war against the atrocities of the British; in the East Bengal, Fardizi movement was initiated by Pir Shariatullah of Faridpur against the oppression of new Zamindars, Mahajans (money-lenders), and planters who were the stooges of the East India Company. A similar anti-British movement started by Mir Nasar Ali of Chandpur in now West Bengal was also regarded as the Wahabi movement.

Syed Ahmed, Haji Shariatullah and Mir Nasar Ali met Abdul Wahab Neijidi in Mecca and agreed on principles to lead their followers for the upliftment of the Muslims as they realized that the decadence of the Muslims was due to the overcast of superstitions and influence of alien religions. Above all, the Quran is the highest truth to follow and the true Muslims should try to establish it. These were the dictums to be followed by all the Wahabis.

This simple faith of pure Islam propagating Islamic justice and equity to each and all, motivated a large number of oppressed peasantry to embrace this and muster courage under the banner of the Wahabi movement to fight against oppressive Zamindars and tyrannical planters. In due course, imbued with the political motives, the Wahabis inspired the rural people to revolt against the atrocities of the British government.

In the north Syed Ahmed Brelhvi organized a militia to wage war against the Sheik mandarins' beastial rule over the Muslim peasantry in Sindh. But he was killed in the battle, and his army was routed out.

Earlier Syed Ahmed had been successful to establish a free state in the far North-western corner of India with Sitana as headquarters by proclaiming Jihad against the British. This incident inspired others to take up arms to wipe out the British.

Enayat Ali and Vilayat Ali of Patna, Karamat Ali of Jaunpur and Zainuddin of Hyderabad started anti-British movement. In fact, the history of the Wahabi movement at least from 1831 to 1858 owed a lot to the Ali Brothers. After 1847, the Wahabi movement assumed its real anti-British, anti-imperialist character.

In Bengal too, under the "leadership of Mir Nasar Ali, popularly known as 'Titumir', many peasant youths mustered their strength to revolt for the cause of Muslim ryots oppressed by the indigo planters and Muslim Zamindars of Purnea district. As a result, on 17 November, 1831, Barasat uprising was held. In the two successive battles, the European planters along with their few hundred sepoys were totally routed by thousands of armed peasantry with swords, spears and other indigenous weapons.

Finally on 3 December, 1932, Titu's army met a British detachment consisting of 10 regiments of N.I. troop of horse artillery with a few guns at Narkelberia now in West Bengal but superior British power ultimately decided the issue. Titumir was defeated and died a hero's death in the battlefield. The next in command, Golum Masum along with 300 followers was arrested. Masum was hanged and many others were transported to Andaman to serve the life term.

After Nasar Ali's significant role in the anti-British Jihad and resplendent revolt, his son Mahamed Mohasin, commonly known as Dudu Mia put on his mettle to take up the cudgels against the flagitious British and championed the cause of oppressed peasantry of East Bengal, instigating them to take up arms against all corruptions and exploitation of the landlords and European indigo planters. But in the battle, Dudu Mia was defeated and imprisoned in the Alipur jail of Calcutta in 1847.

Though he was released after quelling the revolt of 1857, he died as a firebrand hero leaving behind a revolutionary legacy to the freedom fighters to come.

The Wahabis, unaware of the great impact of the revolt of 1857, regimented their forces and garrisoned them in many places, viz., Patna, Agra, Delhi, Hyderabad, etc. Indeed, some of the leaders of the revolt of 1857 made use of the organizational base prepared discreetly by the Wahabis. The popular basis of the Wahabi movement stands vindicated by its well-knit and integrated organization spread throughout the length and breadth of India extending from Dacca to Peshawar. Though in the Wahabi movement, mainly the Muslims were involved and all the victims were the Muslims, the Hindus also showed sympathy but did not participate actively. Notwithstanding, many Hindus were arrested on the charge of sedition.

Wahabis in Andaman

Andaman is solemnly regarded as the land of martyrs because numerous freedom fighters, right from the great heroes of the revolt of 1857 down to the fiery terrorists of the early part of the 20th century were either hanged or put to inhuman torture while incarcerated in Andaman.

Though the Wahabis fought valiantly, they were crushed and defeated to the superior firearms of the British. During 1863 and 1872 there was a series of arbitrary trials and all ring leaders being convicted on the charge of treason, were either put to gallows or transported to Andaman to serve their terms.

Among those transported to Andaman, some of them were settled in the villages, in and around Port Blair. Dr. R.C. Mazumdar rightly remarked, "... a large number of Wahabi prisoners was sent there (Andaman), neither the total number (of Wahabis) nor details of individual prisoner are available". ('Penal Settlement in Andamans', p. 144)

However, from "Who's Who in Andamans"[36] and other sources we have got some references of a few Wahabis settled in Andaman. In the book of Rashida Iqbal, "Who's Who...", only 16 names of the Wahabis are available and among them, only two settled in Andaman, three died and the rest went back to their native places on being released.

Indeed, the period between 1863 and 1872 was condemned for a number of summary trials by which all ring leaders of these seditious community were arrested.

Ambala trial in 1864 and Patna trial in 1865 were closely inter-linked. Yahiya Ali, brother of Ahamedulla, and Muhammed Jafar, both of Patna trial, and Muhammed Shafi

Lahori of Ambala trial, all were sentenced to death, but later transported for life to Andaman.

Ahmedullah, son of Illahi Baksh along with his compatriots Fayez Ali, Yahiya Ali and Furhat Ali was convicted for anti-British activities during and after the revolt of 1857. Ahmedullah was sentenced to death on 27 February, 1865 at the end of Patna trial but commuted to transportation for life and he reached Andaman on 15 June 1865. After 16 years of tortuous sufferings, he died on 21 November, 1881 at Viper Island and buried at Dundus point.

In Malda trial of 1870, Amiruddin, son of famous Wahabi leader, Rafique Mondal and resident of Pabna in East Bengal was convicted on the charge of conspiracy against the British government and transported to Andaman for life in 1872. He was released on 3 March, 1883 and possibly settled in Andaman.

In Raj Mahal trial of 1870, the famous Wahabi leader, Ibrahim Mondal of Islampur now in West Bengal was convicted on the charge of sedition inciting the people of Rajshahi, Bogura, Rangpur, Dinajpur, Malda and was sentenced to transportation for life to Andaman.

Earlier in 1869, Amir Khan and Hashmatdad Khan, residents of Patna and leather merchants of Calcutta were arrested on the charge of collecting silver coins from other traders for the purpose of remittances to Sitara in support of Wahabi movement. In the Patna trial, they were sentenced to transportation for life to Andaman in 1872. On being released in 1878, it is said that they settled in villages near Port Blair.

In Patna trial, Tobruk Ali, resident of Pabna in East Bengal, was tried and sentenced to transportation for life to Andaman. Due to his good behaviour, he was appointed Muharrar at convict station and after 10 years of penal servitude, was released in 1883.

Yahiya Ali, a devout Wahabi leader was transported to Andaman in January, 1866 to serve his term. He was a highly educated personality and could not sustain the brutal torture inflicted on him at Viper Island. He succumed to these oppressions and died. He was buried at Aberdeen village, Port Blair on 20 February 1868.

Abdul Rahim Sidiqpuri, resident of Patna, a staunch adherent of Wahabi movement, was charged of his involvement in anti-British activities and sentenced to transportation for life. He was brought to Andaman on 25 December, 1867. Because of his good behaviour, he was engaged as a Muharrar at the Settlement hospital. He was released on 3 March, 1883 and settled in Andaman as a shopkeeper.

Sher Ali, a valiant Afghan, son of Ulli, Kukikhal by caste murdered flagitious Col. Polak and was sentenced to transportation for life. He was sent to Andaman on 15 May, 1867. As a reward for his good conduct, he was granted ticket of leave on 15 May, 1871. He settled at Hope Town and earned his bread by doing barber's job but in his blood and soul, an indomitable urge of taking revenge against the oppressive British was burning althrough. When the news of the visit of Lord Mayo spread, he hit upon a plan to console himself. On 8 February, 1872, he risked his life and stabbed Mayo to death. Instantly he was arrested and hanged at the gallows at Viper Island on 11 March, 1872. In some scribbles, though Sher Ali was addressed as a Wahabi, yet no evidence is available to suffice the proof in support of the claim.

Since 1864, the Wahabis were transported to Andaman. Among them, the most famous leader was Mohd. Jafar Thaneshari.[38] He was a firebrand freedom fighter and sentenced to death on the charge of sedition, later the Punjab High Court commuted the death sentence to transportation for life. He was brought to Port Blair along with other Wahabis,Yahiya Ali, Mohd Safi Lahori, etc., on 11 January, 1866 and incarcerated at Ross Island. Due to his nobility and personality, he was made Mir Munshi at the Chief Commissioner's office. He was granted ticket-of-leave for his good conduct and married a Hindu female convict to settle in Andaman. He was released on 9 November, 1883 after 18 years of penal servitude. He went back to Ambala and wrote "Kalapani ma'ruf beh Tawarikh, Ajiba" in Urdu which is considered the most authentic treatise of those horrible days in Andaman.

Another great personality regarded by all was Maulavi Ahammed Allah who expired on 20 February, 1868 and buried in South Point seashore where Mazar of Fadl-e-Haqq Khairabadi[39] still exists today.

No doubt, many Wahabis were sent to Andaman as convicts and they had to spend there many years to undergo rigorous punishment as to their terms. Some of them could not endure the beastial torture inflicted on them in the name of the jail administration and expired; many of them, after the expiry of the term of punishment were released and went back to their native places, and a few settled there infra dig and passed away unsung and unnoticed. Today it's very difficult to identify the scions of their great progenitors. Ostensively they mingle with the local people and with the passage of time, they attribute to the growth of the 'local born' society and contribute to the development of a homogeneous culture of the islands,

ENDNOTES

1. Published by Directorate of Education & Culture, A.N. Adm. Port Blair, 1998.
2. Supra, previous chapter, Endnotes.
3. Convicted on the charge of murder of Magistrate W.R. Moore, involved in the revolt of 1857.
4. A small island close to Port Blair, first gallows 'Kala Kuthri' was built there, first open air jail constructed there where chain-gangs were kept. Sher Ali and others were hanged at Kala Kuthri at Viper Islands.
5. 'Penal Settlement in Andamans' by Dr. R.C. Mazumdar, Pub: Gazetteers Unit, Deptt. of Culture, Ministry of Edn. and Social Services, G.O.I., 1975., p 140.
6. 'Provincial Gazetteers of India, Andaman and Nicobar Islands', 1908. p 63.
7. Administrative Report, A.N.I., 1905-06, p 47-49.

8. 'Notice of Nicobar Islands', P. Barbe, Selection of Records, Vol. 77
9. 'Folktales of Nicobar', by Rabin Roychowdhury, Pub. Sahitya Akademi, New Delhi.
10. In Nancowry Island, penal settlement was started in June, 1869. N.A.I., Home Deptt., Public Branch, A. Progs. No. 19-20, April 1871.
11. N.A.I., Home Deptt., Port Blair Branch, A. Progs. No. 48, Jan. 1874.
12. Census, 1951, Appendix - A. XLV.
13. All India Radio, Port Blair Station, an interview of Satish Mathur regarding his experience, broadcast on 22 Oct, 1985. who came to Andaman in 1924 and landed at Mayabunder on being transported.
14. "Colonization in the Andamans, a Note by the Inspector General of Forests", G.O.I., Published on 21-06-1949.
15. Census, 1951, Appendix-A, XLV.
16. NA.I., Home Deptt., Port Blair Branch, A. Progs No. 28-40, July 1906.
17. Ibid.
18. Ibid, A. Progs. No. 80-93, December, 1910.
19. Legislative Council Progs, 17 January, 1922
20. N.A.I, Home Deptt. Resolution No.20/26. Jails., 27 February, 1926
21. The Mopillahs of Malabar, a valiant Muslim community revolted against the British in 1921. After suppression, many of them were sent to Andaman.
22. Roland Miller's 'Mopla Muslims of Kerala', Orient Longman, 1976, p. 42, 109, 114, 116-117.
23. N.A.I., Home Deptt. File no. 20/26 Jails, Oct. 4, 1926.
24. Summary in the Report of the Indian Statutory Commission, Vol, IV, Part 1, p. 367, 402.
25. N.A.I., Home Deptt. File No. 451/24 jails. Oct. 4, 1926.
26. Bonnington, M.C.C., 1932, Census of India, 1931, Vol. ii, Part I & II, p. 41-50.
27. Crooke, W., 1896, 'The Tribes and Castes of North West India,' vol. I. Calcutta, Government Printing Press.
28. Bhargava, B.S., 1949, "Criminal tribes : A Socio-Economic Study of

the Principal Criminal Tribes and Castes of Northern India," Lucknow, Universal Publishers.

29. Ayyangar, A., 1951, 'Criminal Tribes Act,' Enquiry Commission, 1949-50.

30. Jarawa: a primitive tribe of Paleolithic age, native of Andaman, once very hostile and belligerent, now quite friendly.

31. State Archives, Port Blair, File no. S/43, 20 February, 1948.

32. State Archives, Port Blair, File no. S/4, 20, February, 1948.

33. Ibid.

34. Ibid. Report of Dy. Commissioner, December, 1949.

35. Ibid.

36. "Unsung Heroes of Freedom Struggle in Andamans, Who's Who," by Rashida Iqbal, Pub: Directorate of Edn. & Culture, A.N. Adm., Port Blair.

37. Mayo, Lord, the Viceroy of India, 1869-72, assassinated in 1872 by Sher Ali, a Pathan convict at Hope Town, near Port Blair while he was on a visit "to improve the defective system of Government in the convict settlements of the Andaman Islands."

38. Mohd. Jafar Thaneswari in "Penal Settlement in Andamans" addressed as Mir Jafar Ali Thaneswari by R.C. Mazumdar and stated, "Another mutineer, Mir Jafar Ali Thaneswari, spent twenty years of penal servitude in the Andamans. p. 143.

39. Fadl-e-Haqq Khairabadi: Supra, previous chapter.

5

PROVENANCE OF PARTITION OF INDIA

History of the Partition of Indian Union teaches us a lesson precisely that the Act of Partition should never merely mean the physical or terrestrial division of this sub-continent but it cuts through the corporate living of many thousands of people who passed through the orgy still bearing the umpteen pangs of the vivisection of Mother India, dividing overnight the whole population of the country into two distinct, indelible groups—the residents and the uprooted, abysmally addressed as 'refugees'.

The Partition was a trauma that haunts us till today, not only as the memory of horrifying sequel of events—a million dead, seventy five thousand women abducted and raped, but also as a permanent score that incites the poignancy between three nations—India, Pakistan and Bangladesh.

Indeed, trauma in both the private and political domains is something which neither be acknowledged nor assimilated and must therefore be repressed in the hope of forgetting. How then does one acquire understanding of the traumatic events? The sequels of the Partition pervade the present, not as traumatic memory but as odious nightmare that perhaps nothing on earth or even the galore of bright future can subside the fissiparous trauma.

The history of this period is well documented by some authoritative scholars such as Louis Fischer, Allan Campbell-Johnson, Pandrel Moon, Leonard Mosley, Stanley Wolpert and other renowned Indian historians like V.P. Menon, Jasmin Khan, A.J. Kamra, Ajit Chaterjee, Anita Inder Singh, Yuras Samad but it is not relevant to recount the same in toto except to the extent germane to the theme of this book which concerns only with the migration and settlement in Andaman.

Indeed, in India the communal riots were the main cause of forced migration culminating in refugee movements as documented by many authors.

Moulana Abul Kalam Azad[1] in his 'India Wins Freedom,' remarks, "...sixteenth August, 1946 was a black day, not only for Calcutta but for the whole of India...This was one of the greatest tragedies of Indian history and I have to say with the deepest of regret that a large part of the responsibilities for the development rests with Jawaharlal".

Wolpert[2] reports, "... as many as 16000 Bengalis murdered between August 16 to August 20, 1946".

Indeed, August 16 was to the Muslims a day of Direct Action and it turned violent only in Calcutta. Even the then Chief Minister of Bengal, H.S. Suhrawardy said, "Muslims need not be bound by non-violence and violence would be directed at Hindus". In fact, for three or four days dead bodies littered in heaps everywhere at different stages of decomposition... there was a felid smell all around... the air was thickened with the stench of putrifaction.

'Direct Action' was followed by the carnage of Noakhali in East Pakistan which began on 10 October, 1946 and surpassed all facets of genocides. It was beset when Bengali Hindus were busy worshipping the goddess of wealth, Lakshmi, usually celebrated as 'Kojagari Lakshmi Puja'.

Arther Henderson told the House of Commons on November 4, 1946 that the dead bodies in Noakhali, (now in Bangladesh), and Tipperah (Tripura) districts had not yet been counted but according to estimates, would cross the three figures. Over ten thousand houses were looted. In

Tipperah itself, 9895 persons were forcibly converted to Islam in Noakhali's... the number of converts was greater.

"Thousands of Hindu women were abducted and married to Muslims against their will... to convert Hindu women Muslim broke their bangles and removed their 'happiness mark's of marriage ('Sindur') on their foreheads. Hindu Goddesses were smashed and the Hindu temples desecrated. Worst of all, Hindus were made to slaughter their cows and eat meat".[3]

Indeed, the nightmarish sequel of the Partition in East Pakistan was horrible and horrendous. There was complete devastation. Mutilated persons and severed limbs, charred remains of rotting corpses and houses, were to be seen everywhere. It was as if an earthquake or an explosion had tumbled and destroyed the whole country.

V.P. Menon[4] condemns the occurrences and accuses, "... the west Pakistanis alone or even primarily, are responsible for the persecution of Hindus in East Bengal".

In fact, before the Partition, occasional hostilities were reported and quickly escalated into communal riots which the lumpens and anti-socials would take advantage to yield gains. Still no Hindus thought of leaving their ancestral home nor dreamt of migrating to a new land. But storm of tragedies befalling on East Bengal at regular intervals forced them to realize the ineffable reality. They had to bear with the unbelievable trauma of three blood-squeezing and spine-chilling experiences. They were the Bengal famine of 1943, the Great Calcutta killings of 16 August, 1946 and the third one, the gruesome Noakhali carnage of October, 1946.

In consequence of all these occurrences, the last but not the least, the Partition of India made millions of minority group especially the Hindus, destitute and homeless, having been forced to leave their home and hearth and compelled to cut off all social entity with their natal villages and to flee to India being penniless.

The Partition of India created "a problem group" heading to mass migration in either parts of traumated India of 1947 and the member of the group is "invariably and essentially someone who is homeless, uprooted, a helpless casualty, diminished in all his circumstances, the victims of events for which, at least, as an individual, he cannot be held responsible."[5]

A refugee by and large is a victim of India's vivisection owing to the Partition and it was an obligation to succour and rehabilitate the victims of communal passion upsurged in a spoof in East Pakistan that India was pledged to honour. Officially considered that a person, who had migrated before the end of June, 1948 was to be classified as a refugee and he was required to have registered himself as such before January, 1949. However its choice of dates by which only those who crossed the border before the end of June, 1948 were registered as refugees, was a deliberate act of policy intended specifically to deny refugee-status to the hundreds of thousands who were compelled to move to India in later years.

In the statement of Government of India, 1957, the grave situation created by the Act of Partition and subsequent mass migration of the affected people are expressed very tangibly in the following lines, "Because of our vast population, it is sometimes difficult for us to get into perspective of the implications of the mass migration of the people from Pakistan into India in 1947. If we can imagine, however, what would have happened if instead of a few hundred thousand people who fled from Europe to Britain during the dark days between 1934 and 1939, the number of refugees had included the whole population of Norway or Denmark, we can get some idea of the problem which faced this country in 1947". This was indeed the reality. Catastrophic circumstances prevailed immediately after and before the official declaration of the partition between India and Pakistan.

However, Act of Partition was never a hasty decision but it evinced a long trajectory of history since 1922 projecting a litany of past events confiding communal violence and feuds terminating peace and harmony.

Over the years, the communal problems in India became an explosive issue both to the Hindus and the Muslims. Political agitation, communal fratricide and above all a national crisis choked eventually the normal life and living of the common people of the country between 1945 and 1946. Communal frenzy gathered momentum especially after the General Election of 1946 and the demand of a completely Muslim State to be known as Pakistan gained a solid foothold among the Muslims of India. In the early part of 1947, the British government in New Delhi felt the ominous impact of a complicated and almost a morbid situation in which the Indians were busy in fratricides, the Indian Princes were falling out among themselves, the Police Forces and civil administration were on tenterhooks and the British became skeptical and full of foreboding.

On 23 March, 1947, in the meeting with the then Viceroy, Lord Mountbatten, Nehru reiterated his famous tripartite proposals for Punjab to be divided up on communal lines with a central authority to deal with certain major non-communal subjects and Nehru's proposal seemed to be the abetment to the Hindustan-Pakistan division.

Till 14 April, 1947, Mountbatten was awaiting full and frank views of the Governors of all provinces on the draft of his "Partition Plan" of which the cardinal features noted by Campbell-Johnson, are as follows:

(a) that the responsibility for the Partition, if it comes, is to rest fairly upon the Indians themselves,

(b) the provinces generally speaking, shall have the right to determine their own future,

(c) Bengal and Punjab are to be partitioned nationally for voting purposes,

(d) the pre-dominantly Moslem Sylhet district of Assam is to be given the option of joining the Moslem province created by a partitioned Bengal,

(e) general elections are to be held in the North-West Frontier Province.

Earlier in September 1944 both Jinnah and Mahatma Gandhi had long discussions for a united India with no results as Jinnah was adamant for the partition. Again on 6 May, 1947 they had the conversation on the question of India and Pakistan soon after the complete "cessation of British suzerainty over India".

Gandhi did not agree to the principle of partition as that was 'not inevitable' but Jinnah was obdurate to demand Pakistan as 'inevitable' as it was 'the only practical solution' of India's political deadlock. Nehru and Patel succumbed to the charisma of Lord Mountbatten and accepted the Partition in spite of Gandhi's insistence that '... Independence should come first and partition, if necessary, afterwards'. Against their concerted will, Gandhi had nothing to do but to remain as mute witness of the terrible ordeal of devastation and denouement leading to mass scale murder and migration.

On 2 June, 1947, the leaders of the Congress and the Muslim League discussed the provisions of the Plan and concurred with the Plan so that division should be made on the basis of citizenship which in its turn would be based on considerations of geography.[6]

Parliament quickly passed the Indian Independence Act which came into operation on midnight, August 15, 1947 resulting to massive migration to India.

CAUSES OF MIGRATION

Before the Partition, East Bengal (the then East Pakistan) was a densely populated State and solely dependent on agriculture and dominated by the Hindu Zamindars or landlords. The Muslims though being majority were mostly landless agricultural labourers so intense hunger for land was incessant in their mind and acrimony tantamount to enmity was fuming towards Hindus.

After the Partition, the scenario totally changed and the infuriated Muslims got the opportunity to satiate their eventual appetence for land. They experienced that if the Hindus panicked, they could sacrifice everything, their land, property and all other terrestrial belongings, but not their religion at any cost so the instruments of eviction drive would be forcible conversions and violence. If the communal tension could prevail and let loose the reign of terror, it would not only give scope to the Muslims to grab the Hindus' lands but also abet to lawless ruffians and anti- socials unleashing on the helpless Hindus and force them to leave their hearths and homes. Indeed, this course of eviction and perdition went on unabated on a regular basis following fallouts of political repercussions.

If we compare the Census Reports of 1941 and 1951, the truth will come out. According to the Census of 1941, the Hindu population was 28 per cent as against 70 per cent of the Muslim population but in 1951 because of communal violence, the Hindu population decreased alarmingly to 10 per cent whereas the same of the Muslims grew frighteningly to 88 per cent. The exodus of the Hindus started exactly a year before the transfer of power that took place on 15 August, 1947. This began with the Great Calcutta killings of August 16, 1946 resulting in the sorry tale of mass murder and arson followed by the tragic events of Noakhali. One disaster followed another, each producing gruesome reactions in different parts of the country provoking mass migration of the Hindu minorities who were in the favourite euphemism, 'refugees' or 'displaced persons'.

In August, 1948, the threat of conflict between India and Pakistan over the accession of Hyderabad, had reverberations in East Pakistan driving 470555 Hindus out of their hearth and home. By the end of 1949, the outbreak of the communal riots in Khulna and Barisal of East Pakistan forced 11,72,928 Hindus to cross into West Bengal. All through the following year 1950, men, women, children, the old and invalid were swept in an unending stream from their ancestral homes leading to the peak of the enormous migration. The outflow of forced migration reeled large beyond any imagination.

Meanwhile tension between India and Pakistan rose on the issue of Kashmir. Pakistan Prime Minister Liaquat Ali Khan made a fighting speech in occupied Kashmir shaking his fists. Prime Minister Nehru's response to such threats and the Pakistani action of pushing out the Hindus into India was to put the Indian Army on the borders and to warn Pakistan that any move by it to create trouble would lead to a general war between the two countries. As a result of such a deterrent posture adopted by Nehru forced Liaquat Ali to fly to Delhi and conclude the Nehru-Liaquat Pact signed in April 1950. After the pact though the pace of migration slowed down for the time being, the exodus of refugees from East Pakistan continued with intensity until the end of 1951. There was another spurt in the middle of 1952. The untold miseries owing to economic depression in East Pakistan as well as the wild rumour seethed the destitute that after October, 1952, nobody would be allowed to cross the border without Passport or Visa, resulting in frantic scurry and scuttle among the refugees to leave East Pakistan before it was too late. By the end of 1952, 531440 refugees crossed the border.

This sort of mad rush went on over any trivial pretexts. The unrest over the language issue in East Pakistan in 1955 drove nearly 2.40 lakh Hindus out of East Pakistan. Even the adoption of a fanatic anti-Hindu Islamic Constitution played as a lethal instrument to push the unfortunate Hindus over the Indian border. Again a mass exodus took place in 1964 when the Hazrat Bal incident turned into the mass killings of Hindus in Dacca and other areas in East Pakistan. Even in 1971 when Bangladesh won Independence from the claws of Pakistan, about 7.3 million refugees fled to India.

Apart from these lawful migrants, there were many more who crossed the border stealthily either with forged documents or none at all. There is no device to take stock of such illegitimate migrants who are significantly legion.

Indeed, since the death of Gandhi, the situation of East Pakistan worsened and a one-way traffic of refugees from East Pakistan started and the exodus of hundreds and thousands of them continued through the decades.

Unfortunately the Government of India was reluctant to recognize the influx as permanent. Its policy towards the refugees from East Pakistan was conspicuously different from that in the West Punjab. It took a number of measures to prevent an 'exchange' and to restrict refugee inflow to the eastern region in India. Besides, the Nehru-Liaquat Pact, passport system was introduced to regulate the population movement. Also in 1956, the Indian government introduced another measure, migration certificate to restrict the refugee inflow. Ironically as to the dictum of the Nehru-Liaquat Ali Pact, many Muslims returned to their hearth and home in India that they had left after the Partition but very few Hindus dared go back to their ancestral home in Pakistan. Hence the enormous burden of swarming refugees being heaped on India, particularly on West Bengal, was enhancing the social and economic problems awfully.

Of course, Nehru expected that the exodus could be reversed. His point was that the Punjabis had been driven out from their hearths and homes but by contrast the Bengalees by migrating, by fits and starts, proved that they had the option of staying or of leaving. Even the attitude of the high brows of the government establishments was biased and they infused disparity in treating the West Pakistani refugees and the East Pakistan refugees with much duplicity. Probably, the Government of India did not want to acknowledge all the victims of India's vivisection irrespective of their mother tongue at par. On the contrary, the Government of India felt that rehabilitation for the refugees from East Pakistan was unnecessary and it would be better to persuade them to go back to Pakistan. Indeed, the Govt. of India failed to realize the truth and understand the reality.

Hence the plight of the East Pakistan Hindus was miserable and they were made to feel that they had no place to survive. In India, they were unwanted and in Pakistan they were outcast. They seemed to be cursed with none to call them their own either in India or in Pakistan. The 'divide and rule' policy of the British was quickened beyond all bounds under the Muslim League regime in East Pakistan. When deliberate attempts were made to raise them into a class of 'horrenvolks' and reduce the Hindus to a state of vassalage. Virtually they were reduced to experimental guinea-pigs to serve the ends of both the countries in their political laboratories.[5]

MEASURES TAKEN

However, consequent upon the Partition to deal with the colossal problem due to mammoth migration from Pakistan, the Government of India set up the Rehabilitation Ministry in September 1947 to settle the burning issues relating to relief and rehabilitation of the displaced persons.

The objectives of the Ministry were as follows:

(a) to provide relief and rehabilitation to persons displaced from their original place of residence by reason of the Partition of India.

(b) to sort out custody, management and disposal of property declared by law to be the evacuee property.

(c) to look into payment of compensations to displaced persons for immovable property they left in West Pakistan.

Plans of the Ministry of Rehabilitation were generally carried through the agencies of the State Governments.

The Constitution of India in its Seventh Schedule provides for "the relief and rehabilitation of persons displaced from their original place of residence by reason of setting up the Dominions of India and Pakistan".

On 10 November, 1948, an ordinance was passed to control the admission into and to regulate the movements in India of persons from Pakistan. According to the ordinance, "No person shall enter India from any place in Pakistan whether directly or indirectly unless he is in possession of a permit".

But this ordinance could not hold good in the case of the East Pakistan refugees as they had to enter into the Indian border like human flood as long as there was communal violence.

At a meeting held in the Writers' Building, Kolkata on 2 March, 1950, Mohan Lal Saxena[8], the then Minister of Rehabilitation, Government of India instructed the representatives of the eastern States, i.e., Tripura, Assam, Bihar, Orissa and West Bengal to restrict the government work only to relief (Trankarya) rather than the rehabilitation (Punarbasan) for two reasons.

Firstly, since a great percentage of people came to West Bengal having left behind their land and they were likely to return to East Pakistan so the government should do nothing that would help in developing any permanent stake on their part in the land of their refuge.

Secondly, since the crisis had occurred suddenly, no one knew its exact dimension and the government could not take any responsibility.

Saxena was in favour of establishing the relief camps in border areas to facilitate their quick return to East Pakistan. He is believed to have made a case for keeping surveillance on the refugees so that they could not melt into the local populace. As a sequel, about 32,000 Muslims who had left West Bengal before 31, March, 1957 came back to West Bengal and reclaimed the land already occupied by the refugees of East Pakistan whereas very few Hindus dared go back to their own hearths and homes in East Pakistan. Hence the old as well as new refugees made the social and financial condition of West Bengal worst to bear any more human burden.

Indeed, the influx of refugees to West Bengal in 1947 seemed to be a mere trickle in comparison with the angry, swirling torrent of refugees that poured into East Punjab so it had become easier for the Government of India to tackle the problem of the West Pakistan refugees by all means but for the East Bengal refugees, the influx was not a sudden spate but a perennial rush stretching over decades and the movement basked like ebbs and tides epitomising an unending trail. It was really a Herculean task to surmise that maelstrom of fleeing mass and to encounter it.

Rehabilitation measures were not taken up in West Bengal until the mid-1950 because the shortage of fund and resources made the government very reluctant to accept refugees from East Pakistan. However, according to the time of their arrival, the government had to categorize them into two groups:

1) Those who migrated between October, 1946 and March, 1958 were designated "old migrants." They numbered 4,11,7000, of whom 31,32,000 stayed in West Bengal for rehabilitation. When the refugee inflow declined substantially during 1957 and 1958, the government decided to close all camps in West Bengal. Out of the total of 45,000 camp-families, only 10,000 families were eligible to settle in West Bengal and the rest were to be sent to other States.
2) The second category was of those who arrived in West Bengal between April 1958 and December 1963 and were not eligible for relief or rehabilitation. They numbered 61,000 of whom 55,000 stayed in West Bengal. In 1961, owing to the terrible disturbances in East Pakistan, mass exodus resumed. Hence those who migrated between January 1964 and March 1971 were designated "New migrants" and they numbered 1,114600. They were considered only for the government relief if they agreed to settle outside West Bengal.

However, 6,00000 preferred to remain in West Bengal even without any government assistance. It is found from the estimate that the total refugee population in West Bengal would be around 6 million up to 1973.[8]

SETTLEMENT OUTSIDE WEST BENGAL

Indeed, West Bengal had already been over-populated with a population density of 800 persons per sq. mile. Besides, the majority of the displaced persons was agriculturists and West Bengal had very little of land left for agricultural settlement or to accommodate millions of the refugees.

Moreover, the reluctance of the Central Government and its niggardly and half-hearted help to the refugees from East Pakistan created further obstacles to successful rehabilitation.

U. Bhaskar Rao, himself a seasoned bureaucrat expressed his angst against higher-ups and conformed his bonhomie towards the refugees, "...what one needed here were virtues alien to bureaucratic routine—sympathy, understanding, great compassion, the urge to succour and sustain, attributes almost of divinity. ...Here one dealt with human sufferings, strove to erase its memories and to instil in their place a sense of security and well-being joined to self-reliance and self respect".[9] Unfortunately this sort of attitudes had never been shown to the East Pakistan refugees and the high-brow officials did not realize, "....the refugees in the East (East Bengal) came from a different milieu, the influences that moulded their lives were different".[10]

Indeed, it was the tireless national endeavour to set the victims back on their feet and absorb them into the fabric of the community.

Without considering the miserable condition of the East Pakistan refugees, the Government of India announced, "...no able bodied male immigrant...capable of earning his own living be given gratuitous relief either in cash or in kind for himself as well as members of his family for more than a week from the date of their arrival...."[11]

Moreover, in the government circular, dt. 25 November, 1948, the official definition of a 'refugee' had been clarified that only those persons who had managed to reach West Bengal between 1st June, 1947 and 25 June, 1948 'on account of civil disturbances or fear of such disturbances or the Partition of India' were to be entitled to relief and rehabilitation.

Subsequently, another order of December, 1948 specified the government policy that no refugee would be registered after 15 January, 1949.[12]

In consequence of the directives of the Government of India, the Government of West Bengal notified that by 31 October, 1949 all relief camps in West Bengal must be closed down. Later the closing date was extended till 31 December, 1949. It was further clarified that "As soon as lands have been allotted and tents offered and railway warrants issued, refugees are expected to move to their new places of settlement. If they do not, they unnecessarily hold up rehabilitation. It should be made clear to them that by doing so they cannot continue the life of the camp which shall positively be closed.[13]

Thus the nocuous attitude of the Central Government aggravated the mental agonies of the refugees and enervated the spirit of the social activists by exercising apathy towards the wretched displaced persons. "For many years past, it has been the fashion to speak of the refugees from East Pakistan as a creature apart. Often he is held up as an object of derision and contempt.[14]

Indeed, the West Bengal's economy due to paucity of resources, already under heavy pressure, was in no shape to bear the strain of refugees' relief and rehabilitation. When the overcrowding in West Bengal assumed impossible proportion in 1954, a decision was taken to send the refugees to the neighbouring States.

Considering the scope of settlement in Andaman and keeping in view the proposal of Dr. B.C. Roy, the Chief Minister of West Bengal, it was further decided to settle at least a few thousands of East Pakistan refugees there.

Consequently in March 1949, the first batch of 202 refugee families was sent to Port Blair for rehabilitation. The transportation of the refugees, despite the provocation of the Communist Party of India and also due to the spread of wild rumour about the forbidden land, 'Kalapani' went on as to the quota specified by the Government of India of which obvious aim was to cleanse West Bengal of a disgruntled population liable to be infected with the virus of Communism.

Though refugees played a key role in the development of the Left-wing politics in West Bengal yet the relation between the refugees and the C.P.I. was rather instrumental, not congenial. The Communists persuaded the refugees to oppose the settlement in Andaman and instigated to demand resettlement only in West Bengal with a view to winning their confidence and exploit it in the ensuing election to be held in 1952.

In 1950, the Union Home Minister Sardar Vallabbhai Patel went to Calcutta to have a first hand knowledge about the impact of Nehru-Liaquat Pact. On 18 April, he informed Nehru that the opposition leaders were on the spree to catch fish in the murky pool of politics. He mentioned that "People have an eye in the next election (1952) where refugees would have votes. They do not hesitate to adopt a policy which would break the back of Bengal".

Indeed Patel's apprehension had been turned out true but the reality was something else. Prof. P.K. Chakravorty remarked, "It is a travesty of truth to say that the refugees were unwilling to go outside West Bengal for rehabilitation. They were sent to Uttar Pradesh and Andaman & Nicobar Islands. They did not desert their rehabilitation sites. They made good there. They cleared virgin forests, reclaimed waste land and prospered. They found the land in Andaman Islands to their liking, in spite of the dangers that lurked in the virgin forests. Once they succeeded in overcoming their initial reluctance to cross the seas, the refugees willingly left for their new homes in the islands... for carrying out for themselves a new country in the image of the old".[15]

But the Central Government restricted the inflow of the migrants to the islands on various pretexts. Obviously the government did not quite relish the idea of the islands developing into an appendage of West Bengal. The motive becomes clear from the statement of the Union Labour and Rehabilitation Minister, R.K. Khadilkar in the Rajya Sabha on 3rd December, 1974 in reply to a question raised by Dr. R.K. Chakraborty. The Minister said, "...so far as the Andamans are concerned, I have said earlier that it is a special category. We want to develop it in a different way. I want to say one thing. The Ex-Army people have got a colony there. We must look to the defence side also"[16].

Consequently the settlement of the East Bengal refugees in Andaman had been stopped. Had the flow of migrants been allowed to continue, the solution of the economic rehabilitation of the refugees might have been easier and the Dandakaranya Project would have been unnecessary.

Ignoring the instigation and propaganda, the refugees who dared settle in Andaman, by dint of hard labour and relentless exertion, they have won the fate. Overcoming all adversities and despondency, they have become minions of fortune. Their scions are now objects of envy of others because of their success in life and respectability in the society.

ENDNOTES

1. Azad, Abul Kalam, Former Union Minister, in his book 'India Wins Freedom' transliterated by Humayun Kabir, pp. 170.
2. Wolpert in his book, "Jinnah of Pakistan," p. 286
3. Mohanlal Saxena took over the portfolio on June 8, 1948 and changed the name of the Ministry of Relief and Rehabilitation to Ministry of Rehabilitation, dropping the word 'relief' in 1949.
4. V.P. Menon : Secretary to the Union Home Minister, Sardar Vallabhbhai Patel, author of "The Transfer of Power in India," p. 318.
5. "The Refugees in the Post World War", by J. Vernant, 1953.
6. 'Mission with Mountbatten' by Campbell-Johnson, Allan, New York, 1951.
7. 'A Tale of Woes of East Pakistan Minorities'. 1966, National Library, Calcutta.
8. Source: "Refugees in West Bengal. A Study of the Growth & Distribution of Refugee Settlement within C.M.D". By Pranati Choudhuri, Centre of Studies in Social Sciences, Cal-29.
9. U. Bhaskar Rao, 'The Story of Rehabilitation', pp. 2-3.
10. Ibid, pp. 38.
11. Memo No. 5610 (13) F.R. from the Secretary, R&R Deptt. Govt. of W.B. dt 22 Nov. 1948.
12. Memo dated 20 Dec, 1948 in GB. IB 1838/48.
13. Memo. No. 8637 (13) Rehab, Govt. of W.B. dated 9 Dec.1949.
14. U. Bhaskar Rao "History of Rehabilitation" pp. 148
15. 'The Marginal Men', by Prof. P.K. Chakravorty, Pub. Lumiere Books, 1990, p. 230.

6

Prelude to Refugee Settlement in Andaman

The success of any colonization has been achieved in any country by an attempt of the settlement comprising even number of males and females but in the case of Andaman during the British regime, the penal settlement was strikingly characterized by an overwhelmingly large number of males but the number of female convicts was extremely negligible.

In the later days the convicts after the expiry of their term of sentence were allowed to settle in these islands either by bringing their family from the mainland or by marrying female convicts incarcerated in the 'Randi barrack' at Port Blair. Indeed, the penal settlement commenced during the tenure of Col. Farrar who was the Superintendent of British establishment in these islands from 1923-31.

During pre-Independence times, Andaman, originally a land of autochthones, was made a haven for desçendants of convicts, known as the Andaman Indians or Local Borns consisting of people from all communities including Bhantus, Moplas, Wahabis, Burmese, etc.

Only after the Independence, attempts were made for all round development of the islands by offering scope of settlement to the former East Bengal refugees and in due course, to Tamil repatriates from Burma and Ceylon, Malayali, Telegu, Ranchi and other migrants.

The conditions prevailing in these islands were considered favourable for new settlement and the Partition of India on 15th August, 1947 made the situation more viable. So the Government of India had to sort out a systematic approach for the resettlement of East Pakistan refugees in the islands.

At the beginning, the Punjab delegation was invited to visit Andaman for estimating the suitability of the island for rehabilitation of the West Punjabi refugees but it was resolved that the environmental conditions of Andaman were in deep contrast and adverse for settlement of the Punjabi refugees from West Pakistan and the proposal was discarded officially.

On the contrary, a number of delegations, team of experts and experienced officials expressed their favourable opinions for the suitable schemes welcoming agricultural settlement in the islands and considering the feasibility of the islands, they suggested rehabilitation of refugees from East Pakistan.

In this matter, a very useful study which formed the framework of the colonization scheme for Andaman being assigned by the Government of India was made by H.R. Shivdasani. As to his observation, it was decided that about five thousand agricultural refugee families might easily be settled there. He further opined that the Andaman Islands, having been scarcely populated and enough land area being available without affecting the depleting aborigines, were quite suitable for the rehabilitation of refugees, partly at least.

PHYSICAL FEATURES

To implement the colonization scheme, the topography of the islands was taken into consideration. Total land area of the Andaman Islands is 6408 sq. kms which has to be reckoned with as a limiting factor and 75 per cent of it is covered by rich tropical forests. The rainfall though mercifully more or less continuing over nine months of a year creates unpredictable anxiety but with proper soil and water conservation, the land can be made arable for paddy cultivation.

Keeping aside the forest land about 1300 sq. miles, the reserved area for the aborigines about 500 sq. miles and the barren areas of small islets, only an area of 226 sq. miles, was available during initial phases of colonization.

The islands' notable feature is their archipelagic layout. The terrestrial potentiality as well as its submarine territory containing various corals, shell fish and other mineral wealth of the sea all around the islands and in particular its strategic importance is to be considered seriously.

All these factors are squarely related to the colonization scheme. There are various economic, political and strategic overtones quite peculiar to this territory which should not be forgotten for realistic land and sea utilization plans.

However, during the initial stages of settlement in 1950s, the Andaman Islands were chosen whereas the Nicobar group of Islands which is only 120 miles away from Port Blair was not considered for colonization because some of the Nicobar Islands were by then overpopulated and needed dispersal of these tribal population to some other islands for their own rehabilitation. This problem deterred the colonization process.

Moreover, if the colonization scheme was thrust upon the Nicobarese, the natural growth of these tribal populations would be deterred leading to terrible consequences as they would be exposed to some degenerative diseases emanating their physical existence at stake as well as their age old culture and tradition would face the threat of extinction. So Nicobar was not then considered for colonization.

But the situation of Andaman was obviously favourable so the Government of India made plans to settle some of the refugees in Andaman taking into account the climate and the soil of Andaman being similar to those of East Bengal. Besides, the land was virgin and deserted by the old settlers so there might be no possibilities of any clash with the local people as they were concentrated only at Port Blair and nearby villages.

LAND-PEOPLE RATIO

The Forest Department welcomed the prospect of colonization as a means of securing a permanent labour force in place of the floating labourers which was available only at that time. But for various reasons the proper action was not taken beyond the steps of establishing one or two forest villages. Under this situation, the proposal to settle a large number of cultivators in the islands and to develop the potential resources of the soil to the utmost was accepted by the Government of India keeping in mind as to how much land should be deforested and reclaimed to implement the colonization plan.

According to a note made by the Inspector General of Forests, Government of India, on 'Colonization in the Andaman Islands', an analysis of the land area of the region considering different aspects of the land use pattern is mentioned below:

TABLE

Description		*Area in sq. miles*
Old settlements & secondary Jungle	–	40
Jarawa reserve	–	190
Sentinel Island (Tribal area)	–	20
Little Andaman (Tribal area)	–	290
Inland Waterways (Tribal area)		80
Unproductive forests	–	100
Unworkable islands	–	60
Mangrove forest	–	200
Accessible timber forest	–	1420
Total area of Andaman	–	**2400**

Regarding Little Andaman, it was remarked in the note that these 290 sq. miles may be made available for forestry and settlement in the course of the next 100 years considering the docile nature of the Onge tribe. Besides, a large reserve of some 500 sq. miles of forest which was inhabited by aboriginal Onges who numbered only a few hundred souls and evidence showed that they were dying out slowly. So this vast area might be utilized for colonization without affecting the interest of the aborigines.

Hence, chances of all round progress and development of the islands seemed to be a possibility only after colonization of migrants and the settlement might be a success if it was done in the desolate areas of Middle and North Andamans and also in some villages of South Andaman.

In Andaman, only East Pakistan refugees were sent in consultation with the Government of West Bengal. The medley of these refugees included middle class landowners with some education as well as illiterate agricultural labourers. At the beginning, they were misguided and reluctant but when the government announced its decision to offer cultivable land and other assistances to each family who would willingly settle in Andaman, these despondent and destitute people were enthusiastic to move there. There were some interesting instances of these men stranded in railway stations or camps persuading forlorn women to become their wives or daughters in order to register themselves as their families which were mandatory to seek settlement in Andaman. Thus many of them could ship themselves as family units at the government expense and were settled there. During the Second Five-Year Plan, some 1200 displaced persons accompanied by their families were sent to Andaman and over 20,000 acres of land for paddy cultivation were acquired for their settlement.

During the British regime, the agriculture and work of unskilled labour formed the main occupation of the ex-convicts who were allowed to settle in Andaman. Thus the development of linear settlement pattern took place on both the sides of the roads. Though the seat of administration was in Ross Island, Aberdeen village had become the main centre of day to day activities.

Dr. S.T. Das remarked, "The free-settlers (ex-convicts) were compelled to take up agriculture or any other occupation which in majority of the cases, were not in harmony with ancestral occupation......As regards agriculture, only rice cultivation has so far been taken up. Now government job has diverted more than 50 per cent from agriculture"[1].

In due course, there was a further decline in the agricultural occupation at the cost of government services.

The break-up of the total population is as follows:

Labour, skilled and semi-skilled - 33%

Agriculture and plantation - 29%

Office work, trade and commerce - 38%

Hence a great decline in the agricultural activities gave rise to an unbalanced economy but the decline in the growth of population significantly made the situation favourable for further settlement in Andaman.

The population density of the islands was only 7 per cent per sq. mile in 1941 whereas in the other States, the figures were too high. The following table shows the contrast.

TABLE

State-wise Distribution	*Density of Population (Sq. miles)*
India as a whole	284
Kerala	901
West Bengal	776
Orissa	243
Rajasthan	120
Andaman and Nicobar	7

During 1941-1951, there was a great decline in the population considering the daedal variation from 14.41 per cent to 8.41 per cent which attributes to a large scale migration of Burmese and other nationals to their own countries after the attainment of the Indian Independence on 15th August, 1947. Hence the scope of colonization was ample and opened the door for refugee settlements in Andaman.

LAND RESOURCES

Andaman is under a deep mantle of forest cover and occupies an area of 2508 sq. miles. The land resources for colonization and for the development of agriculture can be obtained by the clearance of the forest but the optimum area of forest that be cleared, is a controversial topic.

The logical assumption to ensure the economic well-being of a country is that a minimum percentage of its land surface would be under forest but it cannot be applied to the local areas or regions of that country and it can only be applied to the country as a whole. Hence, Andaman must be taken in isolation in evaluating optimum per centage of land under forest.

Shivdasani opined, "The Andamans cannot be regarded as a country by itself. It is a part of India and the average figure of 25 per centage of forest for a country cannot be applied to these islands. To consider the deficiency of forest area in other parts of the country, these islands cannot be kept entirely under forest".

Shivdasani further remarked, "Exploitation and development of any area specially one which is detached and has restricted communication with the rest of the country and the world at large, make it necessary that the area should be self-sufficient in respect of the labour required for utilization of the forest and also in respect of its food requirements. Therefore, land within the forest area has to be made available to fulfil these requirements".[2]

According to ecologists, at least 25 per cent of the land of a country should be left under forest cover. Others oppose to this view considering the special conditions of these islands and emphasize that at least 50 per cent of the land should be under forest cover.

Hence, out of a total area of 2500 sq. miles, 1300 sq. miles should be left for the forests and 1000 sq. miles may be utilized for agriculture and industrial development. It seemed that nearly 5000 agricultural families may be settled in these islands.

Besides the availability of arable land, another crucial point to be pondered is how to protect the existence and preserve the identity of the aborigines without affecting their age-old culture. Hence the areas where the aborigines inhabit must be kept out of colonization scheme. The total area to be set apart for them may be roughly 500 sq. miles which represents about 20 per cent of the total area of the islands.

However, considering all the environmental factors and prevailing issues like the rights of the aborigines and that of the old settlers and in particular, the suitability of settlement, Andaman was finally chosen to solve, partly at least, the immense problem of refugee rehabilitation.

As the total lands of the Andaman and Nicobar Islands belong to the Government of India, the Administration is authorized to acquire lands for colonization purposes. According to British India Regulations, "...all the land is vested in the crown and is held at fixed rent under license from the Chief Commissioner on certain conditions which among others, make devolution and transfer subject to the consent of the Chief Commissioner and authorize him to determine the occupation on compensation at an year's notice or breach of the conditions.[3]

After the Independence, the same regulation has been put into practice so the allotment of lands to the new settlers bore no changes or charges. Hence the reasonably estimated area for refugee settlement was planned to be reclaimed through the clearance of forests and the land should be made available keeping in mind the following facts:

(a) Total area of Andaman	–	2508 sq miles
(b) Area reserved for aborigines	–	500 sq miles
(c) Area of small islands not to be colonized	–	430 sq. miles
(d) Area left out not to be colonized	–	52 sq. miles
(e) Total area not to be colonized	–	2282 sq. miles
(f) Area to be colonized - (a-e)	=	226 sq. miles

Hence, according to the nature of the lands, the colonizable area of 226 sq. miles containing around 142370 acres has been classified specifically in the following groups:

(a) Valley land for paddy	–	37,730 acres
(b) Flat slopping land for paddy	–	53,850 acres
(c) Higher slopping land for fruits, vegetables, homesteads	–	38690 acres
(d) Land for coconut plantation	–	12100 acres
Total area	**–**	**142370 acres**

Considering the availability of land and its suitability for colonization, the Andaman Islands, particularly South, Middle and North Andamans had the highest potentialities to be colonized both in the river valleys due to perennial supply of water for paddy cultivation and in the coastal lands for coconut, and arecanut plantations. On survey, eleven valleys had been identified as suitable for colonization in Andaman. As many as eight valleys are in Middle Andaman, two in North Andaman and the last one in Havelock Island.

The Forest Department has underlined the probable pattern of land-use under the following heads:

(a) flat paddy land,

(b) terraced paddy cultivation,

(c) fruits, vegetables, homesteads, cattle grazing, and

(d) coconut plantation.

In the following table, the four regions earmarked for refugee settlement have been arranged according to the availability of land, keeping in view the above mentioned land-use pattern---

TABLE 4

Regions	*Flat paddy Land*	*Terraced Land*	*Homesteads Land*	*Coconut Plantation*	*Total Acres*
South Andaman	3100 acres	5500 acres	4200 acres	1300 acres	14150
Middle Andaman	25035 acres	28600 acres	13600 acres	4525 acres	73760
North Andaman	7440 acres	12200 acres	13290 acres	4230 acres	37160
Baratang Island	2160 acres	7500 acres	5600 acres	2040 acres	17300

The first settlement was initiated in March, 1949 in South Andaman on the readily available land in the old settlement areas, deserted either by the ex-convicts or by Burmese and other nationals. Afterwards, attention for settlement was shifted from South Andaman to Middle and North Andaman for obvious reasons.

IMPLEMENTATION OF THE COLONIZATION SCHEME

Although there was no dearth of land in Andaman during initial settlement, it was not found easy to implement the colonization scheme successfully. Indeed, it was not related to rehabilitation alone but some human factors, i.e., emotion, tradition, culture, heritage, etc., would have to be considered earnestly. Besides, the functioning and the progress of the colonization scheme would be determined by the degree of materialization of the working scheme for settlement, i.e., food and shelter, communication facilities, occupation, training for self-help projects, etc.

The main activities with regard to the planned settlement are given below:

(a) Availability of Land

The climate of Andaman is wet and humid like that of East Bengal. The soil is humus and hence quite fertile. For the agricultural community, the rehabilitation in these islands is suitable. In fact, due to farsightedness in the planning of colonization, the settlement has become successful and the displaced persons from the erstwhile East Pakistan grow golden corns in abundance in the virgin soil of Andaman.

According to the colonization scheme, each refugee family would be given 5 acres of cleared land for paddy cultivation and other 5 acres of unclear forest hilly land for homestead and kitchen garden.

Shunning all dalliances and reluctance, the refugee settlers engaged themselves in hard labour and by dint of their relentless perseverance; the settlers could shape the virgin land of Andaman as to their homeland and Rangat, Diglipur, Neil, Havelock and Little Andaman have been turned into the granary of the territory. Significantly, with the passage of time their descendants have prospered in life not only by tilling the land or doing plantation alone but also by qualifying themselves as doctors, engineers, professors, teachers, scientists entrepreneurs and for other white collar jobs.

(b) Inclement Weather

In the Andaman Islands, the rainy season persists almost throughout the year. Only a few months in the summer remain dry so that the clearance of forest and reclamation of land may be done during that period but must be over before the onslaught of rains.

Indeed, the settlement work used to be undertaken during the dry season from November to April. Generally the refugee families were settled by the month of May so that they could acclimatize themselves with the new environment and start cultivation work with the beginning of the rainy season.

(c) Government Assistance

After reclamation of the land, transit camps made of local materials and situated near the jetty, were made ready to receive refugees just after their disembarkment. Later, they were shifted to their allotted sites in the permanent settlement area.

During the period of their stay in the reception camps, the government assistances as mentioned in the letter No. 91 (2) RF/49, dated 7 April, 1949 of the Deputy Secretary, Ministry of Relief and Rehabilitation, Government of India were offered to the new settlers as stated below:

(a) free passage,

(b) ten acres of land, free of cost to each family,

(c) exemption of land revenue for the first two years,

(d) paddy seeds,

(e) agricultural equipments

(f) two plough-animals

(g) milch-animal

(h) two bags of super phosphates, etc.

Moreover, each family was granted a monthly allowance of Rs. 30/- per adult and Rs. 15/- per child below eight years up to a maximum limit of Rs. 100/- for 9 months. For the construction of one's own house, house building materials worth Rs. 1200/- and Rs. 300/- for labour charges were given to them.

Every agriculture family selected for settlement in Andaman was granted an ex-gratia amount of Rs. 1050/- and a loan of Rs. 1730/- repayable in ten annual instalments to meet all other expenses.

However, the above said facilities were offered to the first batch of the settlers but to the later batches, loans were sanctioned under different heads on a varying scale.

(d) Responses of the Refugees

Though the terms of settlement in Andaman were lucrative and alluring, yet the reluctance of the refugees was obvious and persistently developed due to many factors.

During those days, the great hindrance would pose an insurmountable difficulty to reach Andaman because of the great distance by more than 1200 kms from Kolkata separating Andaman by the fathomless sea, 'Kalapani' and this spine-chilling sobriquet was usefully synchronized with the ghostly penal settlement. Moreover, concocted rumours and lesser known facts about Andaman, the forbidden land, would create panic and make the hapless refugees suspicious about the land of gruesome nightmares.

Besides, in the mainland, especially in West Bengal, displaced persons from East Pakistan developed a growing tendency to savour the fraudulent charms to the relief, meant for the refugees and long exposure to the charity of doles and enjoying the luxury of idleness made them somehow dalliant and demoralized. Once a refugee found asylum in a familiar milieu, he would display a strong reluctance to move out. He along with others resisted official attempts to dislodge them. Often he met the government persuasion to transport him to settlement sites outside West Bengal with a sullen hostility and with every stratagem of evasion.

But in the case of Andaman, at the beginning they had been provoked and misguided by the comrades of the Communist Party of India but gradually they became convinced by the earlier settlers and were allured by the government proposal and assistances. Thus the settlement got momentum.

(e) Encounter with Autochthons

The original inhabitants of the Andaman Islands are the primitive people, i.e., Jarawas, Great Andamanese, Sentinelese, and Onges. With the passage of time, the Onges and the Great Andamanese have become docile but the Jarawas of South and Middle Andaman as well as the Sentinelese who live in North Sentinel Island in isolation, remained hostile all through. With the progress of the refugee settlement, the peaceful life of the Jarawas had been affected and disturbed, particularly by the thundering sound of the heavy bulldozers and earthmovers deployed for reclamation of the forest land. They became vindictive because of the encroachment in their own land and their angst and animus found expression in their aggressive activities through attacks and raids on their neighbouring refugee villages. Naturally, the government had to chalk out plans for rehabilitation of the refugees in the sites far away from the tribal reserve areas in Middle and South Andaman to avoid encounter with the tribal Jarawas. Moreover, several outposts of the Bush Police have been set up bordering the tribal area in order to preserve the aborigines and to protect the refugees.

(f) Transport and Communication

Almost after sixty years of the initiation of the colonization schemes in Andaman, even today, the hazards of communication between Port Blair and the settlement villages in Middle and North Andamans have not yet been kneaded away and the settlers of far off areas are still to depend on waterways or to trudge through the jungles.

At the early days of settlement, the settlers had to waddle through canals infested with crocodiles during ebb tide carrying all their belongings as head load or by using yoke to carry kids and heavy loads. The journey was so strenuous and sedulous that the migrants would become exasperated and despondent. Even to fetch water from springs, streams or rivulets, they used to trek long distance. For rations and medicines, they had to bear with those sorts of travails.

During those days, inter and intra island communication facilities were nil and the settlers had been suffering from a feeling of isolation and banishment.

(g) Topographical Hazards

After clearance of the forest land, the stumps of the huge trees were studded and strewn all over the field occupying nearly 25 to 50 per cent of the land causing thorough cultivation impossible because to cut out the stumps or to burn them off was not an easy job for the handicapped settlers. The undulating nature in Andaman flaunts soil erosion as a result of deforestation and torrential rainfall. To check the erosion, bunds were needed to be built up all along the agricultural fields. To mitigate the physical conditions, terrace cultivation was to be adopted. Unfortunately the refugees of East Pakistan were not accustomed to it. Hence, despite their all out efforts and hard labour, the produce was not satisfactory.

In Andaman, the villages were set up in the midst of jungle surrounded by dense forest so during the harvesting season, swarms of insects, flocks of parrots and bands of deer happened to be a constant menace and to harvest the ripen corns would seem impossible at times.

(h) Social Stratagem

At the beginning, the selection of the refugees from the mainland transit camps for the settlement in Andaman was made in a hectic manner but not discreetly at the face of political stalemate. While considering the settlement of the agriculturists, there was no plan to send fishermen, barbers, priests, carpenters, potters etc. The medley of people selected at the outset for the settlement in Andaman included mostly middle class landowners with some education who ultimately deserted Andaman and tried their luck in West Bengal but the illiterate peasants had to stay back. Thus the colonization scheme was primarily imbalanced. To develop a balanced social structure in such a cut-off place like Andaman, at least a few educated people should have been sent there. Hence the social entity does not grow. To the contrary, the new settlers did not adapt themselves to the new environment in the right spirit. The villagers in complete destitution developed misunderstanding leading to quarrels that would threaten the harmony and social amity.

(i) Discontent among the Local People

The first phase of the settlement was started in South Andaman for the availability of already cleared and cultivable land deserted by the ex-convicts and other repatriates. Moreover, the area was suitable for settlement because of its proximity to Port Blair town. But hindrances arose out of the discontent and objection of the local people living in the neighbouring villages and that quite often led to clash of interests between both the parties. The constant protests leading to processions, demonstrations and representations made by the local people drew the attention of the government and ultimately plans for further settlement in South Andaman were stopped.

It is interesting to note that once these local people at the command of the British mercilessly drove away the original natives of the islands, the aborigines, at the point of guns to make room for their own settlement. But with the passing of time, they have become the overlords of the land and begun to raise their voice to resist further settlement. Of course, they have their own pleas and reasons to protest.

However, solely due to the continued resistance and opposition of the local people, the Government of India gave up the plan to extend rehabilitation programme in South Andaman and thenceforth the emphasis was given to further settlement in the distant islands in Middle and North Andamans. Thus the translation of the colonization scheme became easy and fast.

(j) Efforts of the Officials

The refugees from East Pakistan unfortunately being truncated and brutalized by a stark animal existence, ventured desperately merely to seek a shelter and faced the destiny to be terminated. Indeed, they would belong to a new breed of homo sapiens! They became the marginal men, who were not inhibited by the values and morals of the settled society. They were uprooted and led a peripheral life. Being despondent and allured, they wished to settle but they had no idea about Andaman, rather they were scared of the forbidden land, 'Kalapani'. So necessary feedbacks and proper briefings about the prospect of rehabilitation there should have been imparted prior to the dispersal.

The government officials who were incharge of the settlement process were not acquainted with the language and customs of the refugees. The communication gap was the root cause of disbelief and reluctance. Later, these problems were depleted because of persistent efforts of some Bengali knowing officials of Andaman-Nicobar Administration, viz., S. Raha, S.K. Pal, Priten Roy, etc., to stimulate the growing willingness of the refugees to settle in Andaman.

ENDNOTES

1. "The Andaman & Nicobar Islands : A Study of Habitat, Economy and Society"— by Dr. S.T. Das. Sagar Publication, N. Delhi-1
2. H.R. Shivdasani: Report on the Possibilities of Colonization etc., G.O.I., Ministry of Home Affairs.
3. 'Local Gazetteer—The Andaman & Nicobar Islands,' Calcutta - 1908, Govt. Publication.
4. 'Land and People of the Andamans'—by Prabhat Kumar Sen, Pub: P.G. Book Mart, Calcutta-9.

7

Progress of Settlement

Since 1946, the persecution and perdition inflicted on the Hindus of East Pakistan got tremendous momentum in the wake of the Partition of India which resulted in a large scale migration of refugees form East Pakistan to West Bengal. The rush and surge in an unending torrent of panicked people plunged into West Bengal for asylum had already strained the resources of the West Bengal government. The major hurdle for resettlement of this human cargo was the paucity of land so the scope of absorption of all refugees in West Bengal was quite impossible. It was a national problem so the Government of India had to confront it and sort out plans to disperse them over a widely scattered area of the Eastern Zone and even beyond.

But the refugees were antithetical to the plans of the government over their eviction from West Bengal. In this predicament, the refugees posed to pamper the whole process of sending them outside West Bengal. They demonstrated a sullen hostility towards every stratagem of evasion.

The government, of course, did not accept the argument that since the refugees were Bengalis, they were to be settled either in West Bengal or in Bengali speaking areas preferably contiguous to West Bengal. Further the Government of India refused to consider language as the principle of reorganizing the States of the Indian Union on the ground that it would

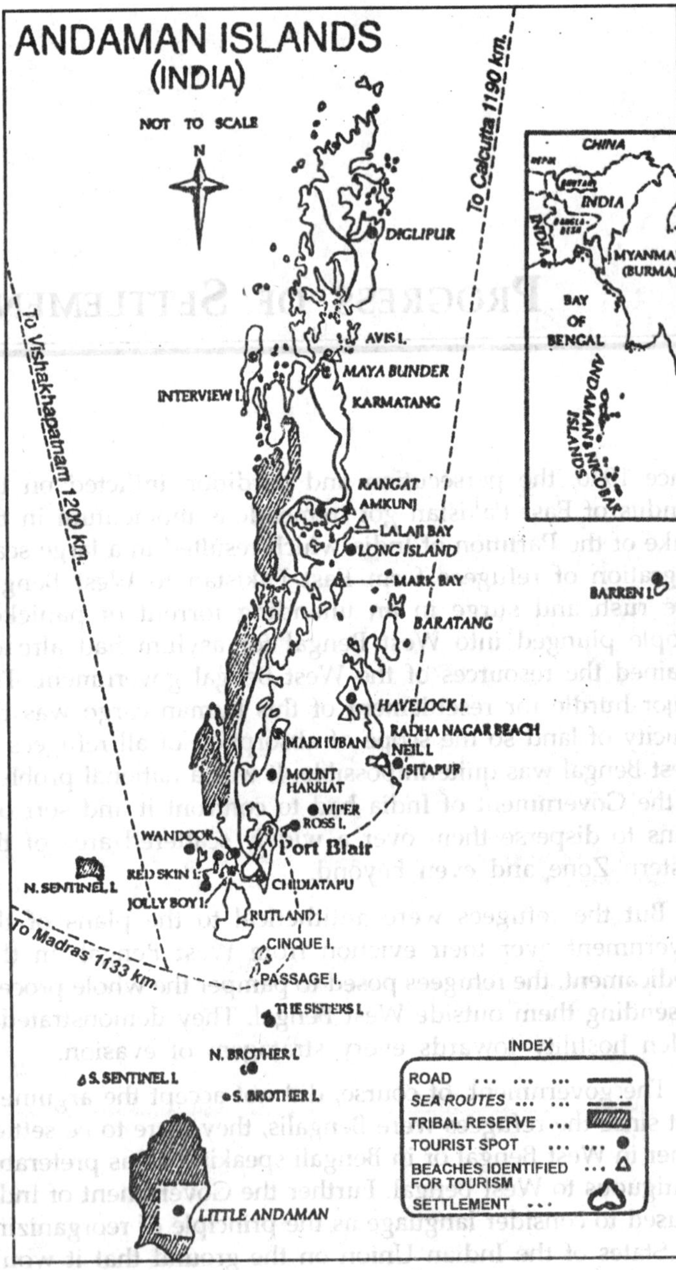

Settlement in Andaman

contribute to linguistic parochialism and ethnic chauvinism.

The much-touted J.V.P. Committee published its report in which it pleaded against the reorganization of States on the basis of language demands. So the government decided to send the excess of refugees to the neighbouring States of West Bengal for rehabilitation without considering the language demands.

In this regard, on December 30, 1947, N.C. Srivastava, Deputy Secretary, Government of India, sent directive No. R&R-4 (9)/GOI/ Ministry of Relief & Rehabilitation to all Provincial Governments explaining their responsibilities to share the burden of emergent refugee problems.

Unfortunately, the response of most of the States was not encouraging. From the official reports kept in the files, Nos. 351/49 & IDM 868/49 available in the State Archives, West Bengal, it is learnt, "while most of the States were aversive towards the displaced persons, the Andamans were conducive for their settlement".

The apathetical attitude of the reluctant States did not skip the notice of the Central Government. Time and again the refugee problems drew the attention of the Members of the Parliament and created commotions on the Floor evolving delectable discourses drooling over the issue.

On April, 1949, L.K. Maitra put the star-marked question in the Parliament, "The refugees from East Pakistan feel that they have no place in the whole of India today. They are like the wandering Jews. If they are to get any shelter outside West Bengal, they have to go to the Andamans, the erstwhile Penal Settlement".

Mohanlal Saxena, Union Minister for Relief and Rehabilitation replied, "Every Provincial government is a unit for administrative convenience. Provinces are not the patrimony or the paternal property of anybody. It is the property of every single Indian and he should be entitled to every inch of space in any part of India".

Referring to the polemic role of the Communist Party in exploiting the helplessness of the refugees in its favour, Shri Saxena said, "It is rather unfortunate that in the matter of refugee rehabilitation, party politics has come to play. It is most detestable... the question of refugees has been a pawn on the chess board of our politics. We must now try to take the wind out of the sails of these political agitators who want to make politics capital out of miseries of the refugees. I know, it is impossible to achieve anything spectacular in a short period. But if we set about this work of rehabilitation in a planned manner, I think, we can make much headway".

In the discourse, Shri Maitra interrupted, "But a planned scheme is necessary. Mere verbiage, mere platitude will not help us".

He further stated that despite the directives of the Central Government, certain Provincial governments were not cooperating on the question of dispersal of refugees in different provinces. He remarked, "So far as Eastern Pakistan refugees are concerned, Bihar, Assam, Orissa and other neighbouring states were set apart and they were not meant for the reception of the refugees from the Western Pakistan. But what happens when the Provincial Governments refuse to accept any refugees from East Pakistan and the pity is that the Central Government cannot force them to accept some of these displaced peoples from East Pakistan. If they do not do that, the Centre has got adequate powers to make them do it......As I told you, my people are forced to go to the Andamans for shelter. Nothing can be more painful. I hope, you realize the psychological effect of that".[1]

Ultimately, all the Provincial Governments agreed to accept refugees for rehabilitation in their States but considering the prospect of settlement in Andaman for readily available limited but cultivable lands for allotment to the East Pakistan refugees, the Government of India agreed to the West Bengal Government's proposal to rehabilitate them there.

According to the Census of 1951, colonization of these islands was suggested early in 1948, "...as at that time about 3000 acres of abandoned holdings were available for settlement".

Thus colonization programme of these islands commenced more as a programme of rehabilitation than that of colonization or development. All through such colonization schemes have in most cases retained their original complexion of rehabilitation. It is significant that the first scheme of settling around 450 East Bengal refugee families during the years 1949 - 1952 in the vicinity of Port Blair was actually sanctioned by the Ministry of Rehabilitation, Government of India.[2]

ROLE OF GOVERNMENT OF WEST BENGAL

Dr. Bidhan Chandra Roy, the then Chief Minister of West Bengal was eager for the refugee rehabilitation in Andaman but to have a first hand knowledge about the prospect of the settlement, he made arrangements for the visits of the Ministers to the islands.

In October,1948, an exploratory party headed by Nikunja Bihari Maity, Minister of Relief & Rehabilitation, Government of West Bengal visited Andaman and after a careful survey, the party members were unanimous in their opinion that the islands were admirably suitable for colonization of displaced families. Under the instruction of the Minister, a government press note was released by the Deputy Relief officer, S.C. Chatterjee stating, "Whoever wishes to go to the Andamans at one's own will, the Bengal Government intends to help them but it has no intention to compel them and allure them to go to the Andamans".[3]

Subsequently a team of experts including four unofficial members was sent to Andaman to survey the whole situation prevailing there. In its report, it was clearly stated that presently the islands were undeveloped. Roadways and transport system was not proper. The condition of agriculture, industry and trade was not good. It was further remarked, "In spite of all these drawbacks, there are plenty natural resources and their potentiality is also immense. If attempts are made judiciously, within no time, the Andamans will be converted into a full grown, well-flourished and prosperous country".[4]

It was observed, "Andaman is not insalubrious and soil is suitable for agriculture. Its climate and rainfall are not epinosic. The islands are covered with dense forest having no wild beasts and venomous reptiles. In the whole islands, out of total 8293 sq. kms of land, only about 50 sq. kms have been brought under cultivation, so enough lands are available".

Under these circumstances, the government started to recruit the willing refugees and asked them either to meet S.C. Chatterjee at his office at 10 A, Aukland Road or to send applications by post.[5]

On January 11, 1949, the Government of West Bengal released a press note explaining the objectives of settlement as desired by the Government of India. It was decided to send two hundred refugee families of East Pakistan to Andaman for settlement. Primarily agricultural families along with a few carpenters, blacksmiths, potters., etc., would be sent there.

Further, it was stated that by January 29, 1949, the application for settlement in Andaman must reach to S.C. Chatterjee and by February, 1949, they should be ready to sail for Andaman by the ship, *S.S. Maharaja*. In the application form, they should furnish the following information:

(a) Name of the applicant (b) Father's name (c) Present address (d) Previous residence—village, Post Office, Police Station, District, etc. (e) address of his own house, if any, (f) Total members of the family: – Name of each member, age, relation with the applicant (g) Previous and present occupation and (h) Skill in any special job.

However, the Government of India was also eager to send refugees to Andaman. H.V. Iyanger, Secretary, Ministry of Home Affairs, visited Port Blair to gather information about the possibility of settlement. On January 5, 1949, he broadcast his own experience and assured all possible help to the displaced persons from East Pakistan.

GOVERNMENT ASSISTANCE

On February 17, 1949 during the question hours, Union Home Minister, Sardar Vallabbhai Patel answered that in the Andamans, there was no scarcity of drinking water. According to the land revenue regulation, the land would be distributed firstly on lease and after 5 years of cultivation, the settlers would get tenancy rights. Besides, they would be entitled for agricultural loan.

As regards facilities to be given to the settlers, N.C. Srivastava, Deputy Secretary, Ministry of Relief and Rehabilitation explained them in his letter No. R & R-4 (9)/ GOI/Ministry of R & R, dated December 30, 1947 addressed to all Provincial Governments:

"It is realized that displaced persons resettling on land, may need assistance in various ways. They may need seeds and bullocks or agricultural implements. In some cases, they may even need food and fodder for a period and assistance to build or repair houses.

"...that the G.O.I. feel that in most cases the help is likely to take the form of repayable loans like the Takavi advances, the technique of which is generally well known to Revenue officers.

"It is realized that in addition to granting resettlement loans, refugees may have to be fed in the village till the time of the next crop and for this purpose, an absolute free grant may have to be made to them. The Government of India will be prepared to share this free grant with the Provincial Governments".

Further in the letter, some more suggestions were made for consideration---

(a) For security of repayment, loans may be given as far as possible to groups.

(b) Resettlement may be facilitated if persons coming from the same village are resettled in close proximity to one another .. (All) will be jointly responsible.

(c) To check misuse, assistance may be given in kinds .... assets may be hypothecated to the government.

(d) The assistance may be given in instalments.

(e) In considering, resettlement of agriculturists, the village artisans (like carpenters and blacksmiths) may not be overlooked.

In conclusion, the most practical advice was forwarded, "Refugees who are being sent to the provinces, have been uprooted from their home and land, and have undergone untold hardship during evacuation ....sympathetic treatment is called for".

Under these guidelines, the Government of West Bengal framed the scheme of reliefs and facilities to be offered to the refugees settling in Andaman. Accordingly, Deputy Secretary, G.O.I., Ministry of Relief and Rehabilitation issued a D.O. Letter No. 91 (2) RF/49, dated 7 April, 1949 in consequence of the Government Press Note released on January 11, 1949 ascertaining the loans and the grants as under:

(a) Free passage for journey from Calcutta to Port Blair.

(b) Ten acres of land in the settlement area to each family, free of cost.

(c) Remission of revenue or taxes against the holdings for the first two years.

(d) Maintenance allowance @ Rs. 30/- to each adult and Rs. 15/- per child under 8 years of age subject to the maximum of Rs. 100/- per month for each family for 9 months.

(e) Free ration to each family from the date of sailing for three months with the provision to extend the period for next six months.

(f) Two plough animals and one milch-cow or buffalo to be supplied.

(g) Paddy seeds, agricultural implements and two sacks of super phosphate as fertilizer, free of cost.

(h) Half an acre of lands to artisans and non-agriculturists for construction of houses and also financial assistance at par the same admissible to the agriculturists for a period of 3 months.

(i) All families to be given sufficient building materials free of cost.

From time to time the scheme of the facilities has been revised and certain conditions have been added to extenuate the demands of the settlers.

On December 28, 1950 the Chief Commissioner, Andaman Nicobar Islands in his letter repeated the scales for the cultivator families as under:

(a) House building loan -Rs. 900/-

(b) Purchase of bullocks -Rs. 700/-

(c) Purchase of implements and utensils -Rs. 130/-

(d) Purchase of seeds, manure -Rs. 100/-

(e) Maintenance allowance for 6 months -Rs. 360/-. The total of all such loans and grants amounted to Rs. 190/-

Besides these concessions, the displaced persons to settle in Andaman was provided with-

(a) Passage money from Calcutta to Port Blair travel -Rs. 90/-

(b) Diet charges during voyage -Rs. 5/-

(c) Cost of utensils given by Govt. of West Bengal -Rs. 38/

Apart from these, each settler family was assured of 5 acres of plain land for cultivation and 5 acres of hilly land for plantation. All these facilities allured refugees to settle in Andaman.

Under these circumstances, following the recruitment procedure, 202 East Bengal refugee families were finally selected to send them to Andaman. On 14 March, 1949, many distinguished persons including Dr. B.C. Roy, the Chief Minister of West Bengal went to the Khiderpur dock to see off the first batch of 132 refugee families going to Andaman.

To encourage them, on behalf of the Government of West Bengal, 100 beasts of burden, buffaloes and 50 she-buffaloes, a number of spades, axes, scythes, ploughs, tumblers, jute-sacks, ropes and other household materials were given for the use of the settlers. Besides, to prepare lands suitable for cultivation, Bulldozers, D-7 Cater Pillars, D-4 Cater Pillar Tractors, 800 mounds of super phosphates were also donated. Assuming that the agricultural families of the first batch might cultivate 2000 acres of land so the Government of West Bengal gave them 4000 mounds of paddy seeds. Even some utensils for daily use such as lantern, cauldron, plates, glasses, corrugated sheets, bolts, nails, hinges, and hammers were also supplied. For their recreation and entertainment, some musical instruments such as Tom Toms like rural drum, 'Khol', cymbals like 'Kartav', or 'karatal' in Bengali, tobacco, bidi, hubble-bubble like 'Hoonko', etc., were also distributed. Even each able-bodied man was supplied with one set of canvas shoes donated by the Bata Company to tread in the jungle.[6]

Just after the dispersal of the first batch of refugees for rehabilitation in Andaman, on April 10, 1949, Nikunja Behari Maity, Minister of Relief and Rehabilitation, Government of West Bengal, broadcast on All India Radio with a view to assuring the refugees of favourable conditions and suitable atmosphere for their settlement in Andaman. He said, "I am glad to inform that about 200 refugee families volunteered for settlement in the Andamans and have already sailed (14 March, 1949). We are daily receiving more and more applications for settlement in the Andamans which unfortunately we are not in a position to grant at the moment till the Government of India agrees to such large scale colonization programme".[7]

The radio message of the Minister bears the proof that refugees were enthusiastic to seek settlement voluntarily in Andaman. The Government of West Bengal requested the Central Government to approve the scheme of further settlement of refugees. Ultimately the Government of India agreed to send more refugees to Andaman. A specific rehabilitation programme was chalked out. Then the process of selection of the refugees, eligible for resettlement in the islands was initiated according to the norms set by the Central Government.

On arrival at Port Blair, the refugees were taken to the general wing of the Cellular Jail for a few days to acclimatize with the islands. Then they were sent to different settlement areas for rehabilitation. There each family would be allotted ready-made house with floor made of timber planks raised to 7ft above the ground to avoid the surge of water due to heavy rainfall, its walls made of bamboo stick or lattice, and the roof covered by G.I. sheets, having slopes on both sides from the centre. Apparently the house looked like a thatched hut common in East Bengal. All these houses were generally agglomerated in one place. The village with their huts scattered hither and thither in the midst of greeneries reminds one of the peaceful villages of East Bengal where the refugees hailed from.

On March 14, 1949, the first batch of 132 refugee families set out for Andaman by *S.S. Maharaja* from the Khiderpur jetty where Dr. B.C. Roy, the Chief Minister of West Bengal was present to bid farewell to them with the clarion call: "You are the first batch being sent to Andaman as free citizens of the country to establish a colony of Bengalees there and prove your patriotism once again after the freedom fighters of the country".[8]

That was the beginning of a new era of settlement in Andaman and the refugee families of the erstwhile East Bengal were rehabilitated in the villages around Port Blair in South Andaman.

ENDNOTES

1. *Hindustan Standard,* dt. 1 April 1949
2. State Archives, Port Blair, File No. 19-4/59-PQ & 19-4/74-PQ
3. File No. PN 1321 (200) Pub, Deptt. of Publicity, W. Bengal
4. *The Ananda Bazar Patrika,* most popular Bengali daily, pub. from Calcutta, dt. 19 Jan, 1949.
5. Ibid.
6. *The Hindustan Standard,* a well-known newspaper, pub. from Calcutta, dt. 14.3.1949.
7. *The Hindustan Standard,* a reputed newspaper from Calcutta, dt. 10.4.1949
8. *The Light of Andaman,* Port Blair, Issue Pub. on 28.8.04

8

Settlement in South Andaman

South Andaman is comparatively a small island having been populated mostly by the descendents of the convicts since the beginning of the penal settlement and provides less quantity of vacant land available for further settlement. Still South Andaman is the most alluring region and has been attracting all along the outsiders to settle there because of the importance of Port Blair, which is not only the capital city of the Andaman & Nicobar Islands, but also the main trading centre for all provisions and domestic items controlling inter-islands trades. It provides all amenities of urban life and good communication facilities, not only for inter-island ferry services but also island and mainland voyages.

The climate of South Andaman is wet like that of East Bengal and the soil is as fertile as that of East Bengal. The rainfall is about 130° favourable for paddy cultivation. The settlement areas were covered with dense vegetation and interspersed with wide open valleys having the access to streams and springs for water, so paddy cultivation and coconut, arecanut plantation are possible.

However, possible areas of settlement in South Andaman available at that time were as follows:

(a) Shoal Bay East –2000 acres (Kalatong to Yeratong)

(b) Sukhanala area –2000 acres,

(c) Burmanala to Chiriatapu –1950 acres,

(d) Putatong –2700 acres,

(e) Shoal Bay West including Jirkatang, Pachang, Buratogu Jig, Miletilek and Girjutilek –4500 acres.

All these areas, once inhabited by the aborigine Jarawas, and in later years resided by the Burmese who repatriated to Burma after the Independence, have been earmarked for the settlement of refugees and other migrants.

During the first year of settlement, 202 refugee families were resettled in the villages such as Hamphraygunj, Monglutan, Chouldari, Wandoor, Maimyo, etc., lying at a distance of 10 to 12 miles from Port Blair. On March 14, 1949, the first batch of 132 refugee families consisting of 495 heads sailed from Calcutta by *S.S. Maharaja*. Among these 132 families, there were 50 cultivators, 22 weavers, and 34 carpenters' families, most of them hailed from Faridpur, Barisal, Noakhali, and Dacca.

Dr. Bidhan Chandra Roy, Chief Minister of West Bengal was very optimistic about the prospect of rehabilitation of refugees in Andaman. So in order to boost up their morale, he himself reached the Khiderpur dock along with the Minister Nikunja Bihari Maity, Smti Renuka Roy who later succeeded Shri Maity as Minister and Hiranmoy Banerjee, the Commissioner, Relief & Rehabilitation Department.

Dr. Roy inspired them with a soul-stirring speech, addressing them as harbinger and messenger of a new life: "Today is a remarkable day for us and for West Bengal. In spite of turmoil and hurry-scurry, these many people are ready to go to an unknown land, Andaman. The reason is that they are pioneers; messengers of a new life as they are determined to build their new home in the new island. In our childhood, we would think that Andaman is a place for banishment where murderers and criminals were sent. Those days have gone. Now the terror of the jail has a ghostly tale of yesteryears. Andaman has now been suitable for settlement. Once there Netaji Subhash Chandra Bose hoisted the national flag and these people want to glorify the islands as Subhash Dweep".[1]

Initially there was great reluctance on the part of the refugees to go farther than West Bengal. The reasons have been discussed elaborately elsewhere. However, Smti Renuka Roy, the then Minister of Relief & Rehabilitation, Government of West Bengal, expressed her anguish against the subversive politics of the opposition party, "... the role played by the opposition party politicians of West Bengal at the Centre and in the State Assembly was negative and did not help increase the facilities for a large number to be accommodated in the State. If adequate arrangements had been made outside West Bengal, would it not have benefited the refugees? If these politicians had supported these measures instead of opposing them even before they could make headway which is once again what they did"?[2]

"Against all these odds, the first batch of refugees reached Port Blair on March 17, 1949 under the supervision of an efficient officer from the department of Rehabilitation, Government of West Bengal. They were received by the Commissioner, Upen Ghosal himself and they were treated so well and placed so quickly on suitable rehabilitation sites that they wrote back to their friends and relatives to join them".[3]

Thus the refugees could ignore the political propaganda and were eager to move to Andaman being motivated by their own people who had been settled there earlier. They intimated the other refugees living in different camps in West Bengal in favour of the settlement in Andaman.

The Government of West Bengal was also very sympathetic towards the refugees who volunteered to settle in Andaman. Even the concerned minister and others left no stones unturned to beseech the Central Government to extenuate the hard and fast terms of settlement so that the rehabilitation could be hassle-free.

Hiranmoy Banerjee, Secretary to the Government of West Bengal wrote a letter No. 8909, Rehabilitation, dated Calcutta,

16/19 December,1949 to the Joint Secretary, G.O.I. entreating to assuage certain terms of settlement in Andaman:

"The recruitment is to be made from (the East Bengal refugees) actual tillers of the soil who are usually economically very poor and having struggled hard after the Partition, are not in a position to raise a capital of Rs. 3000/- which is expected to be provided by each family from its own resources according to the new scheme of G.O.I." Shri Banerjee wrote further :

"... You were pleased to agree to waive this bar in order to allow the Government of West Bengal to grant them loans and grants according to the schedule approved by the G.O.I., admissible to cultivator refugees..."[4]

From another notification No. U.O. 214 (200) Pub., Directorate of Publicity, dated February 25, 1950, it is learnt, "A batch of 30 of East Bengal refugee families (sailed) by S.S. Maharaja on Friday.... Each family was provided with agricultural implements, cooking utensils, two mosquito curtains, ration for the journey, dhoti, Saree, blankets and other garments and a cash dole for sundry expenses for a month". Even Vasantlal Murarka, M.L.A. donated one hundred pairs of Dhoti and Saree to the settlers.

As a personal gift from His Excellency, the Governor of West Bengal, one hundred rupees in cash and some sweets were distributed among the children before embarkation (for Andaman)[5].

No doubt, the government assistance was adequate and the attitude was also sympathetic. Similarly some of the government officials under the AndaNico Administration rendered yeomen's services by extending compassion and sympathy towards the refugees. They would come to Calcutta on duty to recruit the refugee families who were willing to go to Andaman and after scrutiny; they were put to medical examinations before embarkation. During the sea voyage, the officials from Port Blair, namely S.K. Raha, S.K. Paul, P.L.D. Roy, etc., would accompany the refugees to boost up their morale.

In the State Archives, Port Blair, there are several official documents preserved as the proof of the excellent services of those Bengali officers during the initial period of settlement.

In one letter no. 27/10/348/B1, dated 30.1.1952 from M.G. Raja Ram, Deputy Commissioner, AndaNico Islands, it is stated, "A batch of 12 families of refugees from West Bengal, is expected to arrive from Calcutta by S.S. Maharaja on February 3, 1952. McMuller will assist S.K. Raha who is accompanying the refugees and will escort them up to the Aberdeen Jetty in R.C.L. and take them within quarters in the Cellular Jail".

Indeed, the wing No. 2 of the District Jail (Cellular Jail) was used as transit camp for a few days for rest till the refugees were sent to different rehabilitation sites.

In another letter from the Chief Commissioner, A.K. Ghosh to the Refugee Rehabilitation Commissioner, Government of West Bengal, dated 27 February, 1952, it is said, "I shall be grateful if you will depute a responsible officer of your department to take around Shri B. B. Chakraborty (himself a refugee) teacher, Government High School, Port Blair, to the place where 24 families will be assembled for selection".

On May 25, 1952, M.G. Raja Ram, Dy. Commissioner, AndaNico Islands wrote to S.N. Sen, Personal Secretary to the Chief Minister, West Bengal, "I am happy to report that the 150 families which we have recently received from West Bengal by selection by one of our Tahsildars, are doing quite well and are taking to their task of rehabilitation quite cheerfully and honestly[6].

In spite of their acumen and sincerity, some drawbacks still remained that created problems in successful settlement in Andaman. Though mostly agricultural families were selected, some non-agricultural families also were surreptitiously included because of their persuasion and also some inadvertence on the part of certain indolent functionaries. Consequently those non-agrarian people could not adjust with the new environment and failed to engage themselves in physical labour in the fields. They were imprudent and inept. Under this strain, they were getting impatient and fastidious. Ultimately this group comprising middle class literates numbering around one hundred and fifty deserted the settlement and went back to Calcutta. The repatriation of these refugees set a derogatory example and hampered the progress of colonization in Andaman.

By the end of 1949, when the quota fixed by the Government of India for West Bengal was exhausted, Hiranmoy Banerjee, Commissioner, Department of Relief & Rehabilitation, proposed to send more refugees to Andaman, but it was rejected instantly. On the contrary, the Ministry of Rehabilitation expressed disapprobation and disgruntled on the repatriation of Bengalee Refugees from Andaman, and dissented on the proposal of sending more refugees to Andaman.

However, being persuaded persistently by the Government of West Bengal, the Union Minister agreed on the condition that the refugees would go to Andaman at their own expenses. But the Minister realized later that it was absurd for the penniless uprooted people to bear the expenses and withdrew the order. In due course, the Government of India decided to send some more refugees to Andaman and it was communicated to the Government of West Bengal through a telegram on January 25, 1950 by the Under Secretary, Home Department, Government of India, "Rehabilitation Ministry has agreed after discussion with West Bengal Premier to allow 120 families from here (West Bengal) to go to Andaman this year. The first batch of 30 families will arrive by February sailing".[7]

Accordingly 30 families reached Port Blair on February 24, 1950. Subsequently the batches of refugees came to Andaman in phases by different sailings and the policy of the Government of India changed with the passing of time. Sometimes, discrepancies resulted into the outburst of the refugees who demanded that the government assistance should be equal without considering the dates of arrival in Andaman.

From the note of the Chief Commissioner, AndaNico Islands, dated 3rd May, 1950, it is learnt that "The Govt. of

India in the letter, dated 10 February, 1950 have authorized the West Bengal Government to change the amounts which may be paid to the settlers under the various heads provided the total amount does not exceed Rs. 2000/- per family.

"...the G.O.I. has committed us to take 120 families this year (55 of whom are still due). There is no reason why we should not take these 30 families, the G.O.I. wants to send."

Again on May 12, 1950, referring to some arrogant settlers, A.K. Ghosh, Chief Commissioner, AndaNico Islands said, "I have also met on two or three occasions, a deputation of these refugees who came here on 17th April, 1950. To begin with they seemed contended and appeared to know the conditions under which they had been sent by the Government of West Bengal to the Andamans, namely that they would be granted loans totaling Rs. 2000/- per family and they would be expected to clear the virgin land containing scrub jungle. They have become more grasping and obstreperous with the passage of time ... they heard from the refugees who came last year that the very generous terms were granted to the original batch of settlers by G.O.I. They now demanded exactly the same terms and conditions, namely free cattle, free house building materials, free maintenance for 9 months and cleared land.

"...G.O.I. is not prepared to repeat those terms....they are being incited by one or two self-appointed leaders, chief among them are Nirode Bairagi and Pandit Baidya. Instead of sending the entire batch back by this sailing of the Maharaja, we should repatriate these two so-called leaders and their families..."[8]

Indeed, at their instigation, the other settlers demanded to supply articles as per the scale given to the earlier batches such as plates, two cauldrons, cooking vessel, grinding stones 'shil-nora', drum, buckets, two axes, spade, crowbar, two 'dah' choppers, three sickles, mosquito net, lantern, blanket, two mats, 4 bundle tin, plough cattle and milch cows.[9]

The situation became very stern and acerbating because of their adamant attitude. The Chief Commissioner,

AndaNico Islands was so annoyed for the nefarious activities of 'two self styled leaders' that he took immediate action to send them back to Calcutta and intimated Hiranmoy Banerjee, Relief & Rehabilitation Commissioner, through Police Wireless, D.O. No. 1/732/50 dated 12 May, 1950, "...returning to Calcutta by this sailing of the Maharaja, Nirode Bairagi and Pandit Baidya with their families numbering nine in all out of last batch of settlers sent to Andaman on 14 April. These settlers won't accept terms offered and demanded the same concessions as offered to the earlier settlers sent last year. These two men being repatriated are ring leaders inciting the others to put forward impossible demands. We expect improvement after their departure. If remain still adamant, shall be compelled to repatriate them by following voyage.

"... This is intolerable and if continued, will lead to refusal of any settler from West Bengal in Andaman. If you send any more people in response to my telegram, dated 3rd May, please see personally that settlers are properly briefed".[10]

COLONIZATION SCHEME

However, in spite of such sporadic incidents, the settlement work went on undeterred and progressively. In successive batches, many more refugees arrived at Port Blair willingly in order to settle in Andaman under the colonization schemes.

According to the memorandum No. 2007 from the office of D.C. to the Chief Commissioner, dated 10 July, 1950, "...65 families arrived in February and April, 1950 and settled in different villages in South Andaman during 1950. Again in May and June, 1950, 54 families arrived, of them 30 families imported on condition to work in the labour force".[11]

By July 1951, the total number of the refugees settled in South Andaman in eight successive batches was more than 384 families. Till 1962, the population increased and the number rose to 565 families in South Andaman.

On October 13, 1950, the Secretary to the Government of West Bengal wrote a letter to the Secretary, Government of India regarding the progress of the settlement of East Bengal refugees in Andaman as follows:

"The Chief Commissioner of AndaNico Islands had a discussion with us and he says that he will be able to take the following families for resettlement in Andaman in the November sailing:

(a) Carpenters - 50 families
(b) Blacksmiths - 5 families
(c) Washermen - 2 families
(d) Cobblers - 3 families
(e) Fishermen - 12 families
(f) Potters - 1 family
(g) Weavers - number not specified
(h) Businessmen - 10 families.

In a rejoinder, dated December 28, 1950, with reference to the above mentioned 83 families of artisans resettled in Andaman, it is remarked that "The Chief Commissioner of Andaman & Nicobar Islands will be in a position to rehabilitate in addition to this number (83), another 150 families of good cultivators".

Though the refugee settlement in Andaman began in March, 1949 yet the colonization scheme was initiated in 1953. Under this scheme, refugees were brought from West Bengal in various phases and went on till 1961.

Regarding the prospect of rehabilitation in the Andaman & Nicobar Islands from 1949-1963, K.N. Butani, Development Secretary, Govt. of India, prepared 'A note on the Prospect of Rehabilitation, 1949-63' and observed, "Under the old colonization scheme, 2861 migrant families from East Pakistan consisting about 12000 persons were settled in these islands between 1949 and 1963, and were allotted 5 acres of cleared land for paddy cultivation and 5 acres of unclear land for homestead and horticulture. These families are reported to be well off and happy.[12]

From the "Monthly Progress Report on Resettlement of Refugees" of East Pakistan in South Andaman villages, the distribution of refugee population is noted in the following table for March, 1953.[13]

Name of the Village	*Population*	*Adult*	*Child*	*Total*
Aberdeen	34	18	14	34
Garacharma	14	10	4	14
Sipighat	39	20	19	39
Nayashahar	36	21	15	36
Homfregung	63	36	27	63
Mongluton	51	34	17	51
Guptapara	65	37	28	65
Wandoor	168	82	86	168
Chouldari	290	192	98	290
Port Mout	21	11	10	21
Ograbaraj	4	2	2	4
Namunaghar	21	13	8	21
Tushonabad	23	17	6	23
Hobdeypur	2	2	6	2
Manpur	113	73	40	113
Collinpur	52	33	19	52
Tample Mayo	27	20	7	27
Herbertabad	75	58	17	75
Tirrur	7	4	3	7
Mathura	70	46	24	70
Brindaban	18	13	5	8
Ferrarjung	144	111	33	144
Shoal Bay (E)	30	24	6	30
Shoal Bay (W)	43	38	5	43

With a view to accommodating more refugees in South Andaman, a project was initiated by the Chief Conservator of Forest, AndaNico Islands for clearance of jungle and the progress report titled "Five Year Plan for Development and Colonization of the Andaman islands" was submitted to the Chief Commissioner.[14] Forest extraction and clearance was performed as under:

Chriatapu Centre	*Extracted*	*Unextracted*
Chiriatapu, Sukhanallah, Dulalnallah Block	800 acres	600 acres
Monglutan, Asha Pradip Block	300 acres	300 acres
Mohannallah Block	900 acres	N.A.
Dalip Block	Nil	200 acres
Rangachang, Burmanalla Block	Nil	2000 acres
Shoal Bay Block		
East Shoalbay	1000 acres	500 acres
Madhuban	NA	600 acres
West Shoalbay Area–	.	
Alipore	600 acres	N.A.
Mile Tilek	700 acres	420 acres
Girug Tilek	120 acres	N.A.
Jirkatong	N.A.	1020 acres
Barataga Jig	N.A.	870 acres
Pochang	N.A.	1270 acres

Thus more refugees were resettled in South Andaman with the progress of extraction and reclamation of the forest land. But to meet the challenge of rehabilitation of swelled up refugees from East Pakistan, the Forest Department underwent into further operation of the clearance of the colonial land in South Andaman. In the report of Deputy Forest Officer submitted to the Chief Conservator of Forests on March 5, 1962, it was remarked that in Guptapara-Monglutan area, 30 to 40 acres of flat land and in Collinpur area, 40 to 50 acres of land were available for allotment. Though lands were there in Tirur area, it was Jarawa-infested so it was not suitable for successful settlement.

RECLAMATION OF MANGROVE FOREST

In due course, the scarcity of land in South Andaman not only posed a problem for further settlement, but also failed to fulfil the requirements of the old settlers. To cope with the problems, the Department of Rehabilitation sought to explore other ways for reclamation of land. A Pilot Project was taken up to reclaim mangrove forests. The South and Middle Andamans have a network of creeks around which mangrove forests are found on both sides. This area being close to Port Blair will be easier to open up for further settlements by closing down some creeks which in future can be turned into sweet water lakes where pisciculture can be carried on. In the Sunderban area, such a reclamation project has already been undertaken and the result is favourable.

In Andaman, such a project of reclaiming mangrove swamps was taken up and the land to be reclaimed was as follows:

In South Andaman, Dhaninallah Block	-	300 acres
In Middle Andaman, Cutbert Bay or Potadera block	-	700 acres
In Middle Andaman, Kalsi Block	-	200 acres

But in due course, the settlement plan at Cutbert Bay and Dhaninellah was abandoned because the surface and the sub-surface soil layers were found prone to erosion and not suitable for successful colonization.

The survey at Burmanallah, Lakshminallah and Colbrooke area was undertaken and a settlement scheme was chalked out accordingly. But due to sandy soil and absence of perennial stream, Colbrooke plan was dropped. Hence successful colonization in mangrove forests acted as fillip.

In the meeting of Ministry of Rehabilitation, Ministry of Transport, Ministry of Commerce with AndaNico Administration represented by the then Chief Commissioner, Mahavir Singh and others, held on March 27, 1967, it was decided that "...the Pilot Project for reclamation of mangrove forests should not be given up as large tracts of land in the Betapur Island are covered by mangrove swamps and if we succeed in their reclamation, a lot of land will become available for agriculture purpose".

However, in the 'Note on the Prospect of Rehabilitation in Andaman and Nicobar Islands' by K.N. Butani, it is remarked, "A Pilot Project for the reclamation of 4000 acres of mangrove forests in South Andaman has been drawn up and is being processed for implementation. About 600 families will be settled in this land".[15] Indeed, 200 new migrants, say, refugees were resettled in reclaimed mangrove forest land in South Andaman.

According to the working report, 1950-51 of the Ministry of Rehabilitation, 285 displaced agricultural families from East Pakistan were resettled in Andaman and given financial assistances. A longtime scheme for the settlement of 6000 more refugee families in Andaman in a period of 5 years was under consideration. Consequently in the memorandum, No. 900/ Rehab, dated October 16, 1951, Hiranmoy Banerjee informed A.K. Ghosh, the Chief Commissioner, AndaNico Islands that the scheme to settle 6500 families in the islands had been approved and necessary actions would be taken to implement it.

The following statistical chart shows the population pattern of the displaced families settled in Andaman and the expenditure incurred thereof.[16]

CHART

Total arrival March 1949 June 1953	Families got benefits	No.of Agril. families expenditure	No. of Non Agril families expenditure	House Loan-Amount spent	Loan sanctioned	Total amount spent
550 families Total Heads 2037 Adult 1585 Minor 452	529	For 451 families Amount spent Rs 193427	For 78 families Amount spent Rs 13802	Loan for 230 families Rs. 101925	Rs 617862	Rs 307229

CASES OF REPATRIATION

In spite of sincere efforts made by AndaNico Administration and the liberal attitude attributed by the Government of West Bengal, there still remained certain deficiencies in the recruitment of refugees from the camps in West Bengal that ultimately culminated into desertion.

The objective of the colonization scheme was to settle cultivator families in Andaman but due to carelessness on the part of certain recruitment officials, some literate middle class people, businessmen, artisans, and caste-conscious Brahmins were selected who in no time found themselves misfit to the new environment.

Some stray instances are mentioned below in support of the above observation:

1. Harikanta Pal and Harishchandara Pal, both settlers of Mathura village and potters by profession, applied for repatriation on September 5, 1951 on the ground that "...the soil of this island not being suitable for the earthen pots".

   The Tahsildar of the area reported on September 8, 1951, "He (Harikanta) is not of cultivator stock...one Fatik Sil of Mathura helped him in cultivation work on payment. Until now he has transplanted about 2 acres of land, (he was allotted 4 acres of land at Mathura) he will never be a successful cultivator...

   "He has constructed his house with 6 bundles of G.I. sheet given to him. Out of total grant of Rs. 1400/- earmarked for his rehabilitation, Rs. 1198/- has so far been given to him with the exclusion of passage money and subsistence allowance amounting to Rs. 340/-..."[17]

2. Maharaj Baroi, settler of Wandoor and fisherman by profession, applied to go back to Calcutta on November 11, 1951 by ship as he failed to catch fish in the open sea without dingy. He was allotted about 5 acres of jungle land and Rs. 1000/- which he spent in constructing his house. He cultivated paddy which was destroyed by insects. He appealed to send him back to Calcutta.

   Similarly, other fishermen like Jogeswar Biswas applied for repatriation but the Chief Commissioner, A.K. Ghosh remarked on November, 1951, "Prayer rejected. He can easily earn living by catching fish in shallow water..."[18]

3. Bhuban Mohan Dutta applied, "I came down here (Andaman) as a conch bracelet manufacturer and not cultivator. We were allotted the land for the cultivation at Guptapara...where the land contained large trees and shrubs, clearance of which was beyond my reach.." So he applied to go back but his request was turned down.

4. Similarly the request of Bibhuti Bhusan Das was rejected as the Tahsildar reported, "He is a refugee of 1949 batch, settled at Port Mout, working as veterinary dresser... his difficulties in education of his children ... new school has started at Chouldari....he may easily send his children to that school.[19]

5. In reply to the applications of Nakul Mistry and Brajendranath Mistry, the Chief Commissioner remarked," These two families of 4 members each came with the last lot of refugees that came in April last (1950). They, I find, are completely homesick. They may be repatriated to the West Bengal Government".

On June 5, 1950, the Chief Commissioner wrote a letter NO. 10-16 (a) 50, to the Secretary, Government of West Bengal, "I am directed to inform you that the following refugees who came here in April last are being repatriated by the sailing of the June 5, 1950, as they are unwilling to settle down.

"The following recoverable advances were granted to them in accordance with the terms of the Refugee Rehabilitation Department, letter No. 2511- Rehab, dt. 15 April, 1950. Necessary steps for the recovery of loan may kindly be taken as written below:[20]

CHART

Names		*Advances Given*	
1. Nakul Mistry	- Self		
Kumodini	- Wife	For April, 1950	- Rs. 60
Gopal	- Brother	For May, 1950	- Rs. 60
Haren	- Brother	Sea passage both ways	- Rs. 160
		Total	**Rs. 280**

Names		*Advances Taken*	
2. Brojendranath Mistry	- Self		
Tarangini	- Wife	For April 1950	- Rs. 55
Biren	- Son	For May 1950	- Rs. 55
Pushpa	- Daughter	Passage bothways	- Rs. 120
		Total	**Rs. 230**

6. Some of the settlers sent petitions addressing the Chief Minister, West Bengal, against the indifferent attitude of the AndaNico Administration in fulfilling the terms of settlement as assured by the Government of India. As the petition goes:

"We came to Andaman in 1950 for rehabilitation as artisan families. Most of us were suffering from small pox. These 47 families were sent to 'Ram Pahar' and after recovery, brought back to the Cellular Jail. We went to Andaman as refugees to run our business but we could not do it at a loan amount of Rs. 500/- so the government asked us to start cultivation on scrubbing the jungle.

"On 27th March, each family was given Rs. 1000 in cash and sent to the terrible jungle area, Hatidera, presently known as Guptapara to settle down.

"We planted paddy and vegetables. We spent Rs. 1000/- in constructing our houses, to purchase suitable choppers to cut down large trees. In each family, there are 4 to 7 heads to feed. There are no hired labour, no free school, hospital. Insects and wild rats spoilt the corns.

"The Chief Commissioner does not want to give us the rest amount of the assured money as per the G.O.I. scheme.

"We want, either we are accepted as cultivators and the same facilities should be given to us or necessary arrangements are to be made to send us back to Calcutta but the C.C. told us to go at our own cost. We, however, reached Calcutta on January 4, 1951 and enquired with the office of the Development

Commissioner, Relief & Rehabilitation at Auckland but no action has been taken so far".[21]

Sd/ Dhirendranath Biswas and
other four settlers

7. Another interesting application exposed the imperious attitude of the few refugees who were besotted with their caste-ego.

Basanta Chakraborty, Surendranath Chakraborty and Krishna Kanta Bhattacharjee, all Brahmins by caste, came to Andaman on 31 January, 1951 as refugees and were settled at Phoenix Bay as businessmen. But soon they felt frustrated as they failed to run business on the trade advance given by the government which they thought inadequate and all money was spent on rent and treatment.

Hence they applied on September 27, 1951 to leave Andaman as they had no money and they being Brahmins, were not habituated to do hard labour, nor they knew how to till the land allotted to them as settlers. Besides, they did not come to Andaman to spend their life on physical labour. Had they been in Bengal, they could do various jobs, at least be absorbed in their ancestral services of priesthood. So they should be allowed to leave Andaman at the government expense.

In reply, the Chief Commissioner remarked, "They may be returned but house building material advance be cleared".[22]

However, Surendranath went to Calcutta by the sailing of 9th February, 1952 on the pretext to purchase some articles for running a tailor shop but did not return.

Tahsildar reported on April 23, 1952, "I have reasons to believe that he has absconded from this island without repaying the rehabilitation loan".

Regarding Basanta Chakraborty, the Chief Commissioner remarked, "He has repatriated on April 5, 1952 as he will evidently never settle down in Andaman as a useful member of the society".[23]

And Krishna Kanta also left Andaman stealthily on March 7, 1952. During the period of settlement, there were many more interesting examples that would explain the story of settlement in Andaman. A few of them are cited below:

1. A group of youths applied to the Chief Commissioner, AndaNico Islands, on January 12, 1952 through S.K. Roy, Supervisor, Asansol Polytechnic, Dhadka, Burdwan, West Bengal.[24]

   "...We have completed our technical training under the dispersal scheme of Government of West Bengal in the following trades; Electrical, Mechanical, Welding, Automobiles, Generator Maintenance and Fitting. We are willing to go to Andaman. We are keen to establish ourselves there. We are ready to face any kind of hardship that may come in our way.

   Sd/Hari Shankar Sen
& 12 others

2. Another very touching and emotional appeal made on 12.1.1952 by some enthusiastic Bengali boys to the Chief Commissioner, AndaNico Islands, seeking settlement in Andaman:

   "We are a few wretched Bengali youths. Though we are disappointed and tantalized in life, yet we are not averse of struggling. We are unemployed and becoming burdensome. Our future seems sealed.

   "...We are sons of Bengal. Being indigent we know what hardship is. We have experienced the pathos of Bengal. Today we are distraught and desolate but the Bengali tradition inspires us all along. We have taken oath that we will go to Andaman to start a new life. We want to live on hard labour.

   "Hence we earnestly request you to give us chance to achieve the goal...we swear that we shall not belittle Bengal, nay India".

   Address: Sd. Jiban Krishna Pan
9/2, Radhanath Mullick Rd. & other three youths.
Calcutta-12

3. Even from Pune, Birendra Nath Chakraborty of 1379, Bhavani Path, Poona-2, wrote a letter on April 4, 1955 to the Under Secretary, Ministry of Home Affairs, Government of India.

   "I write back to you again requesting you to select me and my family (with 3 minor children) for a settlement in the island according to the Government 'Five Year Colonization Scheme'. I migrated from Pakistan in December, 1953 leaving my properties and movables there and am still floating with no moorings".

   In reply, the Chief Commissioner remarked, "...the settlement scheme in the Andamans is confined to agriculturists.[25]

Moreover, some of the refugee families who were not recruited for the settlement in Andaman went there willingly at their own in 1952. Some of them resettled themselves even by purchasing land from Sardar Harnam Singh of Namunaghar and lived on cultivation. Considering their tenacity and assiduity, the government recognized these nine refugee families as settlers.

However, it is very difficult to ascertain the total number of refugee population settled in Andaman for the dearth of documents not only in the State Archives at Port Blair but also at the State Archives as well as the National Library, Kolkata.

There are only occasional references, one can collect from the proceedings of the Parliament or the State Assembly, West Bengal and from some official records or personal letters.

In reply to a starred question raised in the Parliament, the Development Commissioner, AndaNico Islands, informed as under.[26]

a)	No. of displaced families reached Andaman till June 26, 1952	-	450
b)	No. of repatriated families	-	85
c)	No. of settlers died	-	3
d)	No. of families settled as agriculturists	-	362

e) No. of families working in labour force – 8

f) Total no. of families settled (d+e) – 370

g) Total heads in 450 families – 1857

h) Total repatriated persons in 88 families – 376

i) Total no. of persons in 362 families (g-h) – 1481

Again on July 17, 1952 during the zero hour of the Parliament, a starred question No. 1848 raised by Arun Chandra Guha, M.P. and answered by Kailash Nath Katju, Minister of Home Affairs is as follows:

(1) Till July 17, 1952, 362 refugee families consisting of 1481 displaced persons from East Bengal settled in the Andamans.

(2) Scheme has already been taken to clear 20,000 acres of forest land during the next 5 years for further settlement of refugees.

Another supplementary question No. 1848 was raised by Shri Dabhi, M.P. "Is it with reference to the scheme of settling refugees or other persons also?"

The Minister said, "I can say, more preference would be given to refugees. If refugees are not forthcoming, anybody else will go".

Under these circumstances, while the Government of West Bengal planned to disperse more refugees to Andaman and accordingly Hiranmoy Bandhopadhyay, Secretary to Government of West Bengal sent a telegram to S. B. Sen, Under Secretary, Government of India seeking approval of and a copy of the D.O. Letter No. 670 SB, dt. 6th Oct. 1952 was sent over telegram to the Chief Commissioner, AndaNico Islands.

The Chief Commissioner's reply to the telegram from the Joint Secretary, Ministry of Rehabilitation, was as follows:

"Your telegram of 2nd October about settling five hundred refugee families in Andamans this year, quite impossible to receive five hundred families by middle

December. Your proposal that refugees live in tents and reclaim lands for cultivation, impractical. Experience of settling East Pakistan displaced families in Andamans shows such people incapable of clearing virgin forests and to put them in jungles without communication and water and other arrangements will only mean their returning to Calcutta immediately as soon as maintenance allowances cease".

The reply of A.K. Ghosh, Chief Commissioner was very altruistic and practical in the true sense of term. In his letter, he pointed out clearly "... we have been able to take refugees from Bengal only because after the war quite a number of ex-convicts returned to the mainland of India, abandoning their holdings here. These holdings are all reasonably near Port Blair; and refugees could be settled on them without any preliminary preparation. But I am afraid, we have very little ready land for allotment now and in future appreciable areas can be made available only by clearing forests, uprooting roots and stumps and making the land ready for cultivation at considerable cost. The Government of India have sanctioned a scheme under which this administration will clear 20000 acres of forest in five years and settle some 4000 families on the land—not all refugees".

He further stated, "I am afraid, the Andamans can do very little to relieve the pressure of refugees in West Bengal. You have many lacs of them on your hands, whereas even over a period of five years we can take at the most twenty thousands. Therefore, ours is really a long term plan for the colonization of the Andamans, not a plan to give immediate relief to West Bengal.

"I am sorry to be so discouraging. But it is better to face facts, and not to do the impossible. To send large numbers of cultivators to the Andamans now will only mean their returning to Calcutta as soon as their maintenance allowances stop, which while not helping you, will mean wasting large sums of government money".

Despite the caution from the Chief Commissioner explaining the practical situation of Andaman, the colonization programme was implemented and refugee settlement was undertaken as per the government plan.

To sum up the whole scenario of refugee settlement in South Andaman, it is better to quote from the Census of 1951 for perception...

"The total number of such refugees enumerated in the current census is 1500. These may be divided in the following categories:

(a) The batch of 171 agricultural families who came and settled down here in 1949 and were given cash doles, seeds, implements and cattle free, costing roughly Rs. 2333/- per family minus the cost of a pair of buffaloes and a milch cow. Seven artisan families also came in 1949.

(b) The batch of 49 agricultural families who came in 1950 and were given advances up to Rs. 2000/- per family for their maintenance, to purchase cattle, implements, etc., to be realized in six years.

In both cases, 5 acres of valley and 5 acres of hills and slopes had been allotted for two years. In a few cases where the family had more than one adult, 7 acres of valley had also been given.

(c) 34 families joined the local labour force in 1950 and for eventual settlement on lands they would clear and reclaim. They were about to be settled on the same conditions as the 1950 batch had been settled.

(d) 47 families of businessmen and artisans who came in January this year (1951), were given maintenance, house-building and business advances up to Rs. 1500/- and ½ acre of house site.

(e) Besides these, 48 young Bengalis, some of whom were even matriculates initially joined the labour force and were working as ordinary mazdoors in other organization. Their performance, of course, was not up to the standard but this was inevitable in the circumstances.

In the report of the Census of 1951, it was further remarked, "This unfortunate section of uprooted humanity is labouring under a very lamentable sense of defeatism".[27]

However, adjustment with the new surroundings is the only means of survival. Rehabilitation was accomplished only when the displaced persons became bodily integrated in the life of the existing society in their new set-up. Whether it was a farmer toiling in the fields for the fruits of his labours or it was a worker earning his bread in a workshop, a displaced person must learn to view his present problems in the perspective of the problems of his non-displaced neighbours. Otherwise, the undesirable feeling of separation or isolation would persist and impede the process of rehabilitation. But due to their determination and power of adaptation, the East Bengal refugees struggled hard in Andaman to earn their bread and dedicated themselves to find a new home there. Thus they became an essential part of an emerging novel society where irrespective of their caste or creed, they would live in peace and harmony. Consequently, these crouched and distressed people, once overshadowed by the horrors and perils of migration, started to breathe with hope and aspirations.

The following table shows a general view of the periodical settlements of East Bengal refugees in Andaman since the first settlement in 1949.[28]

March, 1949	..... 202 East Bengal refugee families
May, 1950	..... 65+54 East Bengal refugee families
January-March 1951	..... 78 East Bengal refugee families
January-March 1952	..... 51 East Bengal refugee families
June 1953	..... 97 East Bengal refugee families
1954	..... 438 East Bengal refugee families
1955	..... 390 East Bengal refugee families
1956	..... 357 East Bengal refugee families
1957	..... 221 East Bengal refugee families
1958	..... 194 East Bengal refugee families
1959	..... 9 East Bengal refugee families

As on 31 December 1960, number of displaced persons in Andaman was 9500 and number of families settled in Andaman was 2400.

According to the Report by Raja Surendra Singh of Nalagarh[29], Adviser (Colonization), Government of India under the title, "A Review of the Colonization Scheme of the Andaman Islands and Prospects of their Future Development", it is stated, "Up to date (31 August, 1962), 3281 families with a population strength of 11581 have been resettled under various schemes and at various intervals since 1949...The resettlement cost per head comes to about Rs. 1529.50 and per family Rs. 5367.80."

ENDNOTES

1. *Ananda Bazar Patrika*, Kolkata, March 14, 1949
2. 'My Reminiscences' by Renuka Roy, Pub: Stree Prakasani, Calcutta, 25, pp 150.
3. Ibid, pp 151
4. State Archives, Port Blair, Acc. No.128/ File No. 1-732/50
5. State Archives, Ibid, Port Blair
6. State Archives, Post Blair, File No. 1-732/52, Vol.1
7. 'Udwastu', by H. Bandhopadhyay, pp. 150-153
8. State Archives, Port Blair, File No.64-319/63-Pub.
9. State Archives, Port Blair Application made to D.C., Port Blair, on 24.2.1950, File 1-732/50.
10. State Archives, Port Blair, File No. 64-319/63-Pub. pp. 75
11. State Archives, Port Blair, Ibid.
12. State Archives, Port Blair, File No-27/158/7632/66, Calcutta, dt. 18.08.1966
13. State Archives, Port Blair, File No.1-616/52 (A)
14. The memorandum number is G/246/806, dated 20/21 August, 1951.
15. State Archives, Port Blair, File No. G-665/1967, March 27, 1967.
16. State Archives, Port Blair, File No D C/1-4/4496/A-2, dt. 5/9 Nov. 1953

17. State Archives, Port Blair, File No. S/44/1/732
18. Ibid.
19. State Archives, Port Blair, No. JR/105, dt.1.4.1952
20. State Archives, File: Land Revenue, Port Blair
21. State Archives, Port Blair, File No. TR/160, dt. 29.11.51
22. State Archives, Port Blair, File/No. S/44/1/732
23. Ibid
24. Office of the Relief of Rehabilitation Commissioner, Govt. of West Bengal, Diary No. 682, dt. 15.1.1952
25. State Archives, Port Blair, Letter No. 29-6/55 (4), dt. April 27, 1955
26. State Archives, Port Blair, D.C. Letter No. 1/4/2563/A-2, dt 26 June, 1952.
27. Census Report of 1951, Government of India.
28. The Report of Ministry of Rehabilitation, 1960-61, G.O.I. Press.
29. State Archives, Port Blair. File No. 173-84/62-G

9

Antithetical Attitude of the Local People

Since the inception of the refugee settlement in Andaman in March, 1949, the islands were found favourable and popular among the displaced persons from East Pakistan. Attempts were made to select mostly agricultural families with a few exceptions keeping in view the rigorous conditions of the region. Notwithstanding, those who went there were reported to be doing well. In all, 663 families had been sent to Andaman and a further batch of 184 families was expected to be sent by June, 1954. Thus rehabilitation in Andaman had shown considerable promise and that entire or substantial quotas for settlement in these islands would, for the next year or two, be reserved for refugees from East Bengal.

Prime Minister Jawaharlal Nehru made a statement in Parliament on 15 November, 1952 that the Government of India recognized the necessity of making planned responses to the refugee crisis.

From the telegram sent by Hiranmoy Banerjee, Secretary to Government of West Bengal, the D.O. No. 670 SB, dated 6 October, 1952, it is learnt that "Indian Government has already sanctioned a large scheme settling twenty thousand people in Andaman during the next five years".

Indeed, the Government of West Bengal was persuading to disperse more refugees to Andaman and Indian Government had sanctioned an ambitious scheme for settling twenty thousand migrants there during the next five years.

But this colonization scheme made the local people, say 'local borns' inimical and their agonies took shape in desperation. The repercussion directed particularly against the Bengali refugees got momentum confronting the government policy and ultimately their reluctance took political shape. The local people were mobilized by a trade unionist and young leader of Andaman, K.R. Ganesh who became the first elected Member of Parliament as a candidate of Congress from this territory in 1967.

During the first phase of refugee settlement in South Andaman, some wild rumours spread that the Government of West Bengal was trying to convert these islands into a territory under West Bengal. Exploiting the rumours, the *Light of Andaman,* a weekly by Paras Ram wrote about a rumour that a stratagem was being intrigued to mellow Andaman as 'Bangalisthan'. This sort of incidious rancour only put fuels to the fire. Naturally the local people became excited. Under the leadership of K.R. Ganesh, they staged 'dharna', sent representation, and conducted meetings to raise their voice against the prevaricated design of 'Bangalisthan.' This matter was also brought to the notice of the Central Government.

However, the source of such rumour, (Bangalisthan) might be a starred question raised in Parliament by Dr. Monomohan Das long back on April 6, 1949, almost at the very beginning of the settlement of the East Bengal refugees in Andaman.

Dr. Das asked whether it was a fact that the Government of West Bengal had sent a representation to the Government of India for incorporating the Andaman & Nicobar Islands within the province of West Bengal.

In reply, Sardar Vallabhbhai Patel, Union Minister for Home Affairs, explained in the negative defying the charge that the Central Government was quite competent to administer these islands so the question of incorporation of the islands with West Bengal was meaningless[1].

Still the local people of the islands had been fuming since then at this development and denouncing the Government of West Bengal for the design.

In the State Archives of West Bengal, housed in Writers' Building, Kolkata, there is a file containing "Records (Home-Political) Confidence". In that file, No.38/55, there is a C.I.D. Report No. 1460/846-54/5, dated January 14, 1955 under the title, "Agitation in the Andamans, opposing the proposal of merger of the islands with West Bengal".

In the report, it is stated, "Andamanese Indian Association" of which K.R. Ganesh was the General Secretary, submitted a petition to the State Reorganization Commission against the merger of the islands with West Bengal. The copies of the petition were sent to the President Dr. Rajendra Prasad and the Prime Minister, Jawaharlal Nehru. On March 10, 1954 while Dr. Rajendra Prasad being the first President, visited the islands, the members of the Association also met him to submit a mass petition[2].

On 18 December, 1954 in the morning while landing at Bambooflat jetty, S.K. Basu and B.C. Sen, Ministers of West Bengal faced an agitation organized by the Andamanese Indian Association. About 100 members of the association under the leadership of Vijay Pal Singh, Secretary, local Congress committee staged 'dharna' shouting blaring slogan "Bangal ke sath milna nahi chahte hain" (We don't want to merge with Bengal)[3].

A pamphlet under the title 'Andaman and Nicobar Islands' was circulated by K.R. Ganesh on behalf of the Association. It carried the message of their angst and languishment over a speech delivered by Dr. B.C. Roy, the Chief Minister of West Bengal on the occasion of renaming ceremony of the ship, 'SS Ray-Andaman' of M/s. P.C. Ray & Co., Mayabunder. It is stated that on that occasion, Dr. Roy expressed his views about the future of the islands as a part of West Bengal[4].

Further, in the pamphlet, the frenzy of the local people got expression over the government policy in appointing only Bengali Chief Commissioners since 1947 i.e., I. Majid, A.K. Ghosh, Shankar Moitra successively to head the Administration of the Andaman & Nicobar Islands which created misconceptions among the local people that the appointment of Bengali officers was just a prelude to the merger of the territory into West Bengal.

In the pamphlet, it was emphasized that considering, cultural and ethnic history of the islands, the hideous plan of merger with West Bengal is abrasive and therefore untenable.

Lastly, it was stated in the pamphlet that the future of the islands would be decided in the following lines leading to prosperity of the territory as deemed by the islanders:

(a) The islands should be granted a separate status as part of Indian Union.

(b) The elected body should be formed to run the administration in place of the present nominated one.

(c) Full civil liberties should be given for the growth of popular organization.

(d) Scrapping of all penal laws prevalent in the islands should be allowed.

This pamphlet was submitted to the President of India, Prime Minister and all parties concerned.

On December 18, 1954 on the ground of Netaji Club at Port Blair, a meeting of the Association was held under the Chairmanship of K.R. Ganesh and it was resolved that considering the geopolitical situation and social, economic and cultural conditions of the islands, a separate entity and status should be granted under the Union of India. Its administration should be run not by the nominated one but by an elected body.

Indeed, the local people of Andaman were recalcitrant and awfully reluctant to accept the refugees on being scared to lose their culture and identity as they might have been outnumbered. But the condition of the displaced persons who had lost not only their temporal assets but also their ancestral identity was too miserable to guess. They were living on tenterhooks. Like the Jews, they moved to Andaman to start a new life where they faced imprecation as they were unwanted and onerous. Nobody thought about the mental condition of the wretched people who had become the victims of the vivisection of India and were treated as shuttle cocks being shunted from one place to another place.

Development of the feeling of 'we-group' and 'they-group' came to dominate in instituting a sharp contrast between the refugees and the non-refugees (local people). The local inhabitants and to some extent the government appeared as the we-group and the migrant people, the refugees were set apart as 'they-group' who had no human choice to exercise their own discretions but to submit to the wills and forces of others who would enjoy the privilege to dictate the terms. It has become evident that a feeling of being unwelcome was persistent among refugees and forced them to live on the mercy and pittance.

In a way, refugees were subjected officially to knavish manoeuvres in the name of charity, benevolence and development. With no fault of their own, they suffered and are still suffering from staggering uncertainty and scathing attacks from all corners, particularly from the local people who should have been their hosts, at least for the sake of humanity. This wretched people, happened to be platters, were sent to Andaman by the Government of India for rehabilitation on the lands belonging only to the government and not to the local people because the original natives of the islands are the aborigines and not the local residents so logically they are also outsiders. Still they raised their voice against the settlement of the destitute refugees and kicked up a rumpus for the mendacious rumour regarding the merger of the islands with West Bengal.

Under these circumstances, perhaps a socio- psychological cleavage became gradually wide to negate the smooth assimilation of the uprooted within the receiving society of the host territory. Hence a successful equation of human values could not be achieved between 'we-group' and 'they-group'. Thus the 'cultural incompatibility' between the

Bengali-speaking refugees and the non-Bengali speaking local people might indulge a great hiatus in order to reduce them into two alien groups within the same ethnic cultural milieu.

Indeed, the reluctance and unfriendly attitude of the local born people had acted upon the refugees adversely. Many of them went back to West Bengal deserting the settlement which sometimes refrained others from going to Andaman. They were hurt by the antithetical attitude of the local people. They always felt that the local people not only put obstacles in their way of minuscule living but also made them feel that they were usurpers rather than guests. Once they were forced to abandon their ancestral homeland in East Pakistan being victims of the power politics followed by the disintegrating communal forces. Again in India, they being condemned in rigmarole surroundings faced miserable consequences. Under duress, they had to agree to the government's proposal for rehabilitation in Andaman but there too, they were forced to feel to be still in the material, social, psychological and spiritual insecurity. Aggression having no scope, the process of regression as consequences of accumulated tension was more visible in their behaviour. In this frustrating situation, the feeling of privation seemed operative and generated a sort of apathy towards the land and people. Instead of extending sympathy, the local born people too raised their voice by propagating the well-smitten diktat that only they belong to these islands and have the sole rights over the land by virtue of their birth and there is no place for any other outsiders.

Indeed, what the local born people apprehended that they would lose their cultural identity if a major community, Bengalis could dominate over them and that the islands would become an appendage of West Bengal but both apprehensions have been proved false. Actually what made them scared was that they would be relegated being outnumbered by the unrestricted influx of outsiders. Though this angst could not be dispelled, yet the influx of outsiders has never been debarred. Presently, the population of the local borns has been reduced to a measly figure. Comparing the rate of growth of populations of different linguistic groups of major communities, such as Bengali, Tamil, Malayali,

Telegu, Hindustani settled in these islands, according to the 1951 Census and the 1991 Census, the magnitude of influx of outsiders can easily be understood.

Though the local born people have become outnumbered, yet their cultural entity is not at stake, rather it contributes to weave a cultural tapestry in unison with all divergent cultures of other communities.

TABLE

Islands' population distribution according to linguistic pattern

Census of 1951	Census of 1991
Bengali - 2363	64706
Hindi - 5114	49469
Urdu - 862	1492
Malayalam - 2815	26075
Tamil - 1573	53536
Telegu - 1044	32979

The total population of the whole territory was 30971 in 1951 but in 2001 it was 314084 and the rate of growth is almost ten times. Despite the phenomenal growth and enormous distinction of different linguistic groups, the unity in diversity still prevails in these islands and presence of different languages does not create any hindrance in the formation of cultural integrity. The people though drawn from diverse social, cultural and geographical backgrounds, live in peace and harmony and at the same time, maintain a separate cultural identity of their own.

ENDNOTES

1. *The Hindustan Standard,* a reputed English daily, pub. from Calcutta, dt. 8.4.1949.
2. 'Andamanian Association' as quoted in the report pub. in *The Hindu* June 2, 1967, later reprinted in the *Andaman Aaj Tak,* dt. Feb. 2004, pub. from Port Blair.
3. State Archives, West Bengal, File no. 38/55,
4. Ibid.

10

Settlement in Middle Andaman

Considering the critical condition owing to the refugee settlement in South Andaman and the vehement remonstrance of the local people, the Government of India changed the strategy of settlement in Andaman and stopped rehabilitation there. Thus the second phase of refugee settlement started and the Five Year Colonization Scheme was taken up to rehabilitate the East Bengal refugees in Middle Andaman and other islands which were virtually no-man's land, inhabited neither by the aborigines nor by the local born people. So the second phase of settlement faced no man-made hindrances but the refugees had to face physical obstacles due to impregnable forest, undeterred wild boars and deer, countless parrots, blighting pests and terrible centipedes, and above all inclement weather, etc. These uprooted people tackled them desperately to facilitate the colonization programme.

According to an official note of Deputy Commissioner bearing No. 27/158/7632/66- Cal, dated, August 18, 1966, it is learnt that the 'Colonization Scheme' started in 1953 and settlement outside South Andaman was set into operation till 1961.

TOPOGRAPHY OF MIDDLE ANDAMAN

Middle Andaman having an area of 1536 sq. kms, now the biggest inhabited island in the Andaman group, is the region best suited for settlement. The river valleys give rise to very wide plains with perennial flow of waters.

As regards the area of the available land, Middle Andaman tops among all other regions. The total area of the cultivable land is around 73760 acres suitable for paddy cultivation, fruits and vegetable gardens, coconut plantation. There are as many as eight river valleys and the biggest one among all valleys in Andaman, the Betapur valley lies in this region. The soil conditions are also very good and average rainfall is less than that of South Andaman so being suitable for paddy cultivation.

Middle Andaman stretching from Kadamtala to Mayabunder is the most alluring sites for human settlement. There are vast valleys like Betapur, Rangat and Happy Valley which was found ideal not only for cultivation but also for successful settlement. Indeed, the west coastal area of Middle Andaman was not suitable for immediate settlement due to thick forest belt, hostile Jarawa inhabitation and absence of any port facilities. And in the East, some area was found undulating and hilly covered with dense jungle, unsuitable for cultivation. But the rest of the region was taken into consideration for the settlement of 4000 families and 8094 hectares of agricultural land available for distribution among them with the objective that an equal area was to be developed by these settlers on their own for growing fruits and vegetables and for home grazing. All these surveys were made by the Forest Department and further analysed by H.R. Shivdasani.[1]

The prospect of immediate colonization depends mainly on location where communication facilities are adequate, water supply is perennial and land area is cleared and reclaimed. Considering all these criteria, it appears that Tugapur, Happy Valley, Rangat Valley, Yol Jig, Bamlungta etc., provide ample opportunities for colonization. Thus the relative merit of the possible areas judged by the amount of flat land available for settlement should be counted first and in accordance with that the following areas viz., Betapur, Boroin Jig and Bamlungta, Bania Khari, Curtbert Bay, Red Creek, Tugapur Waterfall valley, Yaratil Jig, etc., were demarcated for further settlement in Middle Andaman. All these areas fulfilled almost all the favourable conditions of successful colonization mentioned above. These areas were heavily worked to fell trees and to reclaim lands for immediate colonization.

The Betapur valley with a total available land of 15200 acres offers 900 acres of flat land suitable for paddy cultivation. Another advantage is that in this area where the Picharnallah meets the Betapur stream, though interspersed by small hills, is almost level for 7 or 8 miles so ideal for settlement.

Besides, the selection of the Rangat valley was made due to the communication facilities via Yerata Jetty where disembarkation of settlers was convenient. The Rangat valley is about 74 kms. from Port Blair and the clearance of forests was relatively easier due to the nearness of Long Island which had been developed as the headquarters of the Forest Department and happened to be the main centre for the functioning of the colonization activities in Middle Andaman.

According to the memorandum No. 37-219 (2)/59-DH, dated, February 19, 1959, M.V. Rajwade, the Chief Commissioner noted that S.K. Raha, Treasury Officer, AndaNico Administration had been deputed to tour West Bengal refugee camps to recruit refugee families from there. Even Rajani Ranjan Sarkar, a settler of 1949 batch, along with a member of the Advisory Council of the Chief Commissioner was also sent to assist the Treasury Officer and to motivate the refugees to settle in Andaman.

The first batch of the East Bengal refugee families reached the Rangat valley in the month of May, 1953. After disembarkation, the migrants had to complete all official formalities including registration. Later they were provided with all necessary agricultural implements and doles or subsistence allowances. They were also allotted 5 acres of flat land and 5 acres of hilly land.

From the tour diary of A.K. Ghosh, the Chief Commissioner, it is learnt that "settlement of refugees should as a matter of fact begin from Bajlungta, later known as Kadamtala, since Rangat is not accessible for nearly 4 months in a year. The land is good and water is easily obtained".[2]

Hence the first phase of settlement in Middle Andaman began not from Rangat but from Kadamtala, near Uttara Jetty in May, 1953. Within two years from 1953 to 1955, the total number of families settled in different areas in Middle Andaman rose to 438. With the growth of settlement, the population increased gradually. By 1966, the existing families were multiplied and about 3000 families were resettled in Middle Andaman totalling around 6000 settlers in Rangat and Mayabunder areas. Among them about 4000 persons were working at Rangat as P.W.D. and Forest labourers. It had been estimated that nearly 5000 agricultural families could be settled further in the island and about 4000 agricultural families were so far rehabilitated. Indeed, in the first Five-Year Plan, 834 families and in the Second Plan another 97 families were resettled in Middle Andaman.

SETTLEMENT PATTERN

The land-use pattern in Middle Andaman was totally changed after the settlement of East Bengal refugees who were basically agriculturists and accustomed to cultivate paddy in their land in East Pakistan. In Andaman, they got the fertile soil and timely rainfall and by dint of their hard labour, they could yield copious production of paddy crop. Beside cultivation, the settlers would earn being engaged as mazdoors in the government departments on daily wage basis.

According to the Five-Year Colonization Scheme, the settlements were planned as nuclear type and their lands were allotted within the periphery of the respective villages. In the virgin land of the area, they were the first to cultivate paddy and the yield was unexpectedly 42 mounds per acre.

With the success of colonization, more area was being cleared and the settlement spread in the Happy valley extending towards Mayabunder. Meanwhile, arrangements were made to receive migrants from the different communities, i.e., Malayalis, Tamilians, etc., other than Bengalis.

In the newly developed colonization areas, the settlement villages where the East Bengal refugees were rehabilitated, were previously known as Number 5, Number 8, etc., measuring the distance from jetty but later the villages were named after the characters of the Ramayana such as, Dasarathpur, Rampur, Sitapur, Janakpur, etc. Each village with a population of more than 200 heads presents an interesting cultural manifestation celebrating Hindu festivals round the years.

Facilities and Assistance

The Assistant Secretary, Government of India wrote a letter bearing No. 8/3/52-AN, dated May 20, 1953 to the Chief Commissioner on the subject, "Five-Year Colonization Scheme for Development and Colonization of the Displaced Persons from East Bengal", and it states as follows:

"I am directed to refer your letter No. 1/850/53 dt. February 6, 1953 and to convey the sanction of the President to your proposal for settlement in Andaman of 100 families of agriculturists from East Bengal under the Five-Year Scheme for development and colonization of the Andamans.

"Accordingly, each family will be given the following concessions :

(a) Allotment of 5 acres of cleared land for paddy cultivation

(b) Allotment of another 5 acres of unclear hilly land for being used as homestead land for growing fruits, vegetables and as pasture for cattle.

(c) Grant of a recoverable loan up to Rs. 2000/- to meet expenditure on passage from the mainland of India to the Andamans, construction of a hutment, purchase of bullocks, agricultural implements, seeds, manure and maintenance till the first crop is harvested.

(d) The necessary expenditure is met from within the sanctioned budget grant for the Five-Year Colonization Scheme.[3]

For clarification, the Chief Commissioner, Shankarnath Moitra wrote a letter, No. 7/Camp/53 to the Secretary, Government of India, Ministry of Home Affairs as stated below:

"In the present scheme for settlement in the Middle Andaman, each settler family is entitled to a loan of Rs. 2000/- vide circular No. 8/3/52 AN, dt. 20 May, 1953 of the Ministry of Home Affairs.

This sum was given out as recoverable loan under the following heads:

House building	Rs. 500/-
Plough animals	Rs. 700/-
Seeds and manure	Rs. 100/-
Cost of utensils	Rs. 130/-
Subsistence allowance	Rs. 360/-
Passage by sea, etc.	Rs. 210/-
Total	**Rs. 2000/-**

In the above letter, the Chief Commissioner further remarked:

1. "From experience it is being found that the total amount is insufficient and that with the best of intention, settlers find it difficult to repay the entire sum as loan. A person, particularly settler in a new country can hope to repay only such items which are of a capital nature and from which an income can be made. Items like subsistence allowance and cost of passage do not give the settlers any return. These are items which are necessary to pay to a settler in order that he may go to the Andamans and begin life there. It is difficult enough for a settler in a new country to make a living. It is well nigh impossible for him to pay back sums he has spent on his journey, on his food. If government wishes, as a matter of policy to take some colonists to these islands, it stands to reason that the government should pay something to fulfil their wish.

Instead of asking the settlers to pay for everything, it is submitted that these two items—subsistence allowance and cost of passage, totalling Rs. 570/- are in equity not debitable against the settlers but should be treated as an ex-gratia grant from government".

2. "At present subsistence allowance is granted to each family @ Rs. 15/- for adult and @ Rs. 10/- for child per month with a maximum Rs. 50/- for a total period of six months.... the above sum is very small compared to present day prices...the maximum pay of an unskilled mazdoor is Rs. 57/- per month. The cost of living in Andaman is higher than that in the mainland... many things of daily necessities like salt, kerosene oil, etc., have to be imported, paying a freight of Rs. 3/- per mound. The Government servants posted to Andaman are allowed a special pay of 33 1/3 percent ....the special allowance per family may also be increased by a third making a total of Rs. 80/- per month....the subsistence allowance (to the settler) should be paid at least for eight months.

3. "At present Rs. 500/- is granted for house building. It is found from experience that it is not possible to build any kind of living accommodation within this sum....it is proposed that in rural areas, the sum may be enhanced to Rs. 800/-, in urban areas (Rangat) Rs. 1500/-.

Hence, grants and loans per family may be considered as stated below

House building	–	Rs.800/-	Recoverable loan
Plough animals	–	Rs.700/-	Recoverable loan
Cost of utensils	–	Rs.130/-	Recoverable loan
Subsistence allowance	–	Rs.960/-	Ex-gratia grant
Passage etc.	–	Rs.210/-	Ex-gratia grant

For 400 families scheduled in the current year (1953), the cost on accounts of such ex-gratia grant would come to Rs. 4,68,000.[4]

Sd/ S.N. Moitra
C.C.9.12.53

Considering the gravity of the situation, a meeting between the Chief Minister, West Bengal and the Union Rehabilitation Minister was held on July 10, 14 and 15, 1954 and the decision was taken accepting the proposal of the Chief Commissioner, AndaNico Islands.

Accordingly, S.L. Mathuria, Under Secretary, Ministry of Home Affairs, issued a fresh order No. 8/18/54-A.N. on July 16, 1954 under the title, "Additional benefits to settlers in Andaman under the Five-Year Colonization Scheme", written as fellows:

"In suppression of Para 1(3) of this Ministry's letter No.8/3/52-A.N. dated 20 May 1953, I am directed to convey the sanction of the President to the grant of a recoverable loan and ex-gratia grant to each settler family in the Andamans under the Five-Year Scheme for Development and Colonization of the Andamans up to the maximum amount shown below:

Loan		Ex-Gratia Grant	
House building	Rs. 800/-	Subsistence Allowance	Rs. 840/-
Plough animals	Rs. 700/-	(Rs. 70/- per mensum for 8	
Cost of utensils	Rs. 130/-	months in the first year and	
Seeds & manure	Rs. 100/-	for 4 months in the next year.) Passage etc.	Rs. 210/-
Total	**Rs. 1730/**	**Total**	**Rs. 1050/-**

Along with the agriculture families, there were a number of artisans settled in Andaman following the colonization scheme and they were sanctioned small traders' loan to start their own business.

On April 26, 1955, the Chief Commissioner, Shankar N. Moitra observed, "The G.O.I. have now been good enough to sanction the grant of such trade loans with a maximum of Rs. 500/- in rural areas and Rs. 5000/- in urban areas for a total sum not exceeding Rs. 50,000/- in 1955-56.

"It is now necessary to work out a scheme for all villages in the colonization area for setting up:

(a) Small rural industries like smithy, carpentry, pottery, etc.

(b) As regards grocer's shop, on account of small numbers, a cooperative store would not be practical.

(c) In the Middle Andaman, there are three places which could possibly be described as urban areas. These are Rangat, Long Island and Mayabunder. In urban areas, the limit of the loan is Rs. 5000/- in one case.[5]

In the file No. 29-7/55 F, dt. October, 17, 1955, there is a list of settlers of different villages, i.e., Tugapur, Sitapur, Betapur, Kalara, Rangat, Sabri, Kalsi, Uttara, Shantanu, Padmapuram, Bharatpur, etc., who were sanctioned recoverable interest-free loan to run their Bakery, Sweets stall, Smithy, Carpentry, etc.

In connection with the small trading loan, some of the incumbents were very prudent and practical. They applied for loan jointly to start a dairy farm.

Tahsildar (Refugee), Middle Andaman, reported on January 27, 1956 to the Development Commissioner:

"I would suggest that these settlers, Satish Mondal, Nakul Mondal, Sukhnath Halder, Nagen Biswas may be extended a loan of Rs. 2000/- jointly for purchase of milch-animals and they may be jointly and severely made responsible for repayment of the loan. If the scheme proves to be a success, we may open such dairies in the colony areas also by helping groups of settlers with loans for purchasing milch-animals.[6]

Consequently, the Department of Rehabilitation accorded sanction for supply of milch-animals to all the settlers. In the Billyground and Rangat areas, 200 such animals were procured from the mainland and the remaining migrant families were allowed to purchase milch-animals locally and loan assistance was extended to them for this purpose.

However, the temporal condition of the then Andaman was not as prosperous as it seems today. Though the settlers were resolute and assiduous, the progress was stymied for many reasons, administrative as well as situational.

On August 7, 1956, the Deputy Commissioner informed the Chief Commissioner of the pecuniary condition of the settlers despite the ex-gratia grants had been given to them.

He further remarked: "It has been found that the refugee-settlers who came here (Middle Andaman) in 1953-'54 have not been able to stand on their own legs, so more ex-gratia grants may be sanctioned to them".[7]

Under this circumstance, the Dy. Commissioner requested the Chief Commissioner for early consideration so that the refugee-settlers might not face starvation.

The following table shows the details of these families settled in different villages of Middle Andaman up to July 29, 1954.

TABLE

Dt. of Arrival	*No of families*	*Settled at*
19 May, 1953	50	Rangat
15 June, 1953	4	Rangat
15 Feb, 1954	116	Nimbutala, Amkunj
2 April, 1954	35	Nimbutala, Amkunj
25 April, 1954	83	Rangat
25 May, 1954	98	Uttara. Shantanu
2 June, 1954	5	Kamdamtala
3 July, 1954	70	Bumlungta Valley
29 July, 1954	70	Shyamkand, etc.

However, the Dy. Commissioner confessed: "Under the term of settlement, we have to supply them with 5 acres of cleared land for paddy cultivation and 5 acres of unclear hilly land and a pair of plough animals. In fact, we have not been able to give them plough animals in the first two years on the ground that ploughing was impossible due to the existence of stumps and logs lying scattered, that cleared land was ineffective of cultivation and sometimes was necessary to allow the stumps and logs to rot or steadily burnt year by year. The result has been that though 3 crops have been taken up to February, 1956 by the settlers of 1953 and two crops by the settlers of 1954, they have not been able to stand on their legs, partly due to ineffective clearance and partly due to our inability to supply plough animals to all of them.

"We have so far been able to procure 436 pairs of plough animals, vide my letter No.27/8/5122/A-1, dt. 12 July, 1956, and 138 families of 1954 batch are still to be provided with animals....

"With this background and the destruction of crop by pests, wild animals, deer and pigs, and absence of marketing facility for other agricultural produce in the vicinity, I venture to submit that the settlers need some more help from the government this year. In pursuance of my discussion with you in June last, I have issued orders to the Tahsildars to pay to the settlers two months subsistence allowance out of their loan account if there is some balance and report such cases where there is no balance with the loan account.

"In view of the circumstance explained above and particularly to poor crop of the settlers in 1953-'54, and 1954-'55, I request you to move the G.O.I. to sanction 4 more ex-gratia grants, i.e., 16 months in all for all the settlers who came here during 1953 and 1954....very early orders are requested.[8]

The Government of India instantly approved the following facilities and assistance to the prospective buyers of work-animals from the mainland:

(a) 70% of the cost of transport and incidental charges of the animals to be allowed as subsidy.

(b) Free deck/bunk passage will be allowed at the rate of one passage for escorting 5 dry animals.

This scheme also continued in the later phases of settlement in other islands.[9]

Hence the settlers of 1953-54 and 1954-55 batches, settled in Middle Andaman were helped with extra ex-gratia grants in cases of failure of crops and the settlers of 1955-56 batches were resettled in Middle Andaman with all assistances. A number of settlers were sanctioned small trading loans to start their own business.

As it happened in the case of South Andaman settlement, some settlers of Middle Andaman enjoying the benefits of the government facilities and monetary assistance left the settlement either stealthily or with official permission without clearing off the loan amount.

Notwithstanding this sort of deterrence, the settlement in the Middle Andaman was a great success. There is a little difference in the physical conditions between South and Middle Andaman but the basic differences arise out of the isolation of the Middle Andaman and absence of any indigenous settlement there.

Moreover, for the development of the settlement areas in Middle Andaman, the government explored all the avenues besides agriculture so that the settlers could be benefited and one of them was sweet water pisciculture which for the displaced persons from East Bengal proved to be a boon. The Andaman Public Works Department and the Agriculture Department jointly ventured to dig ponds with the labour of the settlers in different villages, i.e., Uttara, Bakultala, Kausalyanagar, Rangat, Harinagar, Kadamtala, Panchawati etc., so that the settlers could culture sweet water fish in those ponds. Selling sweet water fish has become a good source of their income.

The great success of refugee settlement in Middle Andaman bears the proof of the power of their adaptability and assiduity and thereby confutes the blame that the Bengali refugees are indolent and ease-loving. On the contrary, they have proved themselves laborious and gritty. By the dint of their relentless labour and indomitable tenacity, they became successful to start a new life. The factors responsible for the success of settlement in Middle Andaman are mentioned below:

(a) Mostly agriculturists were recruited and resettled in Middle Andaman and they would know how to till the soil to harvest golden corns.

(b) The climate of Middle Andaman is wet like that of East Bengal, the plains and basins of rivulets are fertile so the refugees could adjust and cultivate the land wholeheartedly.

(c) Due to homogeneity of the refugees, a peaceful gregarious society has been developed in Andaman.

ENDNOTES

1. Report on the Possibilities of Colonization etc., Government of India, Ministry of Home Affairs.
2. State Archives: Port Blair, File No. 37-277/59-DH, pp 31, Office of R&R Commissioner, Diary No. 682, dated, 15.1.1952
3. State Archives, Port Blair, File No. 41/326/70-Dev.I, p.1049
4. State Archives, Port Blair, File No.41-326/70, Dev-1
5. State Archives, Port Blair, File No. AN. No.29/7/55, dt. 26 April, 1955
6. State Archives, Revenue Department, Port Blair,
7. State Archives, Port Blair, Letter No. 27/13/5602/A-1, dt 7.8.56
8. State Archives, Port Blair, File No. 5/53-7/54
9. State Archives, Port Blair, File No. 37-277-59-DH

11

Settlement in North Andaman

With the success of the settlement in Middle Andaman, the Government of India decided to increase the quota of the displaced persons for Andaman so that more refugees could be settled there on colonization scheme. Thus North Andaman received attention and gradually the settlement stretched farther from Mayabunder towards Kalighat in 1953 and Diglipur in 1956 in North Andaman setting up new colonies for new batches of refugees.

The scheme of rehabilitation initiated by the then Chief Commissioner A.K. Ghosh was accelerated with equal efficiency by his successor, Shankarnath Moitra. Under his able stewardship, the settlement in North Andaman got momentum and three to four hundred of East Bengal refugees were rehabilitated in a year. Till 1962, 2644 families were resettled in different areas in Andaman.

Though North Andaman seemed to be an important region of colonization and betrayed good prospect, it was not chosen at the beginning due to inaccessibility for dense forest, dangerous meandering terrain and also for the total absence of any sort of communication between North Andaman and Port Blair. Moreover, information regarding the availability of land in North Andaman was then entirely based on the insufficient local knowledge of the forest officers because during the Japanese occupation (1943-45), all their records were destroyed. Hence they had to depend on their impressions and assumptions.

Besides, for felling and clearing of gigantic trees, bulldozers, tractors and other heavy machineries are required for the quick disposal of the logs but to transport the appliances from Port Blair during the initial stage of settlement was quite a great problem because at that time, the only means of transportation was the waterways which always depend on weather condition and that too remained more or less inclement round the year. Further, a motorable road from the only jetty at Ariel Bay to the headquarters at Diglipur was yet to be constructed.

Though the Relief and Rehabilitation Department had tried to select the sites for settlement as far as possible near any source of water, yet some villages would face scarcity of water as all the sources were not perennial. Not for water alone, sometimes for food and medicines or in emergency, the settlers had to cross crocodile-infested canals and creeks to collect them.

Notwithstanding all these hindrances, the settlers did not lose heart but engaged themselves whole-heartedly to keep up their morale in creating a new home in exile, far away from their own homeland in the East Pakistan.

TOPOGRAPHY OF NORTH ANDAMAN

Though no big valleys like Rangat or Baratang are available in North Andaman, coastal plains and river valleys of 'Kalpong'[1] are plenty. This Kalara Valley where the people from Kerala were settled later and the name of the area happens to be known as Keralapuram, is the biggest of its kind in North Andaman with a total available land of 2700 acres and out of which 1500 acres are flat, suitable for paddy cultivation and available in the west of Saddle Peak[2] range which is the source of Kalpong River that flows down the Diglipur valley to supply water for irrigation and drinking purpose.

The areas for immediate settlement in North Andaman had been identified as follows:

TABLE

Area	*Acres*	*Area*	*Acres*
Kalara	2700	Cold Stream Bay	1700
Parangara	2500	Fine Bay valley	1700
Terapa Bolin	2200	Palchtara Bolin	1500
Diglipur	2200	Blair Bay	1500
Taipong	2000	Hudson Bay	1300
Casuarina Bay	1700	Baluri Creek	1300
Teel Creek	1100	Pambroke Bay	1100
McPherson Bay	1100	Beele valley	1000
Hoare Bay	1000	Shallow Bay	950
Coffris Bay	510		

Area between Elizabeth Bay and Cold Stream Bay	-1300 acres
Area between Hoare Bay and Buchanan Island	-1300 acres
Area between Cadell Point and Dundas Point	-1300 acres
Area between Buchanan Island and Stewared Sound Harbour	-1250 acres
Area between Mangrove Bay and Cadel Bay	-700 acres
Area between Teel creek and Kuda Khari	-600 acres

Considering the vastness of area and nearness to the Port as well as availability of reclaimed forest land, Parangara and Kalara valleys were having good prospect of immediate colonization for about 100 families in Parangara and 300 families in Kalara. Of course, the factors determining the prospect of future settlement such as, vast area, location, perennial sources of water, etc. Diglipur area seemed to be the most promising for settlement in comparison to other areas in North Andaman.

Consequently Diglipur is the headquarters of North Andaman. Its area is 884sq. kms. The Andaman Trunk Road is the only road connecting South, Middle and North Andamans stretching from Chidyatapu, the southern-most point in South Andaman to Ariel Bay in North Andaman. Diglipur Tahsil comprises of 30 revenue villages such as Sitapur, Subhasgram, Ramkrishnagram, Madhupur, etc. Almost 90 per cent of the population of these villages is East Bengal refugees and other 10 per cent are the migrants from Kerala and Tamil Nadu.

SETTLEMENT PATTERNS

The Government of India decided albeit at the request of the Government of West Bengal to resettle a part of the East Bengal refugees declared 'excess' in West Bengal in hitherto uninhabited Islands of Andaman.

A high level committee was constituted at the instance of the Government of India in 1956 and the report was submitted in the following year. Its recommendations were accepted and a National Development Council was formed to look after the development of the territory.

The process of resettlement continued unabated till 1964. Financial assistance in the form of loans was given to the settlers to meet the cost of passage from the mainland, to build their houses, to purchase livestock and agricultural implements and also for their maintenance till they were in a position to reap their first harvest.

Some of the settlers were grumbling as there were allegations of irregularities in land allotment as well as release of loans. Sometimes, caste-factor played an important role in influencing, the rehabilitation programme of the Government of India.

The refugees were intended to serve as catalysts of settled agricultural cultivation. They were asked to clear the jungle from their fields and make the land cultivable. In a region where there was hardly any indigenous labour and agriculture had to depend primarily on indentured labour recruited through the Catholic Missionary Society, popularly known as 'Father Chalan', obviously the East Pakistan refugees were looked upon as a cheap and inexpensive source of agricultural labour. So on resettlement in Andaman, the settlers were engaged in P.W.D. and Forest Department on casual basis during the lean period.

From the report of the Estimates Committee of 1961-62 under the Ministry of Rehabilitation, it is learnt that nearly 9000 persons had been resettled in Andaman for all accounts successfully under a scheme of the Home Ministry. The Committee further suggested that the potentiality of the territory was then enormous so more of the displaced persons from East Pakistan should be settled there.

The Ministry replied: "The Andaman Rehabilitation Scheme of the Ministry of Home Affairs, is still in operation and displaced families continue to be sent to the Andamans for settlement under that scheme.[3]

On April 28, 1959, one hundred refugee families consisting of 450 souls arrived at Port Cornwallis Jetty in Diglipur on May 2, 1959 and were resettled at the following villages:

Kirishnapur	–	39 families
Sitanagar West	–	37 families
Sitanagar East	–	24 families

All through the journey right from the refugee camps in West Bengal to Diglipur, they were escorted by the Colonization Assistant, P.L.D. Roy and a senior medical officer from AndaNico Administration. On their arrival at Diglipur, the migrants were served with cooked meal and the second meal was served at the destination, the villages where they were sent to resettle. Along with 10 acres of land, other facilities, i.e., maintenance allowance, seeds, manure, etc., were also granted.

In or nearby villages, arrangements were made to provide some community facilities such as, police outpost to maintain law and order, dispensary for general treatment, extra-departmental Post-Office, primary schools, cooperative consumer stores, etc.[4]

On May 20, 1959, 55 families consisting of 210 souls were brought to Diglipur and resettled at Sitapur village. They were also granted all sorts of assistance offered by the Government of India. Nutrition survey was also conducted by Dr. Ajit Kumar Halder in some villages in Diglipur.

During those early days of rehabilitation in the second half of 1950s, any sort of civic facilities were only to be dreamt of and the reality was disdainful and hazardous but the settlers had to be braced enough to brave the unfavourable situation and cope with the oddities of living to pave way for successful settlement. The places which were once the abode of wild boars and deer, took a new look with the magic touch of the East Bengal refugees. The Chital deer which were introduced during the British period, have multiplied very fast and became a menace for the settlers. Deer abounded in North and Middle Andaman to such an extent that no restrictions had been enacted on their killing during those days. Fish was in abundance and average catch was plenty but due to want of marketing facilities, the settlers refrained from catching fish on a large scale. Moreover, they were not accustomed to deep sea fishing so they did not adopt the venture on commercial basis.

In North Andaman, there were 1700 acres under paddy cultivation and 8000 acres under plantation. About 8000 tons of rice was produced but it was inadequate so 9000 tons of rice and 1000 tons of wheat had to be brought from the mainland. Besides, 1000 tons of pulses were also imported. Though with the support of the Agriculture Department, the settlers underwent training in multiple cropping, despite their interest in a one-crop pattern, the production was augmented. Thus the life of the settlers was somehow peaceful though there were some grievances that got vent at times to express their angst.

Unprecedented Hunger Strike

In the history of post-Independence settlement in Andaman, the most significant incident is the hunger strike called out by the settlers of Diglipur in support of their demands, particularly to write off the colonization loans taken by them.

But due to pecuniary stringency, they failed to pay back. They moved from pillar to post to get redressed and applied to all the concerned officers to waive the loan amount but it was rejected by the administration. Failing to get any relief, they took to the last resort, hunger strike, first of its kinds in the history of the Bay Islands.

In the D.O. letter no. DC/121/68-S, dated June 4, 1968, the Deputy Commissioner informed the Chief Commissioner, Mahavir Singh of the conditions leading to the outbreak of hunger strike in Diglipur that :

"The settlers from East Bengal at Diglipur have started an agitation to press their demand afresh for the write-off of the colonization loans taken by them. Two settlers, viz., Sasidhar Mondal and Rajani Samaddar have been squatting on hunger strike since 25 May, 1968 and processions are taken out daily at Diglipur in support of their demand.....

"....Tahsildar, Mayabunder, had attached the property of one settler of Kishorinagar...all revenue officers were issued instruction by wireless not to resort to coercive measures like attachment/sale of movable and immovable properties of settlers for recovery of government dues...

"The property of the settler attached at Kishorinagar was immediately released. ...42 settlers including Bipad Bhanjan Biswas, a former member of Home Minister's Advisory Committee observed token strike on 17 May, 1968 and began to build up an agitation for the write-off of colonization loan. I had assured that it was not our policy to realize colonization loans and other dues from 2861 families by resorting to coercive measures.

"These settlers have been settled in the Andaman under the colonization scheme. Each family was given Rs. 1730/- as loan, and total expenditure was about Rs. 52 lakhs. The loan arrears @ 4.5 percent is recoverable in ten annual instalments.....the settlers appear to be reluctant to repay the loan.

"The agitation is being actively supported and instigated by Suresh Halder, Secretary, R.C.P.I., Ramesh Mazumder of Diglipur and some supporters of Congress of Diglipur..."[5]

However, the strike continued for 24 days and the news not only stirred up the locality but also created commotion in the arena of politics. Ramesh Mazumder informed K.R. Ganesh, the then Member of Parliament from these islands and requested him to take steps to redress their grievances.

On 5 June, 1965, K.R. Ganesh sent a wireless message in reply to Ramesh Mazumder, worded as under:

"We have supported demands of settlers regarding exemption of loan. Matter was raised by us repeatedly in Advisory Committee. Consequently realization was not pressed upon. In September 1967, Advisory Committee authorized C.C. to study problem and individual cases. For total exemption, matter can only be decided by Cabinet on all India basis. Hence Administration cannot make commitment. 'Satyagrah' has served purpose... focus attention.

"Suggest—send settlers' delegation to Delhi in July during Parliament Session. We shall take up again with G.O.I. Self was down with Chicken-pox—hence regret, unable to come to Diglipur. Pl, reply whether my proposal is acceptable".[6]

Notwithstanding his insistence, the strike and agitation continued until the administration assured of quick disposal of the issue. Thus the strike was called off on 10 June, 1968 at 4-30 hrs.

This hunger strike though called off, had a great impact on the settlers and made them conscious about their rights and strength. In future, whenever the settlers felt some common problems, they put forth the issue in a democratic way to press upon their demands.

On May 17, 1970, the Secretary, R.C.P.I. Rangat Zone prepared a representation addressed to the Home Minister and submitted to the Secretary, Government of India placing two demands:

(a) Settlers to be employed during non-cultivation season.

(b) Bengali should be the medium of instruction from primary to higher secondary level in the areas where Bengali refugees were settled.

Though the previous one was rejected, yet the latter one was accepted and accordingly a school was set-up at Rangat with the facility to study science at the Higher Secondary level in Bengali medium since 1969-70 sessions.

But there were other reasons for their grievances. Regarding the non-fulfilment of the terms and conditions assured them before settlement, some of the settlers of the first batch of 1949 had to submit a mass petition on May 18, 1977 to the Chief Commissioner as stated below:

"We inhabitants of village Ferrargunj... brought to Andaman & Nicobar Islands at the very beginning of colonization scheme, 1949,......reached here on 17 March, 1949...shifted to Manpur camp...allotted 2 acres, 3 acres, 4 acres to agriculturists...we raise the following points for your recommendations:

(a) Not yet allotted 10 acres of paddy land and hilly land.

(b) Not helped in construction of residential building at Ferrargunj.

Signed by

Ramakrishna Chakraborty

& other 19 settlers".[7]

It is just one of the many petitions submitted by the aggrieved settlers against the non-fulfilment of the government commitments and absence of community facilities like water supply, education, medical treatment, etc. The denouement was that a feeling of deprivation being aggravated and a sense of despondency had been fuming among them which sometimes outburst in violent protest, demonstration, squatting and strike. The hunger strike at Diglipur was such an explosion.

COLONIZATION IN BARATANG ISLAND

Baratang Island situated in-between South Andaman and Middle Andaman, though not a big island, possesses a few good areas for settlement. The island being uninhabited and covered with evergreen virgin forests of valuable timber is a commercially viable area but extraction of timber faces a lot of difficulties. Initially human labour was used. Later on, elephants were brought into services and they were utilized for dragging and clearing the logs. During the British period when the tramline was introduced, elephants started to help in loading and unloading timber on the trucks and wagons to be carried away with the help of loco-engine.

Baratang serves a very important role in roadway and waterway communications due to its location. Naturally the island is an ideal place for settlement.

Considering the availability of land, the following areas were identified for further settlement:

TABLE

Areas	*Acres Available*
Para Jig	1500
Ada Jig	2200
From Bomlungta to Flat Bay	3400
Lura Jig	3900
Wrafter's Creek, Ragolachang Creek, Jarawa Creek	6300

Once these areas were totally under the inhabitation of Jarawas and presently some of the areas are still reserved for the tribal. But the remaining areas have been marked for settlement. However, due to area of the island not being sufficiently large, planned settlement must be chalked out.

At Baratang, mostly the scheduled tribe people from Bihar, i.e., Oraon, Munda, Kharia, Santhali, Gondi, etc. commonly called 'Ranchis' in Andaman, were rehabilitated.

According to a circular of D.C., no. RB/111/12/vol/2/71/10698, dt. 6 Nov. 1971, "Every registered settler of revenue villages in Baratang Island has been allotted five acres of paddy land as per the colonization scheme.

"Usually in the Forest Department, mostly 'Ranchi' people were engaged and at the beginning, they were brought to Andaman without their families. But while it was decided to open Baratang Island for settlement, the Ranchis got the priority for they were found quite inured to the tropical climate and epiphyllous forest. Besides, they are hardy and sturdy stock of people accustomed to Jhum cultivation to produce rice and they prefer roots and tubular vegetations available in plenty in the forest".

The Divisional Forest Officer, South Andaman informed the Deputy Commissioner, Port Blair of the "Colonization in Baratang Island—Settlement of Ranchi families", in the following lines:

"As desired by the Chief Commissioner, A.N.I., applications were invited from Ranchi labourers of the South Andaman Division willing to bring their families and settle down at Baratang as settlers".

Applications were received in response to the above circular and fifty one families consisting of 169 heads were selected and settled at Baratang.[8]

This was the beginning of settlement at Baratang Island that went on farther. According to the Census of 2001, the number of households at Baratang was 1292 and its total population was 6062.

ENDNOTES

1. Kalpong is the only river in the whole of AndaNico Islands supplying hydroelectricity.
2. Saddle peak is the highest peak in the AndaNico Islands measuring 732 meters.
3. State Archives, Port Blair. MOR, Letter No.13 (1)/61 Gen/dated December 23, 1961
4. State Archives, Port Blair. Circular No. 27/13(R)108/59, Office of Dy. Commissioner.
5. State Archives, Port Blair-File No. 15-52/68-J(1)
6. State Archives, Port Blair. Ibid
7. State Archives. Port Blair. File no. 33-8/70.J1
8. State Archives, Port Blair, Letter No. 6/76-1786/W.Gunj from D.F.O., S.A., dt. 30 Dec.1959

12

Settlement in Other Islands

During the last three decades since the first settlement in 1949, these islands were subjected to heavy pressure for clearance of forest land, for rehabilitation of displaced persons from East Pakistan as well as to make room for rehabilitation of other migrants from the mainland of India and to facilitate commercial plantation programme in the AndaNico Islands. All these programmes need reclamation of substantial areas of virgin forests and thereby lead to unexpected environmental effects.

In the Andaman district, most of the islands are under a deep mantle of forest cover and whatever land required for agriculture, small scale industrial enterprises and for future rehabilitation must be obtained only through the clearance of forests. To avoid total destruction of forest on the pleas of colonization and to dissuade plundering the eco-system, much emphasis should be given on preservation and aforestation.

The only protective mantle which the soils of these islands can have against all the adverse factors is uninterrupted forest cover which intercepts the rainfall with its heavy foliage and allows it to drip for easy penetration in the soil. This protective umbrella of the forests also protects the soil from the winds and gales. The roots of the numerous gigantic trees give anchorage to the soil thereby preventing its erosion.

ANDAMAN AND NICOBAR ISLANDS
(Distribution of communities)

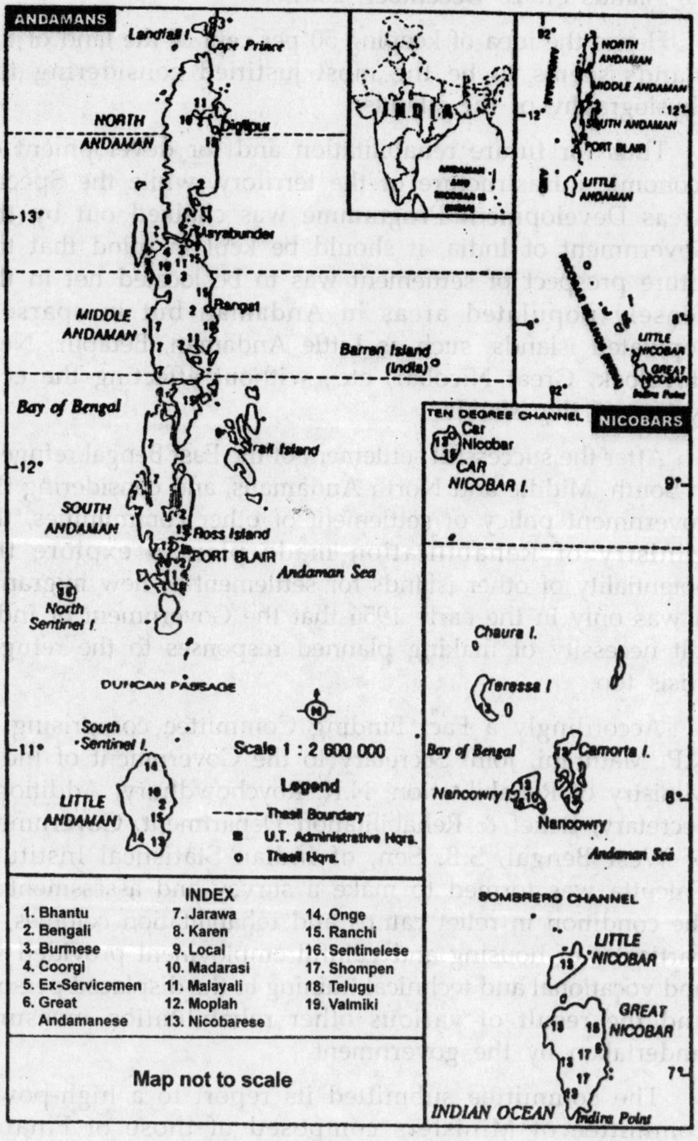

Distribution of Communities

Ignoring all these factors, this archipelago had to bear with the onslaught of the devastating Tsunami that engulfed the islands on 26 December, 2004.

Hence the idea of keeping 50 per cent of the land of the islands seems to be the most justified considering the physiography of the islands.

Thus for future rehabilitation and for development of economic infrastructure of the territory, while the Special Areas Development Programme was chalked out by the Government of India, it should be kept in mind that the future prospect of settlement was to be located not in the densely populated areas in Andaman but in sparsely populated islands, such as Little Andaman, Betapur, Neil, Havelock, Great Nicobar, etc., without affecting the eco-system of the islands.

After the successful settlement of the East Bengal refugees in South, Middle and North Andamans, and considering the government policy of settlement of other communities, the Ministry of Rehabilitation made plan to explore the potentiality of other islands for settlement of new migrants. It was only in the early 1956 that the Government of India felt necessity of making planned responses to the refugee crisis too.

Accordingly a Fact Finding Committee comprising of K.P. Mathrani, Joint Secretary to the Government of India, Ministry of Rehabilitation, N.K. Roychowdhury, Additional Secretary, Relief & Rehabilitation Department, Government of West Bengal, S.B. Sen, of Indian Statistical Institute, Calcutta was formed to make a survey and assessment of the condition in relief camps and rehabilitation colonies, in particular of housing and gainful employment provided for and vocational and technical training to the displaced persons and the result of various other rehabilitation measures undertaken by the government.

The committee submitted its report to a high-power committee of Ministers composed of those of Finance and Rehabilitation, Government of India and the Chief Minister of West Bengal. It prepared a plan of sending the 'excess' refugees to potential areas in Andaman. It expressed the necessity of rehabilitation on a permanent and viable basis.

In the report of Raja of Nalagarh on the 'Colonization Scheme of Andamans and Prospects of their Future Development', published on August 31, 1962, the importance was given to the suggestions of the Estimates Committee of the Parliament, No. 174/300. In the report, it is stated: "The Committee considers that the islands have enough resources to support a bigger population than is envisaged to be settled there in the Second Plan and recommended that a much bolder plan of colonization than the present one should be chalked out by the Ministry in consultation with other Ministries concerned in the lines of the Dandakaranya Scheme'".

Earlier the colonization scheme for East Pakistan migrants was confined to South, Middle and North Andamans. After setting apart lands required for natural growth of population, there was little prospect of settling any new families in these islands. Hence the prospect of further settlements would therefore, have to be located in new areas/islands such as Betapur, Havelock, Neil, Little Andaman, etc.

From the report of K.N. Butani, Development Secretary, Government of India, on "Prospects of Further Settlement of Migrant Families", it is learnt that "These islands have already been indicated by the Prime Minister as eminently suitable for integrated resource development, particularly for the purpose of rehabilitation of migrants from East Pakistan. There is considerable scope for resettlement of additional population. According to 1961 Census, the total population of these islands measuring 3215 sq. miles, is 63548. This gives a density of about 20 per sq. mile as against the all-India average of 392".

Butani further remarks: "The inter-departmental team has visualized that by the end of 1971, the island should be able to support an additional population of about 75000 of which about 15000 would represent the natural growth and remaining 60,000 would be those who moved from the mainland and resettled in these islands. By the end of the

Fifth Plan period, it is proposed to increase the population by another one lakh".[2]

SPECIAL AREAS DEVELOPMENT PROGRAMME

Of course, the scope of opening further settlement areas in South, Middle and North Andamans was limited. Therefore for future operation, it was necessary to think in terms of other islands. The Fourth Five Year Plan envisaged about 61000 acres and major attention would be claimed by the distant islands with the possibility of settlement on the lands available as follows:

Little Andaman	: 25,000 acres of land available
Katchal	: 10,000 acres of land available
Noncowrie, Kamorta, Trinket	: 5,000 acres of land available
Great Nicobar	: 5,000 acres of land available

Some land in the old area might also be opened by reclaiming mangrove forests to the extent of 5000 acres and by intensification of work at Betapur about 3000 acres. Some nearby islands such as Rutland for 6000 acres, Neil Island for 2500 acres and Havelock for 300 acres, might be explored.

At the time of reconstitution of States in 1964, the Ministry of Rehabilitation was made responsible for development of "Such special areas as may be indicated by the Prime Minister from time to time". Of the areas which would be brought under this programme in Fourth Plan, Chanda in Maharashtra and the Andaman & Nicobar Islands hold out great promise. The AndaNico Islands was the first to be declared as the special areas, for they were eminently suitable for integrated development of resources and for the rehabilitation of East Bengal refugees.

The Special Areas Development Programme aimed at building economic infrastructures of selected areas of low population density which were at the same time rich in productive potential. In these islands, emphasis was given not only on agriculture, small trading, fisheries, but on the growth of plantations also.

Of course, since early times, coconut and arecanut plantations have been quite common but not popular enough to be carried on a large scale.

During this stage, an expert team from Kerala visited these islands and felt that rubber and oil palm cultivation held considerable prospects. As they are equatorial crops, plantation of these crops might be tried in the Nicobar group of islands. Further, it was observed that rubber would flourish better over there than in the mainland.

Similarly plantation of red oil palms would be financially viable. In Little Andaman and Rutland Island, operations of red oil palm plantation could be carried on a large scale. The experts of the team opined that AndaNico Islands, especially Nicobar group of Islands are significantly suitable for growing of red oil palm. About 4000 ungerminated pre-heated seeds were brought from Malaysia and seedlings were raised at Port Blair.

Katchal and Little Andaman were found suitable for both crops and Rutland Island was considered basically ideal for rubber plantation. Accordingly, red oil palm factory was established in Little Andaman and rubber plantation projects were undertaken at Katchal in Nicobar and at Mongluton as well as Saitan Khari in South Andaman. It was observed that there were possibilities of eventually developing 30,000 acres of rubber and 30,000 acres of red oil palm plantations on these islands.

The policy for these islands can virtually be called a double-edged sword, one-edge to farm out the rehabilitation programme and the other to foster development not only for the future well-being of those rehabilitated ones but to add to the overall development of these cut-off and far-flung islands. The two words, 'development' and 'rehabilitation' are self expressive.

An inter-departmental team consisting of officers representing the Planning Commission and the Ministries concerned with the important facets of development was constituted by the Ministry of Rehabilitation.

The team was asked (a) to draw an integrated resource development plan for the islands for the purpose of rehabilitating East Pakistan displaced persons and in the light thereof to indicate the programme that may be undertaken to supplement the schemes included in the Fourth Plan in respect of islands and (b) to assess and recommend immediate implementation of selected projects incorporated in the full development programmes of the islands.

Between 5th and 20th February, 1965, the members of the team visited the islands and prepared the outline plan for the integrated resource development of the islands.

As a fillip, in October, 1967, the Office of the Chief Development-cum-Rehabilitation Commissioner was set up at Port Blair. The task of the new department was aimed at opening suitable forest areas, locating suitable lands for farm and plantation crops, clearing jungle and to induct as well as resettle refugee families from East Pakistan, repatriates from Burma and Ceylon, plantation labourers from Kerala and Tamilnadu, and Ex-Servicemen. These people would provide the main source of additional population intended to be absorbed in the islands.

Based on the recommendations of the inter departmental team headed by L.J. Johnson, Additional Secretary, Ministry of Rehabilitation, five projects had been taken up at (i) Betapur in Middle Andaman, (ii) Neil Island, (iii) Little Andaman, (iv) Campbell Bay in Great Nicobar and (v) Katchal in Nancowry Island.

For the year 1968-69, some of the projects with a view to reclaiming about 5000 acres of forest land and inducting 701 migrant families, are mentioned below:

TABLE[3]

Projects	*Area reclaimed*	*Families to be settled*
Betapur (in M.A.)	2050 acres	339 East Pakistan refugees
Rubber research-cum-development station (in S.A.)	500 acres	37 Burma repatriates
Neil Island	1090 acres	141 E. Pakistan refugees
Little Andaman	424 acres	80 E. Pakistan refugees
Katchal (in Nancowry)	875 acres	2 Ceylon repatriates till Nov. 1970
Campbell Bay (In Great Nicobar)	985 acres	100 Ex-Serviceman families

During 1971-'72 about 350 acres in Little Andaman, 500 acres in Great Nicobar and 480 acres in Katchal in Nancowry were reclaimed to facilitate the projects. To work out the projects, a provision of Rs. 111.04 lakhs had been allotted under the revised estimates of 1971-'72 for the Special Areas Development Programme in AndaNico Islands. The provision consisted of Rs. 97 lakhs under grants and Rs. 14.04 lakhs under recoverable loans.

As regards the opportunities in AndaNico Islands as a part of the accelerated development programme under the Special Areas Development Programme, a scheme had been drawn for the development of fisheries in these islands. The scheme envisaged coastal fishing by 100 country boats, off-shore fishing by 160 power-boats and deep-sea fishing by two fishing-cum-processing vessels. Provisions had been made for the proper training of fishermen. In the operation of the scheme, prospective fishermen would be found from amongst such migrants who had experience of sea-water fishing in estuarine areas of East Pakistan and if necessary, selection would be made from the persons of the mainland having aptitude or necessary skill for the various types of fishing proposed to be introduced under the scheme.

Though the prospect of settlement in Andaman consisting of South, Middle, North Andamans and Baratang Island, is not discouraging, yet it cannot justify the possibility of settlement of a high magnitude because of the limitation of natural resources and the scarcity of land to cope with the growing demand. Besides, the forests and marine resources with the limitation of power supply, the development of settlement on the secondary occupation is extremely limited. The only respite is agriculture which can easily make room for intending settlers, of course, in some sparsely populated islands as mentioned above.

In Andaman, there are many small islands but only a few may provide at best 100 acres of flat land for paddy cultivation and this 100 acre plot is considered to be the minimum economic limit for colonization.

Shivdasani observes in his book: "Some (islands) are so tiny as to be of no use while in the rest a fair amount of protective forest must be left standing with the result that the available area will be appreciably reduced.[4]

However, over 1200 migrant families, mostly agriculturists, had been settled in Andaman by the end of 1956. The programmes for the Second Five Years Plan period envisaged the settlement of another 4000 families on 20,000 acres of land to be cleared for paddy cultivation in those monsoon-fed virgin lands.

Considering the potentialities of the islands, the following table shows the future output in different segments:

TABLE

Islands	*Rubber, Coconut*	*Paddy, other crops*	*Total*
Andamans			
Betapur	–	3000 acres	3000 acres
Little Andaman	–	18,000 acres	18, 000 acres
Neil Island	–	2500 acres	2500 acres
Havelock	–	300 acres	300 acres
Rutland	2500 acres	–	2500 acres
Mangrove area	–	7000 acres	7000 acres
Nicobars			
Katchal Island	9000 acres	1000 acres	10000 acres
Nancowrie, Camorta	–	500 acres	500 acres
Great Nicobar	1000 acres	500 acres	1500 acres

It is presumed that out of these 45000 acres, 15000 acres would support about 6000 earners and rest 30,000 would support another 6000 earners bringing the total to 12000 if the SADP worked satisfactorily.

BETAPUR PROJECT

Though Betapur, having a total area of about 58000 acres, is situated in Middle Andaman, yet it was not chosen for settlement during the implementation of colonization scheme in Middle Andaman because of its inaccessibility. Afterwards considering its prime location and ample potentiality, it was included in the Special Areas Development Programme and the first settlement under SADP started at Betapur valley that lies on either side of the Andaman Trunk Road and stretches over a length of about 20 kms. from Rangat to Mayabunder.

In Middle Andaman, a number of river valleys are present and among them, the biggest one in Andaman is Betapur valley which offers 12000 to 13000 acres of flat land, suitable for paddy cultivation. The vast area where the Picharnalah meets the Betapur stream, though interspersed by small hills, is almost level for 7 to 8 miles. The portion is considered suitable for cultivation. The soil is rich and clayey in places. Of course, in the east, 8 miles of Betapur towards Webi, the valley was found to be undulating and the hills were covered with thick forest. This was the most difficult part of the country in the whole Andaman and entirely unsuitable for cultivation.[5]

Role of Rashtriya Vikash Dal

Some of the East Pakistan refugee families who had been initially brought to these islands during 1965-66 as members of Rashtriya Vikash Dal, were settled at Betapur on agricultural land in 1968-69.

At the inception, two hundred migrant families had been selected as 'Sahkaris' under R.V.D. for employment in Andaman where they went without their families. The condition of recruitment in R.V.D. was that Sahkaris would work under the Central and State Governments for the development of the settlement. As and when resettlement opportunities are available, Sahkaris would be released from R.V.D. for permanent rehabilitation. In Betapur valley, Sahkaris were engaged on agricultural operations in the State farm and able-bodied persons amongst them were also engaged on road construction, jungle clearance, felling trees, trolley pullers, etc.

Of course, some 50 Sahkaris, being discharged from R.V.D. were employed in M/s. Jayshree Tea & Industries Ltd., and engaged at its plywood factory, Bakultala but they left the job for low wages and prayed for land to carry cultivation as refugees which was not fulfilled.

As to the report of the Estimates Committee, 1967-68 (page 43), about 2000 acres of forest land suitable for paddy cultivation had been reclaimed at Betapur catchments area and in all 339 Sahkaris were settled there along with their families totalling 1432 heads. Subsequently, the Betapur project was proposed to be handed over to AndaNico Administration for proper management.

Financial Assistance

Among these Sahkari-settlers, except 5 trader families, all others were agriculturists. Each agricultural family was allotted 5 acres of paddy land and one-third acre for homestead whereas each trader family was allotted only two-third acre as business-cum-homestead land. They were granted maintenance assistance as cash-dole and supplied with necessary seeds, seedlings, fertilizers, pesticides and implements.[6]

The following table shows the details of financial assistance offered to the settlers as loan and grant:

TABLE

(a) Assistance as loan	*Approved ceiling*	*Assistance rendered*
For Agricultural Family		
House building loan	Rs. 2000/-	Rs. 1800/-
Purchase of plough animals	Rs. 800/-	Rs. 800/-
Purchase of agricultural implements	Rs. 500/-	Rs. 400/-
Purchase of seeds, manures, pesticides	Rs. 1500/-	Rs. 1200/-
Paddy-bund, soil conservation	Rs. 1200/-	1200/- to 40 families
Sinking wells	Rs. 200/-	Nil
Subsidiary income loan	Rs. 800/- to Rs. 1200/-	Rs. 800/- to Rs. 1200/-
Maintenance assistance	Rs. 225/-	Rs. 225/-
For Trader Family		
Housing loan	Rs. 2000/-	Rs. 2000/- per family, Rs. 800/- to others

Small trading loan	Rs. 5000/-	Rs. 3000/- to 2 families Rs. 2000/- to 1 family

(b) Assistance as grants:

- Cash dole at prescribed rate for 6 months during the first year of settlement
- Subsidised ration for 6 months
- Rs. 25/- in cash to construct temporary hut

Apart from these, considering all other expenses, each agricultural family could be granted Rs. 7225/- towards loans and Rs. 450/- as grants whereas each trader family would be sanctioned Rs. 7000/- as loans and Rs. 450/- as grants. Each agricultural family had to purchase plough animals out of the loan amount.

Community Facilities

Along with the financial assistance, with the progress of settlement at Betapur, certain community facilities were provided.

From Agriculture Department, tractors, power-sprayers, hand sprayers, etc., were made available to enable the settlers to make use of them for cultivation. One 10 acre unit of Soil Conservation Demonstration Centre has been set up at Betapur. A 60 acre Research-cum-Demonstration Farm has been established to train the settlers in modern methods of cultivations. In the farm, the settlers would be engaged as wage earners.

The Andaman Trunk Road was so designed as to pass through the project area to enable the settlers to avail bus services.

A 10-bedded hospital was established at Billyground and one veterinary dispensary started functioning at Betapur covering nearby villages.

One higher secondary school at Rangat, one senior secondary school at C.F.O. nallah, and 6 primary schools in nearby villages were set up under this project.

One Cooperative Consumers Society and one Multipurpose Coop. Society were established to supply general merchandise on controlled rate.

A Saw Mill was also established by the Multipurpose Coop. Society at Betapur to supply firewood and planks to the settlers at subsidized rate. It was inaugurated in February, 1971.[7]

It spite of all these facilities, the settlers had developed a tendency to leave the settlement without repaying the outstanding loan. Some of them even disposed off their movable properties including G.I. sheets given to them from the loan amounts, in order to cheat the government.

However, the Betapur Project had been taken over by the AndaNico Administration with effect from April 1, 1973 and the whole area was brought under the control of the Revenue Department.

According to the report of K.N. Butani[8], Development Secretary, Government of India, "On the Prospect of Rehabilitation", it is learnt that about 1200 persons had been settled at Betapur valley and during 1966-67 about 100 families consisting of about 400 persons got settlement there. The population increased day by day because of the location and fertility of the land. So the project has proved a successful attempt under the Special Areas Department Programme.

NEIL ISLAND PROJECT

Neil Island is close to Havelock Island and 32 kms. by sea from Port Blair. During the early phase of colonization, this small island, only about 20 sq kms in area, though remained isolated and uninhabited, drew attention of the government because of its meadows, valleys, numerous springs and virgin soil. Its close proximity to Port Blair was an added attraction to consider this island for resettlement of East Pakistan refugees.

In 1964, the Inter Departmental Team of Experts visited the island and drew an integrated development plan for it. In its report, it is stated that about 2500 acres of almost flat lands would be available in this island for receiving 86 refugee families immediately. Accordingly in 1964, 100 displaced families were settled in Neil Island.

A high level meeting held on March 27, 1967 at Port Blair, represented by the dignitaries of different ministries at the auspices of Mahavir Singh, the Chief Commissioner, AndaNico Islands, resolved that "in the first instance, only 200 families (from East Pakistan) may be sent to Neil Island... to be given 5 acres of land... to be employed in the clearance of forest land[9].

Consequently, a detailed survey of a 212 hectare site conducted during 1968 under Ministry of Rehabilitation, revealed that flat lands to the extent of 525 acres suitable for regular paddy cultivation, would be available. In view of the limited paddy lands available in Neil Island, it was proposed to induct 175 agriculturist families who would be allotted 1.2 hectare of paddy land and 0.8 hectare of orchard land per family.

Regular settlement commenced during 1968-69. The first batch of 86 families from East Pakistan was settled in the island during 1967 and the second batch of 84 families during May/June 1969. Later 5 more families were rehabilitated there during the first week of July 1969. Out of 175 families, 141 families were allotted at the rate of 3 acres for paddy cultivation and 2 acres for plantation during the year 1969-70.

As to the report of the AndaNico Administration on Rehabilitation Project, dated 23 June, 1989, the following table shows allotment of land to the settlers of Neil Island:

TABLE

Families	*Location*	*Paddy land per family*	*Plantation land per family*	*Total*
59	IIIrd Block	3 acres	2 acres	295 acres
25	IVth Block	3 acres	—	75 acres
6	I & II Block	3 acres	2 acres	30 acres

According to Butani's Report[10] on the prospect of rehabilitation in AndaNico Islands, another 200 displaced persons from East Pakistan were settled in Neil Island in successive years. He further mentioned that about 2000 acres of land were available and about 300 refugee families were likely to be absorbed there.

Since 1967, many more settlers had been settled in Neil Island under various rehabilitation schemes executed by the Community Development Commissioner but the Rehabilitation Department inducted the settlers, and allotted land with other facilities granted by the Government of India. Naturally the tussle between two departments, the Revenue Deptt. and the Rehabilitation Deptt., created confusion and deterred the settlement process.

When the land was allotted, the Revenue Department appeared to deal with matters relating to the revenue administration of the area but the local officers of the Rehabilitation Department were averse to any interference from the revenue agencies on the ground that the areas in question were under rehabilitation scheme.

However, it was felt that the matter should be taken in by the administration with the Chief Development Commissioner to avoid any conflict between these two agencies in the interest of proper administrations.[11]

Consequently, a fresh circular was issued by Dev. Commissioner on May 6, 1971, No. WRB/16/30/4030/71, confirming, "Exemption from payment of land revenue for 5 years has been granted to all settlers under colonization scheme"[12]. Thus the probability of a hitch of concerning interest between both the departments was hashed up.

Community Facilities

Financial assistances such as loans and grants offered to the settlers of Neil Island were almost at par with the same given to the settlers under the Betapur Project.

At Neil, a concrete jetty was constructed to provide berthing facilities for inter island ferry services.

A 10-acre Soil Conservation Research-cum-Demonstration Farm was established to try hybrid varieties of paddy and fruits on the soil of Neil. In due course, fruits and vegetables grown in the island under the supervision of the Farm became a source of income. A scheme to market the surplus produce at Port Blair was initiated to benefit the settlers by reducing the illegitimate intermediary profit.[13]

A nursery was set up at Neil to generate coconut, areca nuts and other seedlings so that they may be distributed amongst the settlers to grow high-yield fruits.

A number of pacca community wells to supply drinking water were dug with the labour of the settlers on payment on daily wages.

The settlers had been given training to take up intensive cultivation to reap harvest twice or thrice a year. After resettlement, the settlers were persuaded to go for intensive cultivation and during 1968-'69, 172 acres were brought under paddy and 35 acres under kharif cultivation. The average yield was 16 to 30 mounds and in the case of transplanted paddy, the yield was sometimes 50 mounds per acre. As regards vegetable cultivation, the produce would be worth Rs. 300/- to Rs. 500/- per acre per season. In the years to come, more and more acres were brought under intensive cultivation. In no time, Neil Island has come to be known the cauldron of agricultural produce.

Grievances of the Settlers

Since long the settlers of Neil Island have been demurring about the unsuitability of its soil for paddy cultivation because it contains sand and calcium more than the normal level.

Even the Estimates Committee of 1958-59 remarked that the agricultural settlers lodged their complaints that due to bad soil condition, there was no likelihood of growing crop in Neil Island. Soil samples had been sent to the Division of Soil Science and Agriculture Chemistry, I.C.A.R. to analyse. The chemical report of the soil pointed that the land is sandy and contains stone particles making it unarable due to want of proper soil conservation measures.

The Committee suggested that fresh probe must be undertaken to find whether the food crops would grow in the island under normal condition and if not, steps should be taken to shift the settlers of Neil Island to other islands.

Consequently, a team of experts headed by Agriculture Advisor, Department of Rehabilitation visited the island during September, 1970 and observed that the soil would require considerable treatment and amendment to make it suitable for paddy cultivation. Of course, it was an expensive proposition because only amendment of soil would not serve the purpose of growing paddy on sustained-basis unless and until irrigation is assured.

There was a proposal from the Government of India that instead of shifting the Neil settlers to Little Andaman or other islands, they might be pursued to settle on plantation instead of paddy cultivation which had been proved futile. But this was a wild suggestion as the settlers were all agriculturists and accustomed only to paddy cultivation. Moreover, at the time of recruitment, they were assured of paddy lands in Andaman. Hence they would not be interested in plantation which was quite unknown to them.

However, the Expert Committee had already recommended for shifting 48 families of Neil Island to Little Andaman but afterwards it was felt that not only these families but all those who wanted to leave Neil Island, might be allowed to shift to Little Andaman during the month of March/April, 1972 so that they could take to cultivation there. And those who would stay back in Neil might be allotted 10 acres of land per family so that they could grow paddy in 2/3 acres for their own consumption and in the remaining land, the settlers would start plantation.

However, as per the report of the Expert Committee, only 95 families expressed their willingness to stay back at Neil and the remaining families were to be shifted to other islands. The 32 families, who were not allotted land at Neil, had already been shifted to Little Andaman during July, 1971. Later, some more families were sent to Little Andaman from Neil Island following the decision of Ministry of Rehabilitation.

Hence, about the land deserted by 48 families or more and reclaimed under the rehabilitation scheme, was vested and 20 per cent of it made available to AndaNico Administration but the remaining land (80%) suitable for plantation would be handed over to the Administration to meet needs of the local people.

LITTLE ANDAMAN PROJECT

Little Andaman Island is about 100 kms south of Port Blair and Hut Bay being the administrative headquarters of it, is situated on the eastern coast of the island. Little Andaman having an area of 282 sq. miles is blessed with several perennial streams. Though the island is thickly forested, yet the landscape is somewhere hilly, and flat lands or valleys are also available.

So far East Pakistan refugee families were resettled in the Andaman group of islands excluding Little Andaman. Most of the known islands suitable for agriculture had already been reclaimed and refugee families had duly been rehabilitated there. But there was little prospect of settling new families any more in those islands so the future settlements would have to be located in left-out islands like Little Andaman and in non-tribal areas like Great Nicobar and Katchal islands. Thus the AndaNico Administration proposed to the Government of India that 10,000 acres in Little Andaman should be kept on lease for the settlement of displaced persons.

The total acreage owing to the clearance in the island would be 60,000 acres of which about 18 thousand acres were cleared during the Fourth Plan. Indeed, the annual clearance rate of timber was about 4500 acres which would yield over 65000 tons of commercial timber to facilitate settlement.

The original natives of Little Andaman are the aborigines, called Onges. Before resettlement of the East Bengal refugees in Little Andaman, there was no permanent civil population besides the tribals. In 1962, in the report of Raja Surender Singh of Nalagarh, Adviser (Colonization), Government of India, a view was held that the condition of the Onges was dwindling and any attempt of colonization or development of the island, will spell the cultural and physical extinction of the Onges.[14] In 1961 Census, the total enumerated estimate of this population amounted to 129 souls including 59 males and 70 females. But in 2001 Census, their number was less than one hundred.

Hence, considering the paramount need of maintaining proper ecological and environment balance and also keeping the ethnic culture of the Onges unaffected, a strategy for future resettlement programme was evolved by the Land-use Committee. According to its suggestions, the scheme of settlement in Little Andaman was chalked out and the project commenced in July, 1969 under the guidance of a survey team deputed by the Department of Agriculture, Government of India. In this operation, nearly 20 sq. miles, around 12800 acres of cultivatable land were surveyed and suitable flat lands were mapped. It was planned to clear about 1620 hectares for settlement of 560 families during Fourth Plan.

Apart from this, an unmapped area of nearly 75000 acres had also shown signs of suitability for agricultural development and out of which about 30,000 to 40,000 acres could be used for paddy cultivation.[15]

The Inter-Departmental Team constituted by the Department of Rehabilitation for drawing the Accelerated Development Programme of this island, emphasized on the possibility of the bulk of developmental activities and stressed on the following plans:

(a) Clearance of 60000 acres of forest land

(b) Settlement of 12000 families on agriculture

(c) Establishment of an integrated industrial complex based on timber resources.

(d) Establishment of a sugar factory with an annual capacity of 60-70 thousand tons.

The Inter-Departmental Team further recommended as follows:

a) About 5000 acres of land in the south-east coast area was earmarked for the settlement of the Nicobarese families from Car Nicobar.

(b) An area of 400 acres was kept aside for allotment to Navy.

(c) An area of 200 acres was allotted for the establishment of a composite Livestock Breeding Station.

(d) An area of 5 kms. radius from a permanent jetty was kept reserved for harbour purposes.

(e) An area of 6000 acres of forest land between the first and the second phases of settlement at Butler Bay was kept reserved for raising red oil palm.[16]

In his inspection note of March, 1970 the Inspector General of Forests noted that there was ample scope for development of plywood, matchwood and sawmilling industries only in these islands, particularly in Little Andaman.

Long back on September 12, 1969, Chief Commissioner, B.S. Butalia sent a D.O. letter No. 8-9/RH to R.C. Soni, Inspector General of Forests for setting up a plywood factory in Little Andaman but it was not established then and there for various reasons, primarily due to red tapism.

Little Andaman is exposed to both south-west and north-east monsoons so the construction of a permanent jetty was very urgent as preliminary requisite to any further work for settlement as well as forest extraction operations. Only in 1973, the jetty was constructed and a breakwater was also completed by 1974.

Besides, motorable roads connecting all the settlement areas had been started soon so that settlement operations could have been organised on a scale bigger than those undertaken in Middle and North Andamans.

Settlement Pattern

In Little Andaman, East Bengal refugees had been settled in a vast area stretching from north-east to south-east regions on both sides of a metalled road constructed from the headquarters at Hut Bay to Dugong creek. Around 400 refugees were granted lands in the settlement villages, i.e., Netajinagar, Ramkrishnapur, Vivekanandapur, etc.

In 1969-70, the Rehabilitation Department initiated the resettlement of the displaced persons. The following table shows the figures of year-wise settlement:

TABLE

Year of Settlement	*Details of Settlers*
1969	26 of East Bengal refugees
1970	22 of East Bengal refugees
1971	32* shifted from Neil Island
1972	43 shifted from Neil Island
1973	126 including 26 small traders
1974	104 including 26 small traders
Total	**353 families including 52 small trader families**

So far 306 agricultural and 15 small trader families were allotted permanent land. Besides, 5 fisherman families were also allotted one acre of land per family. Ten trader families were paid full quota of business loan. Of all, 21 agricultural families still residing in transit barrack at Hut Bay, were yet to be allotted permanent land.[16]

In the Annual Report of AndaNico Administration, 1973, it is stated: "An area of 1071 hectares of lands has been reclaimed in this island (Little Andaman). So far 399 families have been inducted in this island. Out of 399 families, 33 are

*The 32 families shifted from Neil Island during July, 1971 had been temporarily allotted about 4 acres of land per family but in due course, they were allotted full quota of land.

Sri Lanka and Burma repatriates and 366 are from erstwhile East Pakistan. This also includes 26 small trader families. All the agricultural families have been allotted 2 hectares of agricultural land for paddy and other crops and 0.13 hectares of homestead land for the construction of their houses. Each small trader family resettled in urban area has been given 800 sq. yards of land for construction of shop and house. Other small trader families resettled in rural areas have been given additional 2 acres of land for agriculture purposes.[17]

In the report of the Estimates Committee, 1972-73, it was proposed to clear 60000 acres of forest land in Little Andaman for the establishment of an integrated industrial complex and settlement of about 12000 families. The cleared area would serve as a hinterland for the harbour. It was further proposed to maintain suitable tribal reserves for the 'Onges' and to respect their way of life.

Settlement of Nicobarese

In addition, it was also proposed to settle about 300 Nicobari tribal families in the southern portion of Little Andaman Island to lessen the burden of Car Nicobar.

In the report of the Survey Team, 5000 acres of land at south-east coast of Little Andaman have been earmarked for the resettlement of the Nicobari families from Car Nicobar which had already been overpopulated. With the willingness of the Nicobarese seeking settlement in Little Andaman and the readiness of the Department of Rehabilitation to provide land, etc., in an area earmarked for them, the area later known as Harvinder Bay, about 6 kms from Hut Bay, started the settlement of the Nicobarese in Little Andaman.

In an article published in "The Andaman & Nicobar Information", 1976, p 21, issued by the AndaNico Administration, it is stated, "... the Little Andaman Island which hitherto had remained an exclusive home of the Onge tribe, has been opened up for agricultural settlements of so far 337 Bengali families and 15 Sri Lanka repatriate families. Subsequently the Andaman & Nicobar Administration also gave away the South Bay area of Little Andaman to about 150 Nicobar families from Car Nicobar which unfortunately had the effect of pushing the Onge settlement further northwards. In due course, Tamil repatriates from Burma were also settled in Ravindranagar village of this island.

Government Assistance

Under the terms of settlement, the following assistances were given to each agricultural family:

a) Allotment of land :

5 acres of flat land per family for cultivation and 1/3 acre for homestead

b) Grants :

Free passage from mainland

Cash dole for six months @ Rs. 20/- per family

Subsidised ration

Clothing grants

Marriage grants, etc.

All these grants were offered from the date of induction till the harvest of the first crop. Along with these, each settler family was entitled to free medical and educational facilities.

c) Loan per family :

House building	- Rs. 3000/-
Purchase of plough cattle	- Rs. 1200/-
Purchase of agricultural implements	- Rs. 800/-
Agricultural inputs	- Rs. 1500/-
Paddy bunding and soil conservation measures	- Rs. 1200/-
Subsidiary income	- Rs. 800/-
Sinking well	- Rs. 200/-
Total	**- Rs. 8700/-**

d) Assistance to each small trader family :

a) Allotment of land –2 acres for cultivation, 800 yards for homestead

b) Grants - Free passage from mainland to Port Blair
- Cash doles @ Rs. 20/- per family
- Maintenance allowance, etc.

c) Loans - House building – Rs. 3000/-
Business Loan for urban area – Rs. 5000/-
Business Loan for rural area – Rs. 3000/-

Community Facilities

A 50 acre Research-cum-Demonstration Farm with orchard had been established. One 10 acre unit of Soil Conservation Demonstration Centre was also established at Little Andaman in 1973.

A dispensary headed by a medical officer was set up at Hut Bay and upgraded into a 20 bedded hospital. In most of the villages, health centres were also established.

At Ramakrishnapur village, a key village unit with one veterinary Asst. Surgeon and allied staff started functioning. Veterinary services were made available in other villages also.

Post office with wireless communication facility began to function at Hut Bay. Extra-Departmental Post Offices were set up in others villages in due course.

An electric generator for power supply, a sawmill and a red palm oil factory were also established.

Tribal welfare programme for the Onges at Dugong Creek on east coast was taken up under the guidance of Adim Janajati Vikash Samity.

A Consumers' store was established at Hut Bay to cater to the needs of 123 East Pakistan refugee families already settled in agricultural land near Hut Bay by 1970. It would also explore the scope to market 'Onges' products.

An agriculture farm covering an area of 20 hectares was also established in Little Andaman for cultivating rubber, coffee, coco and pepper.

One Research-cum-Demonstration and Seed Multiplication Farm was set up at Hut Bay for studying the suitability of different field and plantation crops under local conditions at the guidance of CARI.

Rice being the staple food for East Bengal refugees and flat land being suitable for paddy cultivation, the settlers began to grow paddy on a large scale. Vegetables and fruits were also grown in plenty. Organised marketing for the surplus produces was arranged at Port Blair and Car Nicobar.

All the settlers would enjoy free medical as well as educational facilities. Two Senior Secondary Schools, one at Hut Bay and the other at Ramakrishnapur, three Secondary Schools at Hut Bay, Netajinagar and Vivekanandapur, a number of Middle Schools and Primary Schools—all these Bengali-cum-other medium schools have been functioning in Little Andaman. The 381 numbers of bullocks, 33 cows, 196 goats, more than 15000 birds for poultry were distributed among the settlers.

However, in December, 1976, a team of Secretaries headed by a Cabinet Secretary visited this island to study the prospect of settlement and observed that after completion of reclamation as scheduled earlier and proper distribution of lands among the settler, no further resettlement was recommended and Special Areas Development Programmes should be directed towards the economic development of the Island.

Indeed, since the inception of refugee settlement in Little Andaman, with the increase of population, the settlers' economic condition has been improving and with the growing knowledge of mechanized farming, the land-use pattern has been changed and the agricultural production has been booming.

SETTLEMENT IN HAVELOCK ISLAND

Havelock, a small island, about 38 kms from Port Blair, provides idyllic resort in the lap of sublime Nature, graced with beautiful virgin beaches and unsullied environment.

For administrative purposes, Havelock belongs to the zone of South Andaman. During the initial stage of rehabilitation, the refugee families were resettled in the periphery of Port Blair in South Andaman and later the settlement extended towards Middle and North Andamans. Simultaneously, considering its nearness to Port Blair and its vast valleys, Havelock attracted the attention of the rehabilitation authorities.

According to the report of the soil survey conducted by the Ministry of Agriculture on colonized area in Andaman, Havelock Island has distinct morphological characteristic in the soil profiles. It includes deep to very deep and well drained soils on hill slopes and high table lands under forest stands and has usually derived from argillaceous or calcareous sand stone. The top soil is dark greyish-brown to black, clayey loam in texture and granular. The sub-soil has a pale olive colour and also clayey so the soil of Havelock is suitable for paddy and vegetable cultivation.

The area reported to be readily available for clearance and utilisation for agricultural purposes, is more than 300 acres. As Havelock was then uninhabited, reclamation faced no problem and the settlers on allotment volunteered to clear the area for their own requirements.

On August 26, 1960, under the chairmanship of M.V. Rajwade, Chief Commissioner, AndaNico Islands, a high level committee meeting was held and it was decided that 1295 acre land would be cleared during 1960-61 to accommodate 259 families, of them 84 East Bengal refugee families would be settled in Havelock Island.

On March 15, 1964, Parliamentary delegates visited Havelock Island and recommended for more settlement.

According to the report of Revenue Inspector, Aberdeen, on March 13, 1965, it is learnt that 29 refugee families had been settled in Havelock at Camp No. 7 during 1960-61 and each family was allotted 5 acre of land for paddy cultivation. But the land being unsuitable for paddy crop, Hemanta Kumar Sil and nine other settlers applied for the change of land. Consequently, they were resettled in new lands and in 1961, 181 settlers in all, were allotted 900 acres of hilly land in Havelock[18].

However, to redress the grievances of the settlers of Havelock Island who had already been allotted lands at Kalapathar area which were found unsuitable for cultivation due to shortage or unarable condition of the soil, the A.N. Administration reallotted them new lands under clause (ii) of Section 146 of Andaman & Nicobar Islands Land Revenue and Land Reforms, 1966.[19] Dhirendra Nath Arindha and 26 other settlers were benefited.

Though Tsunami of 26 December, 2004, hit its grashing teeth on the outfits of the island, it quickly recovers and titivates more glamorous. Now it aptly poses as a tourist destination.

SETTLEMENT IN SMALL ISLANDS

Besides the settlements in South, Middle, North Andamans, Little Andaman, Betapur, Baratang, Neil & Havelock Islands, there are innumerable small islands where the possibility of colonization is doubtful because most of these are very small except a few islands which may provide 100 acres of flat land for paddy cultivation and this 100 acre plot is considered as the minimum economic limit for colonization.

H.R. Shivdasani remarked, "Some (Islands) are so tiny as to be of no use while in the rest, a fair amount of protective forest must be left standing with the result that the available area will be appreciably reduced. On account of the paucity of paddy land, want of communications with the mainland, insufficiency of potable water or similar other reasons, the bulk of these islands can best be used for productions of export commodities, e.g., fruit, coconut etc.[20]

The Forest Department calculated the maximum area of 62 sq. miles being the yardstick for colonization in small islands and its feasibility depends on certain factors such as location whether it's near to the disembarking harbour and enjoys facilities of communications with Port Blair, perennial water supply, available forest lands to be reclaimed, etc.

All the small islands do not fulfil the aforesaid criteria and only a few like Smith Island, Rutland Island and Strait Island, etc., though sparsely populated, may be considered for settlement but their future prospect remains doubtful.

RUTLAND ISLAND

The Island has been surveyed several times, viz., in 1959 by P. Mukundan Menon, in 1962 by M/s Cherian & Cheko and in 1964 by a Rubber Board Delegation led by K.J. Jacob. In all these survey reports, it is stated that about 6000 acres of land mainly situated in the southern half of the island, are suitable for rubber plantation. Besides, perennial sources of water are reported to be available. The utilisation of timber from the 6000 acres of forest land available there would also be done locally.

But due to paucity of flat land for paddy cultivation and the pressure of the environmentalists, the colonization programme was suspended and Rutland along with three nearby islands covering an area of 73.86 sq. miles have been left as pastoral and hunting ground for the Onges.

According to 2001 Census, in Rutland Island only 194 households were there and mostly they were the workers of the Forest Department and obviously belonged to the Ranchi community.

SMITH ISLAND

Smith Island in Diglipur area having an area of 7.9 sq. miles possessing 400 acres of land, is situated in North Andaman and a sand bar connects it to Ross Island of Diglipur.

Earlier lands were allotted to East Pakistan refugees there but they deserted as the island used to be cut off during high tide keeping them isolated and uncommunicated from their own people already settled in and around Diglipur.

However, while it was brought to the notice of the Administration, the Colonization Development Officer remarked on November 18, 1963: "It is desired by the Administration, that the land at Smith Island, abandoned by the Bengali settlers be resettled with Ranchi settlers. There are 125 acres of good paddy land at Smith Islands. 20 Ranchi families are proposed to be settled there as soon as the settlers are available".[21]

Subsequently as to the decision, Smith Island has been turned to become a settlement of Ranchi labourers of the Forest Department and their population is 676, according to 2001 Census.

STRAIT ISLAND

It is situated at 60 kms south-east of Port Blair and remained uninhabited till 1969 when the Government of India decided to resettle the primitive tribe, the Great Andamanese in this island to ensure better health and to preserve their ethnic culture and traditions. The main objective behind the settlement of the primitive tribe is to make them self-dependent by doing agriculture and plantation.

Sometimes they barter their produces or a portion of their hunt for tea, tobacco and sugar from the crews of the ferry boats plying between Port Blair and Rangat via Strait Island. Their number had fallen from 10,000 in 1760 to 23 in 1980 before inching up to 51 in 2005.

HANSPURI

It is also an isolated and totally uninhabited area near Mayabander and only by country boat, dingi, one can reach there.

From the report of the Dy. Forest Officer, D.O. No. NG/64-1392, dated July 3, 1963 addressed to the Chief Conservator of Forests, AndaNico Islands, it is learnt that a few Ranchi mazdoor families applied to settle at Hanspuri. Consequently Selvanus Tirkey and other 7 applicants were allowed to settle there.

SETTLEMENT IN GREAT NICOBAR

Great Nicobar is the southernmost island of the Nicobar group and Campbell Bay is the headquarters of this island where the Ex-servicemen have been rehabilitated.

It has an area of 95571 hectares and is the biggest inhabitable island in the Nicobar groups covering 1045 sq. kms. Campbell Bay is 544 kms south of Port Blair but only 145 kms away from Sumatra. The southern most tip of this island is Indira Point, earlier known as Pygmalion Point. This island enjoys tropical humid climate. Both south-west and north-east monsoons contribute to the annual rainfall varying from 2563 mm to 3672 mm.

Long back in the mid nineteenth century, in spite of prevalent stymied situation owing to lack of transport and communication, dearth of food, absence of medical facilities, impediment of vast sea and relegated life, E. M. Man, Superintendent of convicts, Port Blair during 1868-1871, visited the island and remarked in his book, 'Nicobar Islands with special reference to tribe of Great Nicobar': "It seems merely a question of time for the promising character of these rich lands to be recognized and for advantage to be taken of the opportunity they offer to the energetic colonists. The cocoanut trade, though by no means of negligible value, would sink into insignificance beside the wealth that might be realized from the rich forest and jungle land and the proper cultivation of fertile and practically virgin soil".

Indeed, he envisaged that Great Nicobar Island was an ideal region for settlement of the migrants. What Man predicted, has become a reality and almost after hundred years, Campbell Bay has been selected as the best suitable site for the settlement of Ex-servicemen.

Strategic Importance

The AndaNico Islands are often referred to as the Bay Islands and encircling the Bay of Bengal are the littoral countries, i.e., Mayanmar, Malaysia, Indonesia, Singapore, Sumatra, etc., earlier dominated by the British and during the Second World War, overrun by the Japanese Army.

Since early times, this territory, particularly the Nicobar group of islands had been under the domination of pirates and slave trade along with forest and marine exploits was conducted by them. Though the British gave only secondary importance to the strategic importance of the island, the policy has been changed after the Independence.

These islands represent our frontier sea outposts to cover a vast span of sea which abounds in good fish as well as marine minerals so it is necessary to be vigilant not only to protect vast territorial waters but also to guard our national security.

The AndaNico Islands possess an area of 6 lakh sq. kms as Exclusive Economic Zone and out of it, Nicobar district including Great Nicobar Island covers an area of 3.5 lakhs sq. kms. This vast area cannot be protected merely by deploying Naval fleet so to exercise logistic support, the Government of India thought of a strategy to protect the region by settling valiant people like the Ex-servicemen who have been ennobled by their dedicated services to safeguard their motherland.

Background of Settlement

In 1966, a topographical survey was made under the guidance of Karunakaran, Director General of the Geological Survey of India to explore the possibility of future settlement in Great Nicobar.

However, considering the strategic importance of the island, the Government of India ingesting the survey report, decided to make a plan for the rehabilitation of Ex-servicemen belonging to different States of India.

On March 16, 1967, a meeting was held at the initiative of the Ministry of Labour and Rehabilitation, attended by Jaisukhlal Hathi, Union Minister and Mahavir Singh, Chief Commissioner, Andaman & Nicobar Islands, along with other members.

Hari Singh, Secretary (U.T.), Ministry of Home Affairs remarked: "Some sort of selectivity in the choice of families who moved into the islands for settlement.... in respect of those families officially sponsored by government for settlement in the island. ...general check-up about the physical ability and occupational background for the type of occupation in which they were resettled, would be necessary ... to check their antecedents, etc., from the security angle".

According to the resolution of the meeting held on March 27, 1967, it was decided that before settlement, "...a party of Ex-servicemen could be taken to this island (Campbell Bay) to see things for themselves...A scheme adopted in respect of a similar resettlement programme in N. E. F. A. which was received from the Ministry of Defence, has been sent to the Chief Commissioner for comments...."[22]

Considering all these factors, particularly the strategic importance and potentialities of Great Nicobar Island, a scheme for resettlement of Ex-servicemen from all parts of India was undertaken by the Government of India in 1969.

Ex-servicemen were duly rehabilitated according to the rules of the District Soldiers, Sailors, Airmen Board, formerly known as the Ex-servicemen Association (1958) and the Indian Ex-servicemen League (1960). According to the information from the Assistant Commissioner's office, Campbell Bay, the fresh batch of Ex-servicemen came to the island in 1969. Others, from different parts of the mainland followed them successively in 1970, 1974, 1977, 1979 and 1980.

In accordance with the rules of the District Board, the Ex-serviceman settlers were provided with the travel fare from their respective homes on the mainland to Great Nicobar, free ration for three years, free supply of domestic articles and loans for building houses at concessional rates. To start with, each family was allotted 5 acres of flat land and one acre for residence. But most of the flat lands were found not suitable for cultivation so the Rehabilitation Department took proper steps to select sites. Thus villages of the settlers have been developed on the coastal plain near the sea stretching along north-south coast covering 41 kms.

It was proposed to clear about 610 hectares of land and if possible, 1415 hectares during the Fourth Plan period. A start had been made by clearing 162 hectares. A pilot scheme was initially chalked out for the settlement of 100 Ex-servicemen in 1969-70. Later it was decided to induct 330 Ex-serviceman families from 9 States and to rehabilitate them in 7 villages along the East Coast between Campbell Bay and South Bay as per details given in the table on next page.

TABLE

Statewise Break-up of Settlers

State	Year of Families Induction						Total Families
	1969	1970	1974	1977	1979	1980	
Andhra Pradesh	-	-	5	-	3	-	8
Haryana	-	-	-	5	1	-	6
Karnataka	-	-	9	-	-	-	9
Kerala	-	-	15	7	2	5	29
Madhya Pradesh	-	-	-	5	7	6	18
Maharashtra	-	-	40	6	-	4	50
Punjab	69	31	-	-	-	-	100
Tamilnadu	-	-	45	17	3	6	71
Uttar Pradesh	-	-	24	9	1	5	39
							330

Out of 330 families, 13 settlers left the settlement and 5 settlers died leaving behind no heirs. Hence the number of families on the roles was 312.[23]

As per 1981 Census, the total population of Great Nicobar was 4976 and the number of Shompen and Nicobarese tribes was 474 but as the population swelled up, the number goes up to 7566 and that of the tribals is 955, according to the Census of 2001.

Initially 100 Ex-servicemen families from Punjab were selected by a Selection Board. In its Letter No. 1585/RES/2, dated October 25, 1968 by the Director General of Resettlement, instructed the process of allotment of lands to the settlers according to the rank and file of the personnel as mentioned below:

(a) Officer - 25 acres per family,

(b) J.C.O. - 15 acres per family,

(c) Other rank - 11 acres per family.

Under the Pilot Project, families of the next batch were settled temporarily on 4 acre plot per family. As to the report of the Estimates Committee, 1971-72, it was stated that due to incessant rains during 1969-70 working season, the R.R.O.'s Unit could undertake the reclamation operations only on 56 working days so the total area reclaimed for cultivation till May 1970 was only 500 acres so the allotment of full quota to the later batches was hampered. But in due course, the full quota of 10 acres of lands was allotted to all the families settled in the villages as follows:

TABLE

Villagewise distribution of families[24]

Name of the Village	*Distance from Campbell Bay Jetty*	*No. of families*
Govindanagar	3 kms	62
Jogindernagar	13 kms	49
Vijaynagar	18 kms	80
Laxminagar	24 kms	47
Shastrinagar	35 kms	26
Gandhinagar	30 kms	66
		Total 330

Agricultural Operations

The Project 'Yatrik' reported that enough of valley lands suitable for paddy cultivation were available at Galatia river catchments. Besides, the valley lands were also available between Naryal Tikri and Mataita Anala Bay. It is estimated that about 1000 acres in Galatia catchments and about 850 acres in Mataita Anala area would be available. The total area of level land on the west and north coast, fit for cultivation was estimated as 17800 acres.

The Soil Survey also revealed that enough of cultivable land was available between Naryal Tikri to Indira Point in the east towards south coast and it was expected that with the construction of roads linking west coast with Campbell Bay, the settlement would extend on a speedier programme.

According to the survey conducted by the Government of India and the Rehabilitation Department, AndaNico Administration, it was estimated that about 4650 acres of land on the east coast and 11000 acres of land on the west coast suitable for agriculture was available. By 1981, 1730 hectares of land were reclaimed on the east coast.

For a watershed and a sub-watershed in the area, soil conservation plan had been drawn up and intensive soil conservation measures were adopted.

The settlers were encouraged to adopt diversified cropping pattern in place of cultivation of paddy. Thus sugarcane, high breed maize, pulses, oilseeds, tuber crops etc., attracted interest of the settlers. In due course, all along the sea shore in vulnerable areas, emphasis has been given on casuarina plantation to protect lands from soil erosion. Besides, a large area has been brought under spices and plantation crops, i.e., coconut, arecanut, nutmeg, clove, pepper, etc.

A pair of plough animals was supplied to each settler family for manual cultivation. In the case of death of animal, the Government of India agreed to pay compensation @ 100 per cent of the actual cost of the plough as well as milch animals, died of Liver Fluke in Campbell Bay. Besides, actions were taken to procure the animals locally, otherwise from the mainland.

Irrigation potentialities of the island had been explored by the Central Water Commission of the Government of India and two schemes were suggested as follows:

Name of Scheme	*Area to be irrigated*	*Cost per hectare*	*Total cost*
a) Swaroop Nallah Scheme	400 hectares	Rs. 8072/-	Rs. 52.47 lakhs
b) Prem Bahadur Nallah Scheme	408 hectares	Rs. 8014/-	Rs. 59.14 lakhs

Both the schemes were undertaken for implementation under the Central Water Commission and the Ministry of Irrigation, Government of India.

Pattern of Assistance

The Andaman and Nicobar Administration proposed that each Ex-serviceman family would be allotted 2 acres of paddy land, 8 acres of plantation land and one acre as homestead land The Steering Committee agreed to this proposal and made a plan for settlement of 1000 families.

In the successive settlements, each family was given 11 acres of cleared agricultural land including areas for homestead, paddy cultivation and plantation. The area for cultivation was reclaimed properly with field paths and proper drainage for plot.

An agricultural farm covering 20 hectares was established for multiplication of seeds, seedlings and for cultivation of different crops including rubber, coffee, coco and pepper in order to extend benefits to the settlers.

Initially it was thought that the agricultural operations would be undertaken with the help of small tractor but it was proved futile. Then with the help of Naval authorities, plough animals had been brought and distributed among the settlers but it was still doubtful how far these animals could withstand the adverse climate and maritime environment. Naturally the settlers were encouraged to purchase tractors, power tillers, rice hullers, etc., for their convenience with financial support from the bank.

The settlers were also offered the following assistances as grants and loans:

a)	Free passage from one's hometown to the settlement site at Great Nicobar	- Rs. 700/- per family
b)	Ration grant over a period of 5 years	- Rs. 6375/- per family
c)	Agricultural tools and livestock	- Rs. 3100/- per family
d)	Seeds, fertilizers	- Rs. 3000/- per family
e)	Household equipments	- Rs. 750/- per family
f)	Soil conservation	- Rs. 2000/- per family
g)	Building grant	- Rs. 5000/- per family
h)	Additional loan for house building	- Rs. 3000/- per family
	Total	**= Rs. 23925/-**

In the successive years, the house building grant has been enhanced to Rs. 8000/- in case of Ex-servicemen's families. During 1976-77 while crops had failed, the affected 138 families were sanctioned 50 percent additional ration grant.

Other Facilities

a) For regular communication, Inter-Island ferry services between Port Blair and Campbell Bay have been rescheduled so that there should be three trips of ferry services per month.

b) A temporary jetty and a permanent jetty were constructed at Campbell Bay in 1972 for the convenience of the settlers.

From Campbell Bay, towards north south direction touching the east coast of the island, a tarred road of a length of 45 kms had been constructed. Another metalled road of 42 kms from Campbell towards east west direction was also completed to facilitate the rehabilitation programme. Later roads connecting Campbell Bay to the west coast and also to Indira Point in the south have also been constructed.[25]

Community Facilities

Considering the mental condition of the settlers of Great Nicobar owing to the impact of hard area in the remotest island being totally isolated from their native place, facing all sorts of hardships in an unknown territory, the Government of India took all the steps to provide medicines, educational facilities, transport, communication, etc. To lessen the hardship of the settlers, the following steps were taken:

a) A number of pacca wells was dug in the villages at the proportion of one well per ten families.

b) Survey of water resources in the island was taken up by the Geological Survey of India to find perennial sources of water.

c) Besides, pathways connecting all the plots, two trunk roads of 94 kms linking Campbell Bay with Galatia river in the south and Kopenheat in the west were constructed under Project Yatrik.

d) Conversion of temporary bridges and culverts into permanent ones had been undertaken.

e) A permanent jetty had already been constructed and a break-water to provide all weather berthing facilities in the Campbell Bay harbour was completed.

f) In the island there are two Senior Secondary schools, one at Campbell Bay and another at Vijaynagar, one Middle school at Gandhinagar and 5 Primary schools functioning under the Directorate of Education, AndaNico Islands.

g) It was planned to construct an air strip/helipad in the vicinity of Campbell Bay so that at the time of emergency, transportation of patients, or others might avail the flight. Helipad has already been built up.

h) A 20-bedded hospital under qualified doctors has been functioning at Campbell Bay. There are three dispensaries, one each at Jogindernagar, Laxminagar and Gandhinagar to provide medical treatment to common ailments. Project Yatrik also runs a small field hospital at Campbell Bay.

i) All the villages have been electrified with the help of generators.

j) Banking facilities are available and becoming popular among settlers particularly those who are eager to seek loans.

k) Dairy and poultry farming, and goat rearing seem to be a source of income. During 1970, 100 she-buffalos from Haryana and in 1974, 90 she-buffalos along with 265 plough animals from Andhra Pradesh were brought and distributed among the settlers of Campbell Bay.

Master Plan for Campbell Bay Development

The Chief Development-cum-Rehabilitation Commissioner prepared a Master Plan for the development of a Township at Campbell Bay in pursuance of the Revenue and Settlement Survey. At the outset, there was a plan to induct 1000 Ex-servicemen but to start with, 330 families were settled and subsequently in the following years, the rehabilitation of the Ex-servicemen continued.

In 1976, the Team of Secretaries recommended that 2000 Ex-servicemen's families might be settled at Campbell Bay. To cater to the needs of this large number of settlers, some integrated development schemes for the growth of cottage industries as well as scientific cultivation might be undertaken.

The Syndicate Bank began to advance agriculture loan amounting to maximum 10 lakhs to the eligible settlers towards self-employment.

One sawmill has been installed by a settler out of the loan amount sanctioned by the Bank. There are many rice-hullers owned by the settlers. Shell crafts, artifacts of driftwood, furniture, fruit juice shops, all these have been set up with the support of the Bank.

In 1976, a Border Area Project Centre was set up to chalk out plans for the welfare of the settlers. Under this Project, Mahila Mondals of the villages, Balwadies, Craft Centres and Primary Aid Centres were set up and run by the female members of the villages.

Side by side a unit of Zila Sainik Board has been established at Port Blair to monitor the welfare programmes of the Ex-servicemen.

The government has been trying to achieve the goal of setting up a planned town but the transport bottleneck, the shortage of technical personnel and delay in getting machineries and materials from the mainland often create hazards.

A marked change has also been taking place in the outlook of the Ex-servicemen and the attitude of indifference has gone off. And their active participation in the constructive activities in the settlement area has become spontaneous. Thus the idea of Campbell Bay Township is under due consideration.

Indeed, for the interest of the existing population, the whole scheme of resettlement at Campbell Bay has been reviewed by a team of experts from the Department of Science and Technology. As to its suggestion, the future resettlement plans have been discontinued since 1980 considering the physical hindrances and strategic importance. So under the existing social pattern, the government has been planning for economic development of the settlement area so that the grievances of the settlers may be redressed and they can enjoy the urban facilities.

Response of the Settlers

In the first batch during 1969-70, 100 Ex-servicemen's families, from Punjab only had been settled in Campbell Bay. They are all valiant and proud of their dedicated service for the defence of the motherland, India.

In the second batch of 1974, 138 Ex-servicemen settlers were recruited from different parts of India. They were all strong and stout. They adjusted themselves happily in their new home in the new land.

Despite all the community facilities offered to them, they would face a number of difficulties and express their grievances against irregular ferry services, lack of specialist doctors, want of domestic animals, agricultural problems, etc.

Indeed, the Ex-servicemen's families had apparently volunteered for the settlement at Campbell Bay in the hope that they would get 14.5 acres of land per family as assured at the time of recruitment but after settlement, only 10 acres of land were given to each family that made them aggrieved.

Moreover, they protested against the scheme of allotment on the basis of army ranks. They demanded a uniform pattern of allotment which was not accepted immediately.

Though they were Ex-servicemen, they were settled in the island as farmers and expected to tender their labour in the agricultural fields, allotted to them. Unfortunately most of them were neither farmers nor interested in cultivation. Consequently, a major portion of their fields remained unexploited. Some of them found it more lucrative to carry on business in illicit liquor than to toil hard in the field. In reality, these people have failed to develop attachment with the new environment and many of them have disposed off their holdings and gone back to their native place. But the rest who have adjusted themselves, are now well-to-do.

However, they have certain grievances against the dilatory attitude of the Rehabilitation and Reclamation Organization. As per reclamation procedure, the R.R.O. had to provide main contour bund around the field just after reclamation but failed to do so. As a result, due to heavy rain, the top soil has been washed away. Besides, the R.R.O. had left a number of large stumps or logs on the cleared fields and moved away. But these stumps and logs stood in the way of proper cultivation and 25 to 50 per cent of land was being wasted.

No doubt, there were grievances being fumed among the settlers but in due course, some of them could adjust themselves with the changing situation and were satisfied with the results of their labour.

KATCHAL ISLAND

Katchal is the second biggest island in the Nicobar group and one of the finest islands for extensive cultivation. Its area is 673 sq. miles, suitable for extensive cultivation. It reaches a height of 835 ft. on the eastern side and the hills are composed of calcareous sand stones and marble slate usually formed in deep seas. Otherwise, the island is generally flat, sometimes with swampy ground of coralline diluvium on the north-western portions and sandy alluvium on the north and the south coasts. It has excellent water supply from stream and wells. It is sparsely populated by about 900 Nicobarese living along the coastal fringes. About 1000 acres of land suitable for cultivation and plantation crops are available in the centre region of the island and are best suited for rubber plantation.[26]

K. N. Kaimal, the then Rubber Production Commissioner, made a detailed study of the information available and reported that from the climatic angle, the Nicobar group of islands were the most suitable for rubber cultivation.[27]

During 1959-80, P. Mukundan Menon, deputed by the Rubber Board made an exploratory survey of the terrain and soil condition of various islands in Nicobars. He reported Katchal as the only island having sizeable areas, suitable for opening large scale rubber plantation. The extent of land available in Katchal was estimated to be 10,000 acres.

The Rubber plantation is highly labour intensive. The plantation unit of 1000 acres can provide regular employment to not less than 300 labourers. When the plantation will be in full production, the requirement of skilled rubber tapers alone for such a unit is more than 250. A few months, training and practice can impart the necessary skill in taping to unskilled labour.

After conducting thorough soil survey and assessing viability of rubber plantation, the Department of Rehabilitation, Government of India, sanctioned a project for bringing 6000 acres under commercial plantation of rubber at an estimated cost of Rs. 450 lakhs and it was expected to provide 1000 families of regular employment who would be settled under the project. The rubber-project was implemented through the Rubber Board in December 1967 and a rubber seedling nursery was started in April, 1968 at Kapanga Island.

According to the report presented by the Chief Development-cum-Rehabilitation Commissioner, AndaNico Islands, on "Rehabilitation Programme in Andaman & Nicobar Islands", it is stated that in December, 1967, R. B. Kottayam of the Rubber Board started the rubber plantation with Rehabilitation fund.

On March 15, 1978, 47 Ceylon repatriates were inducted for settlement and 92 adults were engaged as labourers in the farm at the rate of Rs. 8/- per day. Side by side, Red oil Palm plantation on 20 acres was also started and maintained by the Department of Rehabilitation.

The recommendation of the team of Secretaries in December, 1976 was that "Katchal Rubber Plantation is to be expanded to 2000 acres to make it a viable unit".[28]

In the following table, the areas brought under rubber plantation are shown.

TABLE

Pattern of Plantation

Year	*Areas*
1968-69	150 acres
1969-70	250 acres
1970-71	150 acres
1971-72	325 acres
	Total 875 acres

It was expected that an additional area of about 350 acres would be brought under rubber plantation during 1972 sowing season. But the Government of India so far authorized the Department of Rehabilitation, AndaNico Islands, to clear 2700 acres up to 1972 and the total area brought under rubber plantation at the close of 1973 would probably be 2355 acres.

Settlement of Ceylonese Repatriates

Though it was the policy of the Government of India to resettle the Indian migrants from Ceylon at Katchal Rubber Project as wage earners, the Ceylon repatriates were not forthcoming for settlement at such a distant island, Katchal and surprisingly only two Tamil families being the Ceylon repatriates were settled down on Katchal plantation till November, 1970. Naturally the work of the Project was carried on by recruiting labourers locally who used to put forward various demands and had been agitating since long.

Actually a rubber plantation needs regular workers in the ratio of one worker per three acres. Hence, Katchal Rubber Project needed 2000 regular workers when the entire 6000 acres would be brought under rubber plantation. If a family may provide two workers for the plantation, at least 1000 families are needed to be settled. As the Project was rehabilitation oriented and it envisaged settlement of 1000 Ceylon repatriate families to labour strength but till November, 1970, only two Tamil families were settled down and unfortunately suitable Ceylon repatriates of Tamil origin were not interested to settle in Katchal nor suitable Tamil families among Ceylon repatriates, already settled on these islands were willing to move to the far flung Katchal island so the progress of Katchal project was terribly hampered due to shortage of labourers.[29]

Besides the labour problem, there was another urge of disapprobation smouldering among the Nicobarese tribal, natives of Katchal Island, who always count the outsiders as 'encroachers' on their land and have never approved of the activities of raising an alien plantation on their land. They even tried to evict the encroachers by forcibly occupying their land under the Project. When persuasion failed, the government had to apply force to desist them. This was unprecedented because never before in the past, the government came across such a resistance from the tribals in the way of implementing any project.

However, securing their consent, about 22 acres of land have been brought under red oil palm at Katchal and the scheme of palm oil production has been sanctioned.

Government Assistance to Tamil Settlers

a) Each Ceylon repatriate of Tamil origin was allotted free residential accommodation and ½ acre of land for kitchen garden.

b) For transportation from the mainland home to Katchal Rs. 700/- per family

c) To purchase household equipments - Rs. 200/- per family

d) To provide employment to each family, two able bodied members in the Rubber plantation as wage-earner @ Rs. 8/- per day

e) Cash doles for 3 months at the same rate equal to that to East Pakistan refugees settled in other islands.

f) One Primary School of Tamil medium opened, later upgraded to Higher Secondary level

g) One Sub-Post office and one Primary Health Centre opened.

In spite of providing all sorts of facilities, i.e., medical, education, water, electricity etc., the settlers were not eager to settle there. Some of them even deserted and tried to settle somewhere in Andaman. The main reason behind their disinclination may be the tropical climate of Katchal Island and torrential rainfall may seem insalubrious to them. Possibly a constant pang of desire to join their own people might have haunted them. Whatever may be the reasons, the Katchal Project has not turned out to be successful. In the later days, the government has decided not to extend the Project any more and the Tamil labourers of Katchal Project may be settled under Saitan Khari or Mongluton Rubber plantations.

ENDNOTES

1. Sate Archives, Port Blair, File No. F/173-84/62-G. Raja Surendra Singh of Nalagarh, Adviser, (Colonization) Ministry of Home Affairs, Government of India.
2. State Archives, Port Blair, File, 'A Note on the Prospect of Rehabilitation' (1949-'63)/J/RH/9A.
3. Library, National Memorial Cellular Jail, "Special Areas Dev. Prig. Its Scheme & Implementation". Pub. by Deptt. of Rehab, AndaNico Islands, March 1972.
4. Shivdasani, H.R. "Report on the possibilities of colonization" G.O.I., 1949.
5. Shivdasani H.R. 'Report on the possibilities of colonization' G.O.I., Ministry of Home Affairs.
6. State Archives, Port Blair, G-665/1967, 'Colonization in Betapur'.
7. State Archives, Port Blair, 'Colonization in Betapur', File No. G-665/1967.
8. "A Note on the Prospect of Rehabilitation in Andaman and Nicobar Islands (1949-'63)", by K .N. Butani, Development Secretary, Govt. of India.
9. State Archives, Port Blair, Colcnization in Andaman', File No. G-665/1967, p 27.
10. State Archives, Port Blair, File No. G-665/1967, dt. 27 March, 1967.
11. State Archives, Port Blair, Office of Dy. Commissioner, Letter No. 8/26/279, 1970, Calcutta, 24 June 1970, File No. 40-1/70-J(I).
12. Ibid
13. Source: Andaman Nicobar Information, 1976. Andaman &. Nicobar Administration, Port Blair.
14. State Archives, Port Blair; File No. 173-84/62-G, Report Pub. on 31.8.1962
15. Special Area Development Programme, Pub. by Deptt. of Rehab, A.N.I. March, 1972.
16. State Archives, Port Blair, Report of Inter Departmental Team, dt. 2 March 1976.
17. Annual Report, 1973, AndaNico. Administration, p 7.
18. State Archives, Port Blair, Letter No. DFO/1-26/64-Tim/371, dt. 17 May, 1965.
19. State Archives, Port Blair, File No.33-7/70-J (i)/Office of SDO (Adm.), South Andaman, Order No. 339, 27.8.1970.

20. Shivdasani H.R. 'Report on the possibilities of colonization', Govt. of India, 1949.
21. Office of the Directorate of Agriculture, D.O. No. 43-10-DA/63, No. 18, 1963.
22. State Archives, Port Blair, File No. G-665/1967.
23. Booklet: 'Note on Rehabilitation Programme in Great Nicobar', by AndaNico Administration, March, 1981.

    Ministry of Home Affairs, OM No. 21/61/70-ANL, 30 Dec. 1970.
24. Booklet: 'Note on Rehabilitation Programme in Great Nicobar,' issued by A. N. Adm. March, 1981:
25. Andaman and Nicobar Information, Port Blair, 1982.
26. Booklet: The Forests of the Nicobar Islands, p 6, published by the Ministry of Food and Agriculture, Govt. of India, 1954.
27. Ibid.
28. State Archives, Port Blair, "Rehabilitation Programme in Andaman & Nicobar Islands", presented by CDRC, 15 March, 1978
29. Ministry of Home Affairs. OM No. 21/61. 1970-ANL, dated 30 December, 1970.

    Regarding the arrival of 2 Tamil families, the matter was taken up with the Ministry of Rehabititation and the Rehabilitation Minister of Tamil Nadu with the Secretary, Rehabilitation visited these islands in the month of November, 1971 and proposed to send team of Ceylon repatriates to visit Katchal. Consequently the situation improved and Ceylon repatriates of Tamil Origin started to opt for settlement in the Katchal Rubber Plantation.

13

Settlement of Other Communities

The colonization programme was started with the settlement of East Pakistan Refugees in Andaman but the quota of these refugees fixed by the Government of India was exhausted soon. While the government of West Bengal proposed to the Government of India for sharing the swelled up human burden due to fresh swarm of refugees from East Pakistan, by sending at least some of them to Andaman, the Union Home Ministry suddenly came up with a technical reason for not sending more than the prescribed quota to Andaman. The reason was that for Kerala and other states, respective quotas had already been fixed and persons from those States had to be rehabilitated in these islands.

This pretext seemed to be most unreasonable to Dr. B. C. Roy, Chief Minister of West Bengal and to the thoughtful Indians that at a time while the country was terribly suffering from continuous surge of displaced persons into the eastern region, all such silly casuistry should have been stopped. Smt. Renuka Roy, Minister of Rehabilitation, Government of West Bengal remarked, "The refugees from East Bengal to settle in an island environment ideally suited to a riverine people appeared to be the proof of the unsympathetic attitude of the Central Government.[1]

In spite of the appeal and grievances expressed by the Government of West Bengal, the Union Home Ministry took steps to resettle people of other communities from different States, such as Keralians, Telegus, Tamilians, etc., even repatriates from Burma and Ceylon on different colonization schemes in the Andaman and Nicobar Islands.

Indeed, the Central Government did not favour the idea of reforming the islands into an appendage of West Bengal, 'Bangalisthan'. This becomes clear from the statement of the Central Labour & Rehabilitation Minister, R. K. Khadilkar in the Rajya Sabha on December 3, 1974 in reply to a starred question raised by R. K. Chakraborty for further settlement of the East Bengal refugees in Andaman. The Minister replied, "...so far as the Andamans are concerned, I have said earlier that it is a special category. We want to develop it in a different way. I want to say one thing. The ex-Army people have got a colony there. We must look to the defence side also".

Moreover, the Central Government contrived to design the islands as a land of many languages in order to develop settlements of mixed characters, not restricted to people of one particular cultural background. So the government implemented the scheme to induct different groups of people from various walks of life such as fishermen from Andhra Pradesh, cultivators from Kerala and Tamilnadu, plantation workers from repatriates of Ceylon and Burma, some sturdier stock of people, i.e., Ex-servicemen who could provide a good nucleus.

However, due to wilful attitude of the government, the question of settlement of East Pakistan refugees was suspended in 1961 while their population was only 8700 as to the report of the Estimates Committee, 1959-60. Thus the Government of India construed the Special Areas Development Programmes with the objective to make the settlers developed and economically self-dependent. Development means not merely more paddy lands and more economically viable plantations but more forest extractions; more forest and marine produce because in these islands, there is tremendous possibility of development of timber and marine based industries.

The opening of new settlements led to provision of social services on a large scale and, more and more people were brought to these islands in the wake of expanding needs and requirements of labours in the government departments.

There's no system of contracts and work in major departments like the P. W. D. and the Forest Department. This means that labour here has to be employed by the government in a big way and the labourers are mostly Ranchis, Telegus, Tamils, Malayalees. In all, their number is reported to be over 14,000 or more and most of them are on government's pay roll. But for other, private and public establishments, and in shipping, transport, trade and commerce, small scale industries, a large number of labourers are needed.

Till 1951, the population moved up only gradually and then suddenly it shot up. In 1961, it was estimated at 63548 and by 1966, it was about 75000. The increase has been due to an increase in the number of labour hands. There has also been an increase in the number of government servants who have been brought in for manning various schemes. Along with this, 420 families from Madras, Bihar, Kerala, Maharashtra and Burma evacuees came to these islands under the colonization scheme during 1953-1961.

According to the scheme, settlements of East Pakistan refugees and other migrant agriculturists and artisans from different States is shown in the following table.

TABLE

(Distribution of population as to their mother tongue)

Census, 1961

Bengalee	-	13853	Malayalee	-	6628
Burmese	-	1714	Tamil	-	13932
Hindustani	-	8046	Telegu	-	3758
Ranchi (Oraon)	-	2214	Southern Sadri	-	1658
Ranchi (Munda)	-	867	Urdu	-	1897

By 1961, Tamil has become the language of the majority as a single community closely followed by Bengali.

For comparative study, household population by language spoken in the Andaman and Nicobar Islands according to the Census report of 1991 is shown below-

TABLE

	Male	*Female*	*Total*
Bengali	34199	30507	64706
Hindi	27186	22283	49469
Ranchi (Oraon)	5013	4240	9253
Ranchi (Munda)	1681	1264	2964
Ranchi (Kharia)	1378	1120	2498
Ranchi (Santhali)	387	9	396
Malayalam	14152	11923	26075
Tamil	31476	22060	53536
Telegu	18219	14760	32979
Urdu	805	687	1492

Now the picture has been changed and Bengali happens to be the language of the majority as a single community.

However, up to 1964, 2887 families were settled in various parts of the islands. Besides the displaced persons from East Pakistan 157 families from Kerala, 43 from Tamil Nadu, 184 from Bihar, 4 from Maher and 5 from Burma were settled in the islands.

The following table shows year-wise distribution of emigrants of different communities settled in the islands up to March, 1959.

TABLE

Year	*East Bengal families*	*Kerala families*	*Madras families*	*Maharashtra families*	*Burmese evacuees families*
1949	202	-	-	..	-
1950	119	-	-	-	-
1951	78	-	-	-	-
1952	51				
1953	97				
1954	438	35			5
1955	390	37	4		
1956	357	42	-	-	-
1957	221	5	8	4	-
1958	194	6	-	-	-
1959	9	-	-	-	-
Total :	2156	125	12	4	5 = 2302

If we split the population according to the First-Year Plan and Second-Year Plan, the figures come out as follows:

	From East Pakistan	*Kerala*	*Tamil Nadu*	*Burma*	*Ranchi Bihar*
1st Year Plan	1456 families	72 families	4 families	5 families	
2nd Year Plan	1188	53	22	-	120 families
Total	2644	125	26	5	120

During 1966-67, repatriates from Burma consisting of about 980 persons came to Andaman for settlement.[2]

In the following pages, the details of settlement of different communities have been discussed.

SETTLEMENT OF RANCHI

During the British days, a small number of tribal people from Chotanagpur region of Bihar was brought to Andaman to work as forest labour. After 1947, many more came here to work as labourers either in the Forest Department or P. W. D. Being submissive and laborious, they were in great demand. As the recruitment station was in Ranchi, these people are widely called 'Ranchi'. They were usually recruited either by the agents of the Church, known as 'Father-Chalan or by the official of A. N. Administration viz., Osman Ali, commonly called as 'Sarkar Chalan'.

From scattered reports and official notes, it is learnt that Ranchi people used to be brought to Andaman on contract for one or three years and after the expiry of tenure, they would return back to their native places in Bihar.

Satish Mathur, ex-Andaman political prisoner, said in an interview broadcast at A.I.R., Port Blair on 22 October 1988 that he was transported to Andaman on charge of treason and landed at Mayabunder in 1925 to serve his term. At that time, Mayabunder was covered with dense forest. To clear the jungle, labourers from Bihar, known as Ranchis were brought to Andaman as 'Father Chalan'. They were engaged on contract for felling trees @ Rs. 5/- per ton to facilitate the settlement started in 1923 under the British colonization scheme.

To refer the system of 'Father Chalan', the Chief Conservator of Forests informed the Chief Commissioner on November 27, 1948, "This is in respect of a bill for Rs. 3068-3 annas - 6 piece sent by the Roman Catholic Bureau to the C.F.O. on account of feeding charges of the batch of labourers sent to Port Blair in May, 1947 due to delay in sailing from Calcutta. On 13 May, 1947, 94 Ranchi labourers arrived at Port Blair.[3]

In another Memorandum, the Conservator of Forests wrote to the Chief Commissioner, that the total expenditure for sending 194 men, 7 women, 6 boys or girls and 5 babies to Andaman was Rs. 2827/-.[4]

As to the requirements of the A&N Administration, the agent on behalf of Catholic Bureau would recruit Ranchi labourers, and make necessary arrangements to send them to Andaman. The details of Ranchi families are shown in the following chart.[5]

Date & year of arrival	*No. of families requisitioned*	*Actually arrived*
13.05.1947	94 Ranchi Labourers	94
09.06.1948	185 Ranchi Labourers	44
17.08.1948	150 Ranchi Labourers	51
18.09.1948	200 Ranchi Labourers	27

On 20 May, 1959, 40 Ranchi families comprising of 145 heads were brought from Chotanagpur to Andaman and settled at Baratang Island. They were given cash doles of Rs. 70/- per family for one month, and 2 maunds of paddy seeds to each family. Tahsildar with the help of Colonial Assistant allotted 5 acres of cultivable land to each Ranchi family.

The largest settlement of Ranchis is at Baratang, 65 kms away from Port Blair and the settlement villages grow at Para Jig, Lura Jig, Wrafter's Creek, Ragolachang Creek, Jarawa Creek, etc.

Even in some other little islands like Rutland, Smith Island and in some cut off areas like Hanspuri, Ranchi mazdoors were settled, so the saying goes, where there is jungle, there are Ranchis.

Usually they would come in this island as labour force on contract without accompanied by their families. But when they went back after the expiry of the tenure, the departments would face acute labour shortage. So the government decided to settle them on a special scheme, 'Colonization in Baratang Island – Settlement of Ranchi Families'.

A. G. Abraham, D. F. O., South Andaman informed the Development Commissioner in his memorandum No. 6/076-1786, Wimberleygunj, dated December 30, 1959, "As desired by the Chief Commissioner, A&N Islands, applications were invited from Ranchi labourers of the South Andaman Division willing to bring their families and settle down at Baratang as settlers".

In the list of the applicants, there were 20 mazdoors, 20 fellers and 11 mahouts. All were allowed to bring their families in order to settle at Baratang.[6]

From the D. O. Letter 20. RB/111/12/vol.2/71/10698, dated November 6, 1974 addressed to the Chief Secretary, A. N. I., written by the Development Commissioner, it is learnt, "...every registered settler of revenue village in Baratang Island has been allotted five acres of paddy land as per terms of the colonization scheme".

According to the Population Census, 1991, the number of Ranchis belonging to non-scheduled languages i.e., Oraon, Munda, Gondi, Santhali, Kharia, etc., was 15327 in these islands.

Social Pattern of Ranchi Society

Ranchi settlers hailed from Bihar, now Jharkhand, belonged to various tribal and caste groups of their original homeland such as Oraon, Kharia, Munda, Turi, Mahli, Ghasi, Cheek, Dom, etc. The Census of 1971 shows that Ranchi people occupy a distinct place in the linguistic picture of the islands viz., Kurukh/Oraon - 2.79%, Kharia - 1.01%, Munda-93% etc. Each group has its own dialect but everyone can speak Hindi.

Many of these groups are divided further into a number of exogamous clans which have sub-clans also. The clans are all totemic in nature. Culturally Ranchis belonging to different clans and sub-clans are homogeneous in nature.

By religion, traditionally they believe in animism and follow rituals as to their age old tradition but after coming in contact with the propagators of Christianity, many of them have been converted and embraced Christianity.

In their social life, both Christians and non-Christians observe some of the traditional festivals like Karma or Karam, Sarhul, etc. Side by side they celebrate New Year's Day, Christmas, Good Friday along with Durga Puja, Holi, etc.

Obviously the Ranchis belong to the weaker section surviving below the poverty line. In the Fifth Plan, development heads such as 'Welfare of Backward Classes,' 'Labour and Labour Welfare,' 'Community Development' and 'Social Welfare,' all of which might conceivably cater to the needs of these people, are allocated a sum less than 1.5 per cent of the total allocation, hence all these efforts make them self-conscious so that they can aspire for betterment of their own.

However among them, a few persons are well educated and well-placed in political sphere or in government service. Godwin Soren is a well-known Ranchi leader and popular in regional politics.

Benjamin Soren, of course, died young in an accident, was a firebrand leader of Ranchi community. Younger generations have realized the value of education and run after the white collar jobs. Thus gradually a change is shining and they are marching towards a bright future.

In recent years the Ranchi people have started agitations on the demand of the scheduled tribe status with job and free education benefits under the C&D categories of the

Scheduled Tribes Regulation. On 9 August last year, a few thousands of them first staged 'dharna' and serial demonstrations at Diglipur, Mayabunder, Rangat and Baratang were organised between 1 and 3 December but the island authorities desist to consider their demand for fear it will shift the focus away from the protection of ancient tribes.

SETTLEMENT OF ANGLO-INDIANS

During the British regime the Anglo-Indians played a pivotal role in the administration of the Penal Settlement of the islands. Though the Europeans held the key positions, the Anglo-Indians too were entrusted with certain responsibilities.

Sir Henry Gidney, an Anglo-Indian leader of India suggested that to run the administration in a better way the Europeans as well as the Anglo-Indians might be settled in separate villages in the Andamans.

During his visit to Port Blair in 1925, Sir Alexander Muddiman, the Home Member discussed the practical aspects of this proposal with the local authorities. In its resolution of 1926, the Government of India expressed willingness to receive applications for land from the Europeans and the Anglo-Indians. In the same resolution, it was noted that to cope with the tropical climate causing heavy rain, any form of agriculture involved hard physical labour. Besides, the insalubrious climate might act upon the health of the people who were not accustomed to manual work in torrential rain and under scorching sun. Moreover, for them, a plantation required an investment of Rs 5000/-.[7]

However, a few families of the Anglo-Indians, most of them from Calcutta and nearby areas, accepted the offer and came to Andaman for settlement but immediately after settlement, many of them went back to Calcutta because they found the facilities of city life simply absent in these islands. But those who stayed back became contented and happy.

Iqbal Singh remarked in his book, "...a small percentage comprised of Anglo-Indians who had tried to make the islands a colony for themselves, decided to live here and joined the Police department or started their own business or farm". Among them Barnes and Gilda families were well known among the local people.[8]

Further, from the documents available in the State Archives, Port Blair, it is learnt that there was a scheme for resettlement of the Ex-British Army personnel, the Europeans as well as the Anglo-Indians, in Andaman. Publicity of that scheme was ventilated by the General Adjutant, General Branch, Resettlement Directorate, New Delhi and the decision of the Government of India was communicated to the Chief Commissioner, Andaman and Nicobar Islands.

Intending settlers were advised to fill in the application forms printed in Appendix 'A' of the notice and submit the same to N.K. Patterson, Chief Commissioner, A.N.I. who was the first Chief Commissioner of the islands after the reoccupation from the clutches of the Japanese authority in 1945.[9]

In response to the circular, those who applied in prescribed form, were allotted land in Andaman. To cite an example of eagerness among the Ex-servicemen, here is the application of S. M. Laurance of 4569, New Bhoiguda, Secunderabad ½ Division, dated March 28, 1947 addressed to the Deputy Chief Commissioner, A. N. I. - "I have a capital of Rs. 5000/- and as such I shall pay my own and my family's passage to the Andamans and on arrival there, I would like very much to start a Bakery..."[10]

On page no. 295 is a list of settlers who were settled in different villages in Andaman.

Among those settlers mentioned above, only a few stayed back. Even after the Independence, with the growth of population, changing social condition, and political vitriol, they could not cope with and either returned to the mainland or went abroad particularly to Australia where their relations had already been domiciled. Now-a-days, the presence of these Anglo-Indians is almost nil.

TABLE

Name	*Address*	*Dt. of Settlement*	*Grants*		*Villages*
J.C. Berger	Ballard Estate, Bombay	11.3.1947	Farming	Rs. 500/-	Homphreygunj
P.B. Cornelius	Ballard Estate, Bombay	11.3.1947	Farming	Rs. 500/-	Mongluton
J.G. Barnes	3, Canal St. Entally, Cal	10.3.1947	Fruitgardening	Rs. 500/-	Mt. Harriet
T.R. Turner	3, Canal St. Entally, Cal	10.3.1947	Fruitgardening	Rs. 500/-	Mt. Harriet
M. Davis	3, Canal St. Entally, Cal	12.3.1947	Fruitgardening	Rs. 500/-	Mt. Harriet
M. Turner	3, Canal St. Entally, Cal	12.3.1947	Poultry	Rs. 500/-	Mt. Harriet
S.C. Mabert	2, Hare St. Calcutta	17.3.1947	Fruitgardening	Rs. 500/-	Mt. Harriet
O.L. Johnson	Bangalore	17.3.1947	Poultry	Rs. 500/-	Mt. Harriet
L.R. Carbery	15, Free School St. Cal	15.3.1947	Poultry	Rs. 500/-	Mt. Harriet
F.A. Englebright	15, Free School St. Cal	15.3.1947	Farming	Rs. 500/-	Mt. Harriet
E.P. Currran	15, Free School St. Cal	15.3.1947	Poultry	Rs. 500/-	Mt. Harriet
F. Lazare	St. Mary's H. School, Bombay	15.3.1947	Poulty	Rs. 500/-	Mt. Harriet
L. Holdashah	10, Homij St. Fort Bombay	15.3.1947	Poultry	Rs. 500/-	Mt. Harriet
H.C. Ritchie	10, Momij St. Fort Bombay	15.3.1947	Poultry	Rs. 500/-	Mt. Harriet
D.W. Johnson	31, Elliot Rd, Calcutta	24.3.1947	Poultry	Rs. 500/-	Mt. Harriet
N.B. SouthCombe	Sukh Nivas, Pasta Lane Kolaba, Bombay	16.3.1947	Poultry	Rs. 500/-	Mt. Harriet
S.M. Lawrance	Secunderabad	28.3.1947	Bakery	Rs. 500/-	Mt. Harriet
G.A. Pigott	Marine Drive, Bombay	28.3.1947	Flower, Fruit	Rs. 500/-	Mt. Harriet
L.B. Timmins	Mazagaon, Bombay	28.3.1947	Flower, Fruit	Rs. 500/-	Mt. Harriet

TABLE

Name	*Address*	*Dt. of Settlement*		*Grants*	*Villages*
F. Newton	2 Empress Park, Lahore	7.4.1947	Flower, Fruit	Rs. 500/-	Mt. Harriet
S. Freemantle	Dehradoon, U.P.	24.3.1947	Flower, Fruit	Rs. 500/-	Mt. Harriet
C.P. Mariano	Cochin	15.3.1947	Business	Rs. 500/-	Mt. Harriet
C. Rencoule	115 City Rd. Sialkot	10.4.1947	Business	Rs. 500/-	Mt. Harriet
F.B. Lefeuvre	Poona Cantonment	23.4.1947	Sheep, Cattle, Poultry	Rs. 500/-	Mt. Harriet
T.C. Cavroll	North Haven, Ketty, Nilgiri	23.4.1947	Veg., Fruit, Poultry	Rs. 500/-	Mt. Harriet
B. Robinson	Sealdah, Traffic Qrts, Cal.	09.5.1947	Veg. Fruit, Poultry	Rs. 500/-	Mt. Harriet
I.E. Sacharan Gunel	4/B, Bakery Rd. Hastings, Cal.	19.5.1947	Tea, Rubber	Rs. 500/-	Mt. Harriet
S. Lopez	4, Canning Rd. Allahabad	06.6.1947	Poultry	Rs. 500/-	Mt. Harriet
C.L. Ling	34-B, South Rd. Allahabad	17.5.1947	Poultry	Rs. 500/-	Mt. Harriet
A.D. Speechly	Rly. Qrts., Ajni, Nagpur, C.P.	24.5.1947	Poultry	Rs. 500/-	Mt. Harriet
N.H. Thompson	Block No. 293, Tapti Rd. Bhusawel	16.6.1947	Poultry	Rs. 500/-	Mt. Harriet

Assistance and Concessions

In the notings of the file no. 1-133/47 (A), 1947, Port Blair, regarding the concessions to Anglo-Indian Ex-servicemen for resettlement, it is mentioned, "Government has undertaken to contribute Rs. 1000/- towards the cost of settlement of an Ex-serviceman's family if the family is prepared to provide Rs. 500/-. It has been estimated that the total cost for a family to establish itself and cultivate 8 or 10 acres of land includes 8 maintenance charges until a crop has been reaped and the cost of a hut has been estimated at Rs. 1500/-. Govt. is also willing to pay a maximum sum of Rs. 300/- for travelling expenses".[12]

With reference to the letter no. 1-207/46, dated 12 September 1946, it was informed that the Government of India was pleased to approve the scheme regarding the settlement of 100 families of Ex-servicemen in the Andaman and Nicobar Islands and to grant Rs. 1000/- per family settled in the islands, provided that each settler puts up Rs. 500/-.

N.K. Patterson, the then Chief Commissioner stated the details of expenditure in his letter no. 1-207/46, dated 12 September 1946 to the Secretary, Government of India, Home Deptt., New Delhi, as follows.[13]

Estimate of cost of importation and settlement of Ex-servicemen in Andaman assuming that each settler family would consist of 2 adults and 3 children on an average –

Transport charges	–	Rs. 220/-
One pair of plough cattles	–	Rs. 400/-
One plough	–	Rs. 12 and 8 annas
One blade harrows	–	Rs. 10/-
Agriculture implements	–	Rs. 25/-
Cost of seeds, manure, others	–	Rs. 393/-
Cost of living quarters	–	Rs. 500/-

Cost of maintenance of family
until first crops reaped and sold
for six months @ Rs. 45/- (6x45) – Rs. 270/-

Grand Total – Rs. 1830 - 8 annas.

SETTLEMENT OF TAMILIANS

For colonization in the Andaman and Nicobar Islands the policy of the Government of India was, "...persons from Kerala and other places in India had also to be accommodated in the quota fixed for outsiders". Accordingly it allowed other migrants from different States to settle in the Andaman and Nicobar Islands and their quotas were also fixed so that no single community could become a majority in number and command over others.

This open door policy is very liberal for the sake of ideology and ideal for practical purposes but is not easy to implement it.

In the case of Bengali refugees from East Pakistan, they had nothing to lose because they were forced to abandon everything they had accumulated generations after generations. Immediately after the Partition followed by large scale massacre and destruction, they had to leave their homeland. Overnight they became homeless destitutes having nowhere to go but to flee to West Bengal to survive.

By then West Bengal became overpopulated and land became scarce so the East Bengal refugees had to move to other places outside West Bengal as they had no other choice.

Unlike East Bengal refugees, other communities had never faced this sort of catastrophy owing to the partition and had never been forced to leave their ancestral homesteads or agnates and cognates so they were despite the allurement pertaining to the government assistances, reluctant to come to Andaman. Hence the yearly quotas for these people had never been filled up. Even those who came, were not forced to come due to poverty. Moreover they still nurture roots in their State and remain nostalgic althrough, so they refrain from developing any attachment with Andaman.

The settlement of the Tamilians from Tamilnadu were started in 1960 while 17 Tamil families were brought to Andaman and settled at Pudu Madurai and Bajota villages near Pahelgaon in Middle Andaman as cultivators on colonization scheme. Indeed most of them were not cultivators so they were not interested in cultivation and the production of their fields was very poor. Ultimately, many of them left their villages keeping their lands at the mercy of their neighbours. Instead of cultivation, they prefer any odd jobs under the government establishments.

Tamil Expatriates from Burma

But before them in 1950s the Tamil evacuees from Burma were permitted to settle in these islands.

In the memorandum no. 64-380/65 PUB, dt. 5 March 1965, K.K. Warriar, Asst. Secretary to the Chief Commissioner, informed the Secretary, G.O.I., Ministry of External Affairs, "I am to add that during 1954, five Burmese evacuee families were brought here and settled by the Administration under the Colonization Scheme under which East Bengal, Ranchi, etc., settler families were also settled."[14]

From the tour diary of A.K. Ghose, Chief Commissioner, Andaman and Nicobar Islands, it is learnt that he visited the settlement area at Shoal Bay on 14 February, 1950 and commented: "This area may be reserved for settlers from Burma and the Bengali refugees settled near Wandur if water is available".[15]

Thus the Tamil evacuees from Burma were settled at Shoal Bay in 1950. They were allotted 60 acres of paddy land but these 12 families cleared only 24 acres and cultivated about 20 acres so the approximate yield was meagerly 5 maunds per acre because they failed to develop cooperative spirit, on the contrary, they were involved in conflicts among themselves.[16]

These 12 Tamil repatriates uprooted from their holdings in the South Burma after the Karen rebellion, were allowed as evacuees to settle in South Andaman. Initially they were given Rs. 2000/- for their rehabilitation at Shoal Bay and provided shelter in the abandoned camps of the forest labourers. On idling and dalliances, all their money sanctioned as grants and loans was exhausted in buying rations. Such a bad adoption in the resettlement of the people probably took place because of the lack of proper supervision from the Administration.

However, C.S. Jha, Commonwealth Secretary, Ministry of External Affairs, Government of India explained the whole situation leading to the evacuation, in his memo, no. S/411 4/64, 7 August, 1964 as follows:

"The main causes of returning to India were the nationalisation of various segments of the Burmese economy, refusal of visas and Foreigners' Registration certificates, inability to transfer savings to India and arbitrary treatment by the Government authorities.

"From the middle of June 1964 about 200 Indians have been arriving at Calcutta by Air from Rangoon every day. All these were income-tax payers in Burma. The non-income tax payers will be arriving or have already arrived as deck-passengers by ships. The cabins in these ships will be occupied by those who were paying income tax in Burma.

"...Destitute will be carried entirely free of charge... other deck passengers will be charged Rs. 75/- per head as against the economic deck class fare of Rs. 150/-.

"...Concessional air tickets at Rs. 125/-, though fare is Rs. 205/-, liberal custom and import rules are applied to them.

"...The Embassy has estimated the number of Indians returning from Burma during the present exodus about one lakh."[17]

However, some expatriates from Burma and Ceylon of Tamil origin had come down to these islands on their own volition. They were frequently approaching the A&N Administration for allotment of agricultural lands, house-cum-shop sites and other assistance for their rehabilitation.

In reply to their approach, the Government of India informed them that the unsponsored repatriate families, who had come to the islands on their own, cannot be resettled under the special schemes, taken up by the Department of Rehabilitation.[18]

However, the settlement problem of Tamil expatriates from Ceylon was not solved because they came to India as evacuees or repatriate, and not as refugees. For them, as such no colonization scheme was thought of by the Government of India. So, for many years these expatriates of Tamil origin from Ceylon and Burma had to move from pillars to posts to get their grievances redressed.

From the two mass petitions, it will be clear how these people had to struggle for shelter and settlement.

Seeking consent for allotment of land, the Indian repatriates from Burma wrote to the Chief Commissioner, Andaman and Nicobar Islands, on April 22, 1970 as under:

"...We have come back to our motherland India in 1964 and later with no shelter anywhere, we moved to Mongluton (South Andaman)... We are being served with notice of eviction from Tahsildar and a fine of Rs. 200/- each... by 29 April. Hence we appeal to you for mercy.[19]

Sd/Konda Naidu and sixteen others.

With reference to the above letter, Deputy Commissioner, Andaman and Nicobar Islands, reported to the Chief Commissioner, D.O. No. Rev/2/6/10/3216, dt 31 July, 1970 as follows:

"Facts that 24 Burmese Indian repatriates had encroached about 15 acres of land of Survey No.1 of village Mongluton, during February/April, 1970.

"It appears that the persons involved have left Burma and have come to this territory on their own..., have not come as regular repatriates through the Indian Embassy at Rangoon... rules do not permit allotment of land to them".

Indeed, earlier it was notified that as evacuees one must carry the documentary evidences while leaving Burma on or after 1st June, 1963, such as:

a) Passport or travel documents.

b) Letters issued by All Burma Indians Congress.

Moreover, to enable the repatriates with legal documents, to avail all sorts of the government assistances, every family was given identity card. Those who were not having the above mentioned documents, were neither entitled for land, nor for any assistance.

Burma Ceylon Repatriates Association: (B.C.R.A.)

Meanwhile, all these repatriates both from Burma and Ceylon organised "Burma-Ceylon Repatriates Association", housed officially at Phongyi Kyanng (Budhist temple) at Port Blair. On behalf of the Association, T. Sameahy Servai, General Secretary, submitted a representation to the Chief Commissioner, Andaman and Nicobar Islands.

"We are the British Ceylon Indian Repatriates constantly knocking since 1964... to provide the minimum requirements of human beings—shelter, loan, a piece of land...

"We are a section of population from many States of India, i.e., U.P., West Bengal, Bihar, Andhra Pradesh, Kerala, Punjab, Mysore, Tamilnadu. There are more than 1500 families scattered throughout the islands engaged in different vocations...

"...We are totally ignored by the local administration. Hence we demand –

(1) Agriculture land at Rutland, South Andaman or Little Andaman for 50 families for agricultural settlement

(2) Business loan for 40 families.

If the demands are not fulfilled till 25 September, 1972, we will resort to hunger strike".[20]

In response to the ultimatum served by B.C.R.A., dated 24 August, 1972, the Andaman & Nicobar Administration informed that the Department of Rehabilitation, Government of India decided that all the Tamil families who had arrived in India on or after 1st June, 1963 and who had not applied for rehabilitation assistance so far, might apply for grants of assistance by 31 August, 1972. Applications of such persons were invited through the *Daily Telegrams,* only newspaper published by the Administration from Port Blair. Further, the loans to eligible persons would be granted after scrutiny of applications.

However, those who applied for rehabilitation assistance were duly sanctioned.

Of course, N.N. Chadha, Judicial Secretary, Government of India made it clear that according to the existing rule of the Government of India as mentioned in the circular No. 1(7)/65, RH 111, dt. 30 June, 1965, the Burmese repatriates who came to this territory on their own, would not be entitled for the allotment of land though they were eligible for loan assistance.[21]

Eligibility for Loan

But to be eligible for loan, the applicant must be (1) an Indian who repatriated from Burma, and (2) he must be a native of the Territory of Pondicherry and (3) his father should have been a native of the Territory of Pondicherry.

In the notification, it was stated further, "As regards the condition (1) above, attention is invited to D.O. letter no. S1/411/76/64, dt. 7 February, 1965 from Deputy Secretary, Ministry of External Affairs to the Chief Secretaries of all State Governments from which it will be observed that only such persons as can produce the documentary evidence of having left Burma for good on or after 1st June, 1963 are eligible for rehabilitation assistance.

"...If any repatriate from Burma wishes to settle in a State other than one to which he originally belonged to, he may not deserve the facilities and concessions normally admissible to the repatriates from Burma.[22]

According to the criteria for getting business loan, the eligible applicants were sanctioned loans ranging from Rs. 500/- to Rs. 1500/- by the Deputy Commissioner, order no. 325, dated 22 August, 1970. The loan would bear simple interest at the rate of 8.5 percent and it would be reduced to 6 percent if paid regularly. The loan would be recovered in 10 years in 9 annual equal instalments.

Expatriates from Ceylon

Another section of Tamil people was brought from Ceylon for settlement in the Andaman and Nicobar Islands. During the British period, "Malaiyego Tamilargal" or Indian Tamils mainly from Ramnad district were sent to "Venderayvalai" or Sri Lanka as bonded labour but clashes started between the new and the old settlers. After a brief discussion over the issue between Srimavo Banderanayake, Prime Minister of Sri Lanka and Lal Bahadur Shastri, Prime Minister of India, the settlement of Indian Tamils from Sri Lanka started in three phases in 1972, 1974, 1976. Of course in 1970, 70 Tamil families had been brought from Ceylon and settled at Katchal Island to work in the rubber plantation. Now they are above 250 families.

In 1972, 17 Tamil families from Triconomalay, Sri Lanka were brought to Andaman and Nicobar Islands under rehabilitation scheme. Among them, 12 families were settled in the forest area, 28 kms. away from Hut Bay in Little Andaman. The area is commonly called as Ceylon Basti but in revenue papers renamed as Ravindra Nagar. In due course, the number increased to 28. The rest 5 families were sent to Katchal for employment and to settle under the rubber plantation scheme. Later 47 Ceylon repatriates were engaged as labourers in the plantation.

In the second phase in 1974, 22 Ceylon repatriates were settled in this region.

In 1976, 28 Tamil families from Sri Lanka were also settled in these islands. Meanwhile in Saitankhari area under Ferrargunj Tahsil in South Andaman, a rubber plantation covering 500 acres was started in 1965 and 37 Burma repatriates of Tamil origin were brought there to work as labourers and to settle on permanent basis.

Following the settlement of Tamil repatriates from Burma and Ceylon, many ambitious people from Madras started coming to the islands of their own to do business or to seek jobs. They were engaged in various economic activities whatever was available or suitable for them. In search of livelihood, they spread all over the islands and adjust easily with the new environment.

Tamilians are mostly Hindus and only a few are Christians. Murugan, Ayappa, Ayyanar, Vinayaka, Balaji, Mariyamman, etc., are their popular deities and they build temples wherever they settle. During Vel Vel festival, devotees walk on fire to appease deities like Murugan and Mariyamman. The Christians attend churches of their respective sects. Deepavali and Pongal are the major festivals of the Hindu Tamils and the Christian Tamils celebrate Christmas and Good Friday. Mutual participation in the celebrations of others is common in the islands. Many other Hindu festivals, they celebrate are Chittirai Vizha, Karthigai Deepam, Pangani Uttiram, etc.

Those who were settled during the early phases were mostly illiterate but they have realized the importance of education. They have struggled hard to set up a number of Tamil medium schools under the banner of Tamil Education Protection Committee, Port Blair initiated by Tamizar Sangam.

The Tamilians are very conscious about their own culture and tradition. Tamizar Sangam at Port Blair organizes cultural programmes as well as mitigates their common problems.

They live amicably with their neighbours like the Bengalis, Ranchis, Telegus, Malayalis, etc., and develop healthy relations with all.

The first settlement of Tamil evacuees from Burma was started in 1950 with only 12 Tamil families but this population grew very quickly for various reasons, as discussed above and by 1991, it turns out to be 53536 and probably grew to 70,000 by 2005. They hold a very commendable position not only in business but also in socio-political life.

Among the Ex-servicemen families settled at Campbell Bay in 1972, there were 80 Tamil families who have been rehabilitated at Vijaynagar, Lakshmi Nagar, 30 kms. and 35 kms. from Campbell Bay respectively.

Though the Tamil community is somehow orthodox and strictly caste based, in Andaman, they have undergone some changes in their beliefs and practices, and become liberal to accept certain views of neighbouring communities. Over the years, Tamil culture and tradition has intermingled with others and contributes significantly to develop unique island culture in this archipelago.

SETTLEMENT OF MALAYALIS

The settlement policy of the Government of India was to rehabilitate people of other States in the islands so that no community would get the scope of commanding over the society by virtue of its majority in number and thereby would spoil the identity of another community. So further settlement of East Pakistan refugees became restricted and settlement of other communities from the mainland, such as Keralians, Tamilians, Telegus, etc., were started on different colonization schemes.

The people of Kerala, Keralians or Malayalis settled in Andaman during 1953-54, are obviously a migrant population comprising of Nayar, Iravas, Pulayan, Arayan, Chaliyan, etc.

As regards the terms of the settlement of Malayalis who had been settled during 1954-55, the Andaman and Nicobar. Administration had a discussion with the Government of Kerala and it was decided that an amount of Rs. 18,578-43 paisa spent towards the passage expenses and others in respect to the settlement of Malayalis in Andaman was to be reimbursed by the Andaman and Nicobar Administration[23].

During 1961, 20 agricultural families from Kerala were settled in these islands and according to terms and conditions of settlement, they were given the grants and loans. Below is a statement of advances paid to the Malayali settlers during 1953-54 and 1955-56.[24]

TABLE

Settlers brought from	*Expenditure incurred*	*Recoverable amount*
Trivandrum	Rs. 5048- 2 annas	Rs. 4824-6 annas - 3 paisa
Quilon	Rs. 4557/-	Rs. 4332-12 annas
Kottayam	Rs. 2583-4 annas	Rs. 2355-5 annas-9 paisa
Trichur	Rs. 2506-4a-5 paisa	Rs. 2392-3 annas-8 paisa

The details of the migrant families from Kerala, settled in these islands during 1954-56 are mentioned below:

TABLE

Head of the family	*Area/village*	*Age*	*Year of settlement*	*Family members with wife and*
A. From Trivandrum District :				
K.K. Pilliai	Vilavancode	35	1954	3 daughters
K.N.K. Pillai	Perunthanni	30	1954	1 son, 2 daughters
P.A. Damodharan Nampitti	Palkulangara	27	1954	1 daughter
K.P. Nampitti	Palkulangara	55	1954	1 daughter, 1 son
G. Basudevan Pillai	Nedumangad	32	1954	1 daughter
Neel Kantan Bhaskaran	Attingal	34	1954	1 son, 2 daughters
S. Narayan Pillai	Attingal	40	1954	1 son, 1 daughter
Parameswaran Pillai	Muthathura	44	1954	2 wives, 3 daughters 1 son
Bhaskaran Nair	Vanchiyoor	34	1954	2 daughters

B. From Quillon District :

Around 13 families in 1954, 14 families in 1955 and 13 families is 1956 were settled in Andaman.

C. From Kottayan District :

Around 5 families in 1954, 4 families in 1955 and 11 families in 1956 were brought to Andaman for settlement.

D. From Trichur District :

8 families in 1954, 5 families in 1955, 6 families in 1956 were settled in Andaman.

The Kerala Government, however, agreed to bear the transport expenditure for the settlement of Malayalis in Andaman for 1954-1956, amounting to Rs. 2392-3 annas - 8 paisa.[25]

However, in the case of settlement of agricultural families brought from Kerala during 1961, the incidental expenses on each family amounting to Rs. 45/- were debited to the ex-gratia grant of the settler concerned. Of course, in the letter of the Asst. Secretary (Rehabilitation), Andaman and Nicobar Islands, dated 31 January, 1967, the government assistance has been explained in the following lines:

"The colonization scheme among other things, envisages a provision of Rs 210/- ex-gratia towards the cost of passage and Rs. 130/- as recoverable loan towards the cost of utensils to the settler. It is not clear whether the cost of bus and railway fares for bringing families from outlying station (in Kerala) to Madras, is a legitimate charge in the colonization scheme..."[26]

On behalf of the Andaman & Nicobar Administration, it was proposed that while the expenditure on meals and refreshment during journey period was ultimately recovered from the subsistence allowance of East Pakistan settlers, on this analogy, the meals and refreshment charges in the case of the Malayali migrants too might be debited to the ex-gratia grant sanctioned for each family.

In this context, the details of the grants and loans admissible are mentioned below:

a) Recoverable Loan :

i)	Cost of building one's house	Rs. 800/-
ii)	Purchase of plough animals	Rs. 700/-
iii)	Cost of utensils	Rs. 130/-
iv)	Seeds and manure	Rs. 100/-
	Total	**Rs. 1730/-**

b) Ex-gratia Grant :

i)	Subsistence allowance @ 70/- per family for 8 months in the first year and 4 months in the next year	Rs. 840/-

ii) Passage, meals, etc.	Rs. 210/-
Total	**Rs. 1050/-**

As to the report of the Assistant Secretary (Rehabilitation), Andaman & Nicobar Administration, no. 19-4/59 PQ and 19-4/74-PG, dated 19.8.1966, in all 420 families from other States such as Madras, Bihar, Kerala, Mahe, etc., and Burma evacuees under different schemes during 1953-1961 were settled in Andaman.

According to the terms of the colonization scheme, all the settlers from Kerala were treated at par with those from East Pakistan.

Most of the Malayali migrants were settled in Middle and North Andamans and they were allotted 5 acres of paddy land and 5 acres of hilly land. In due course, with the increase of family members, they settled themselves in other parts of the islands either by purchasing land or by securing any job. They are very nostalgic in christening the names of their villages, such as Keralapuram, Padmanavapuram, Dharmapuram, Trivanchipuram, etc.

Malayalis settled in Andaman for more than ten years are recognized under the 'Local' category and enjoy the benefits that go with it in terms of employment, education, etc.

Most of the Malayalis were dependent on agriculture and coconut plantation. But they are very conscious about the modern education and send their wards to schools. Unlike the Tamilians, they never demand to set up Malayali medium school. They usually send their children to English medium schools. Each village has a Primary school and in a cluster of every three or four villages, there is a Secondary school.

They take the facility to uplift themselves. Young Malayalis are not interested in farming and prefer white collar jobs so they are serious about their studies. As a secondary source of income, the settlers not only catch fish or work under Forest, Marine, P.W. Departments, but also rear cattles, start piggery, dairy, poultry business, etc.

Response of Settlers

The Malayalis, though, could adjust with the new environment yet there were certain grievances grunting among them.

Keshava Pillai of Dharampura village in Middle Andaman sent an application forwarded by K. R. Ganesh, M.P. from these islands and the then Deputy Finance Minister, demanding the fulfilment of quota of paddy land and hilly land due to him as a settler on 28 September, 1970 to B.K. Halve, Chief Commissioner for consideration.

On 19 July, 1971, Madhavan Pillai of Keralapuram in North Andaman found his plot not fit for paddy cultivation so he applied for a suitable plot or to allot the plot no. 44 already deserted by the earlier settler.

Against the shortage of land, the following settlers applied for fulfilment of quotas assured by the government.

- Subramaniam of Keralapuram settled in 1958
- Subramaniam Pillai, settler of Padmapuram in Rangat Tahsil
- S.K. Nair, settler of Betapur
- Sarojini of Thoraktang (Swadeshnagar) in Middle Andaman and others.

Indeed, there were about 130 dependent members of Malayali settler families at Betapur area and it needed 650 acres of land so the Administration had to chalk out plans for their settlements. Even against the natural calamities, the Administration took steps for relief of the affected families. As for example, M.C. Verghese, settler of Sivapuram in Middle Andaman was affected by the cyclone of 1967 and granted Rs. 5000/- on 7 March, 1970 to set up a sawmill in his locality.

Similarly, some Malayali settlers of Betapur area including K.M. Mammi of Dharampura and K.V. Verghese of Swadeshnagar were affected by the flood of Rangat river in 1970 and received relief in cash and kind.

The Malayalis are by nature cordial and accommodating. Malayalam is their mother tongue but they pick up local Hindi easily, so can communicate effectively with other communities and maintain healthy relations with their neighbours.

Most of the Malayalis are Hindus. They worship Subramanian, Ayyapan, Bhagavati, Nadal and Gulikan. They celebrate Onam, Holi, Kartik, Ganapati Puja, Diwali, etc.

The Christian Malayalis of Andaman are devoted to the dictums of the respective churches and a Father/Pastor advises them on spiritual matters. They celebrate all the major festivals related to Christianity.

The Malayalis as a whole never shun their own culture and tradition even in these far flung islands. Their own organisation, Kerala Samajam celebrates all their regional festivals including Onam and Durgapuja at Port Blair and takes steps to propagate their own culture and popularise their language.

Besides Malayalis and Tamilians, a number of Telegu fisherman families was also settled in Andaman on the government expenses. Later many of them came on their volition to do all odd jobs and their population grew to a considerable number of 32979 as per 1991 Census. There are other communities too such as Kanna (323 heads), Marathi (539 heads), Oriya (841 heads) Punjabi (1752 heads), Gorkhali (393 heads) etc. Thus due to all their spirit of assimilation and unison, this territory has become a Mini India.

ENDNOTES

1. 'My Reminiscences', by Renuka Roy, Stree Pub., 2005, p 152
2. General Administrative Report, AndaNico Islands, 1966-67
3. State Archives, Port Blair, File no. 334/48, Sl. no. 26
4. Ibid, Sl. no. 44, p 28
5. Ibid, Sl. no. 44. Memo No. E/72/1473, dt 28.11.1948
6. Ibid, File No. G/167-A2, Vol I, 1959-60
7. State Archives, Port Blair, Home Deptt. File No. 20/26 Jails

8. 'The Andaman Story' by Iqbal Singh, p. 180-181
9. State Archives, Port Blair, File no. 8/c. No. 1-207/46, dated, 12 September, 1946.
10. Ibid.
11. Ibid.
12. State Archives, Port Blair F/No. 1-133/47 (A). 1947.
13. Ibid. File No. 1/207/47 (1947) Office of C.C. AndaNico Islands.
14. Ibid.
15. State Archives, Port Blair, File No. 1-792/50
16. Ibid.
17. Ibid. Most confidential No. S1/411/4/64, dt. 7 Aug. 1964.
18. Ibid. F/No. 45-4/70-76/J(1).
19. Ibid. File No. 33-3/73-J(1).
20. Ibid. File No. B.C.R. A/3/71-72, Cal, dt. 24.8.1972.
21. Ministry of Rehabilitation, File No. 33-3/70-J(1), dt. 30 November, 1972.
22. Letter of B.N. Mitra, Under Secretary. Govt. of Pondicherry, No. 1(7)/65-RH111, Ministry of Rehab., dt. 30 June, 1965.
23. State Archives, Port Blair, File No. 37–274/59–DH.
24. Ibid. File No. 1233, dt. 20 Feb, 1967.
25. Ibid. File No. U.O. No. 1233, dt 20 Feb. 1967, from Asst. Secy. (R).
26. Ibid. File No. 19/66 RH-1966/File No. 37-274/59-DH.

14

Administrative Set-up

After the Independence, this island-territory was given the status of a part 'D' State in the Constitution of India. With the Reorganization of the States on November 1, 1956, these islands as a whole became a Union Territory. Thenceforth, the AndaNico Islands continued to be administered by the Union Home Ministry through the Chief Commissioner who used to be advised in legislative and other policy matters by an Advisory Council, constituted by the Central Government. Then an enlarged Advisory Council came into being from 1963 in the name and style of "Chief Commissioner's Advisory Committee" to look after the well-being of the islanders.

During the year 1972-73, steps were taken towards the democratization of the Administration of these islands in order to involve the islands more effectively in the development programmes to be checked by themselves through the democratic process.

The non-official members of the Chief Commissioner's Advisory Committee were elected for the first time from 1972 onwards by Panchayat Pradhans, the Municipal Board, Port Blair and the traditional tribal councils from among themselves with the exception of one member from Great Nicobar, directly nominated by the President of India.

In order to represent the tribes of these islands better in the Chief Commissioner's Advisory Committee, the Government of India decided in October, 1975 that one member shall be nominated each year by the Ministry of Home Affairs from amongst the three tribes, viz., Great Andamanese, Onges and Shompens. In the context of the International Women's year, the Government of India further decided that one woman member shall be nominated each year by the Ministry of Home Affairs for this committee.[1]

Till 1962, the Member of Parliament from this territory used to be nominated by the President of India on the recommendation of the Chief Commissioner, AndaNico Islands. Late Bishop Richardson[2] was the first nominated MP from these islands in 1952. He was followed by Laxman Singh, and then Niranjanlal, both belonged to local born society.

Meanwhile it was decided that the next MP from these islands would be elected and a bill to this effect was passed in 1967. The first elected Member of Parliament was KR Ganesh[3] who also belonged to the local born community and was elevated to the rank of the Deputy Finance Ministry of India in 1969. Since 1972, Manoranjan Bhakta, a settler of Diglipur won all the elections till 2008 as a candidate of Congress. Now the standing Member of Parliament is Bishnupada Ray[4] of BJP.

On the thirteenth year of the Republic of India, the Andaman and Nicobar Islands (Administration) Regulation, 1979 was promulgated by the President of India in July, 1979. Accordingly an indirectly elected council called Andaman Nicobar Pradesh Council was formed.

The Regulation came into force on April 15, 1981. The tenure of the Pradesh Council is for four years. Among the 25 members, five of them are nominated by the Chief Commissioner to act as Counsellors to look after various portfolios, barring law and order and service matters.

On November 12, 1982, the status of the Chief Commissioner was elevated to the rank of Lieutenant

Governor[5] who also acts as the Chairman of the Pradesh Council. Among the five Counsellors[6] of the first Pradesh Council, there were Nalini Ranjan Mondal, a refugee settler of Billyground in Middle Andaman, Nagen Halder, a refugee settler of Diglipur in North Andaman, Abdullah Kutty, a Moplah descendant of Wimberlygunj in South Andaman and other two counsellors were Aberdeen Blair from Nicobar and Shantikrishna from the local borns. The then Member of Parliament, Manoranjan Bhakta became the ex-officio member of the Pradesh Council. This bears the proof that new settlers as well as the old settlers like the Moplahs and local borns would hold a commendable position in socio-political scenario of the then Andaman.

For the convenience of the Administration, the Union Territory is divided into three districts: (i) Andaman district (ii) Nicobar district and (iii) Madhyottar Andaman district. Andaman district is the largest one with its headquarters at Port Blair but in the Nicobar district, the inhabitants are mostly tribals having 107 census villages with its headquarters at Car Nicobar whereas Campbell Bay has only seven villages and all these villages have been brought under Panchayat Raj with the exception of all Nicobari villages where they follow traditional system as the local self-government, headed by the village captain. The entire Union Territory is divided into nine Community Development Blocks of which three are in South Andaman, three in North and Middle Andamans and the rest three are in Car Nicobar, Nancowri and Campbell Bay respectively.

In 1964, the Ministry of Rehabilitation was made responsible for the development of special areas and the first notified special area is the Andaman and Nicobar Islands which was considered to be exceptionally suitable for integrated resources development and rehabilitation. Accordingly in October, 1967, the office of the Chief Development-cum-Rehabilitation Commissioner was set up at Port Blair to implement the programmes under the special areas development scheme.

For the settlement of the refugees, the government announced the exemption of land revenue for 5 years.

According to the notification no. W.R.B/16/30/4038/71, dt. 6 May, 1971, it was announced that there would be no land revenue for 5 years since the settlement of the migrant refugee commenced under colonization scheme.

Over the years while the population of the settlement was swelled up and the dependants of the families were grown up and obviously some of them encroached upon more lands of the government by clearing forests illegally. They started to build their houses on encroached land, commonly called 'Kataidera'. These unauthorized lands are used by the usurpers without paying any revenue. They even enjoy the privilege of ration cards and voter identity cards. Surprisingly due to political pressure, all sorts of civic facilities like electricity, water, education and medical have been provided to them. Attempts from all corners have been made to get these unauthorized land, sanctioned under the Andaman and Nicobar Islands Lands Revenue and Land Reform Regulations 1966 which is the modification of the Land Tenure Regulation, 1926 and later modified further on 19 May, 1946.

According to the Regulation, it explains the power to make grants of land "...to any person for the cultivation of long use crops, construction of building, workshop, for a period not exceeding 30 years, with an option for renewal by a licence in writing permit any person to occupy any land for any purpose, for construction of building, or agricultural works–no right under licence shall devolve by inheritance or be transferred by any manner".[7]

However, the sub-section (1) of Section 88 of the Land Revenue and Land Reform Regulation, 1966 states, "All land in the Union Territory of Andaman and Nicobar Islands is vested absolutely in the government and same as provided by or under this Regulation, no person shall be deemed to have acquired any property therein or any right to or over the same by occupation, prescription or conveyance or in any other manner whatsoever except by a conveyance executed by or under the authority of the Central Government.[8]

It clearly envisages that no one in these islands has an absolute right over any kind of landed property as owner of the said land but some kind of usufructuary right is passed by one. The regulation bars all sorts of "right to or over the same by occupation" so the question of legal sanction of ownership over the encroached land seems impossible. Hence it creates long pending problem and garners socio-political chaos. So the influx continued and encroachment remains unabated.

In fact, in the whole of the islands, the immigrants have not only outnumbered the pre-colonial populations but also marginalized them in all conceivable respects for obvious reasons. The settlement of these new settlers was primarily concentrated in rural areas as schemed up by the government and not by the migrants at their own will and the cultivable land including homestead area was allotted to each family as to the rehabilitation plan chalked out by the government alone. Of course, in the later days, the vagabonds or itinerants of the same language group settled on other sites either by purchasing land from the earlier settlers or by encroaching illegally into the government lands in the remote areas.

The uniqueness of the islands acquired a special dimension on account of its sudden growth of population. Unlike in other instances where the dominant community finds means to take over the mien of economic, political and social life and exercise a commanding position but here in these islands, the situation is exceptional where otherwise marginalized and migrant groups coming from all parts of the country initially as the convicts and later as the settlers become the primal focus of this social dynamics. They have reorganized themselves first as the non-descript social aggregate which has its deep impact in the formation of social categories like the 'Local Borns,' the settlers and the mainlanders considering their chronological periods of their settlements. These diverse components of the human tapestry ultimately culminate into a unique harmonious society.

This can be envisaged if one looks for a morphological contour which is based on the utilization of physical space in juxtaposition with the concomitant economic and socio-cultural milieu of the emerging island society. Indeed the complex population structure epitomizes the essence of Mini India and strives on the march of securing its own Statehood as well as State Legislative.

ENDNOTES

1. Annual Report, Andaman & Nicobar Islands, 1979
2. Bishop Richardson: son of the Captain of Mus Village in Car Nicobar, 'Hachevki' by name, embraced the Christianity and became John Richardson, later elevated to 'Bishop', translated the Bible into the Nicobarese language, and published in 1970. He was the first nominated M.P. in 1952 from the Union Territory, Andaman Nicobar Islands, conferred with Padma Shree in 1965 and Padma Bhushan in 1976.
3. K. R. Ganesh, son of K. Ratnam and Dhanam, born in an ex-convict family from Andhra Pradesh, on 21 June, 1921. He reorganized the Local Born Association and brought out the first ever journal, "Hamari Awaz" from Port Blair. He was the first elected MP from this Union Territory in 1967 and sworn in as Deputy Minister in 1969. Again in 1971, he was elevated as Minister of State for Revenue.
4. Bishnupada Ray, standing M.P. from the Andaman & Nicobar Islands. He was married to a local lady of Port Blair.
5. K. L. Campany, the First Lt. Governor of this Union Territory.
6. Five Counsellors were Nagen Halder from Diglipury, Nalini Ranjan Mondal from Middle Andaman, Aberdeen Blair from Nicobar, Abdullah Kutty from Ferrarganj and Shantikrishna from Port Blair—all elected to the Pradesh Council in pursuance of Rule 21 of Andaman & Nicobar Islands (Administration) Rules, 1981.
7. Andaman Nicobar Manual, 1908.
8. The Andaman & Nicobar Islands Land Revenue and Land Reforms Regulations 1966, p. 15.

15

ANDAMAN INDIANS, THE LOCAL BORNS

The Penal Settlement Regulations of the Straits had been introduced in this settlement (Andaman & Nicobar Islands) in 1868 and rules were made for its jail administration and also for convict-marriages. Since the establishment of the penal settlement, convicts mostly on criminal cases were transported to these islands as life-convicts. During the term, after completion of scheduled confinement periods in or outside the Cellular Jail, the convicts were offered to settle in the islands either by bringing down their families from the mainland or on getting married choosing partner from the female convicts locally.

Earlier in 1862, the Government of India allowed female convicts to become self-supporters and convict-marriage used to be arranged among the self-supporters, male and female convicts[1]. However Intra-convicts marriage sometimes found derogatory to the well-being of the society as it was noticed that a male term-convict who married a female life-convict usually left his wife after his release. This resulted in prevalence of unnatural vice to an alarming extent among the convicts. Due to scarcity of females in the settlement, many women married only in name were forced to adopt pseudo prostitution. According to Merk,[2] Superintendent of Penal Settlement, Port Blair, who in 1904 expressed his opinion to stop the transportation to the Andamans because the life of the prisoners in Andamans was much more unrestrained than that of a prisoner in an Indian jail,[3] and the state of immorality in the settlement was horrifying.[4]

Even Sir Reginald Craddock, Home Secretary to the Government of India in his report of 1914, wrote, "As to sexual morality, the system directly encourages immorality". The natural consequence of such state of affairs was the prevalence of debauchery and venereal diseases to a great extent. In 1918, there were only 233 female self-supporters as compared with 1304 male self-supporters on a ratio of one woman to six men. Hence immorality on the part of women was rampant.

Of course, Captain Man[5] was not in favour of stopping such intra-convicts marriages though leading to sexual perversion but wished to place certain restrictions on them[6]. Accordingly, the Government of India decided to permit only convict of first class i.e., self-supporters to marry. Any self-supporter might marry a convict woman under convict rules if he had the permission of the Settlement Authority and the marriage could be held in accordance with the social custom of both the parties. After duly married, the couple was allowed to settle in the nearby villages on the government assistance. Shadipur, Bimlitan, Aberdeen, Garacharma, Tushnabad, Namunaghar, Wimberlygunj, Mithakhari, etc., are the villages where the married couples were settled.

Thus the settlement grew and the descendants of the convicts happened to be known as 'Local Borns'. Though their parents originally belonged to different regions of India, they, in due course, have been moulded into a homogenous group of community having a unique affinity irrespective of their caste, creed or language and belonging to all streams of Indian culture. Thus they have grown and flourished in and around Port Blair.

In the Census Report of 1951, it has been clearly mentioned who the Local Borns are:

"The main basis of the population (of the Andaman & Nicobar Islands) is what in the old days, was known as

'Local Borns' signifying thereby the convicts settled here and their progeny. This terminology with a rather humiliating connotation, has since been changed and in this Census, all permanent residents of the Andamans who have made these hospitable islands their home, have been recorded as 'Andaman Indians' be he a new settler from East Bengal, a naturalized Karen from Burma or a person born here out of convict ancestry".

But this eclectic view is the latest paradigm and in the earlier days, the plight was quite different. In the Census Report of 1951, the prevailing condition has been discussed precisely in the following lines: "The artificial creation and nurturing of a special community as "Local Borns" were obviously due to the social disabilities to which the early convict settlers were subjected to in those days. But it certainly has created a fissiparous tendency which is very undesirable in the present political context of the country. A feeling of separateness attended with an inferiority complex has crept in, retarding the progress and development of the people".[7]

Population Pattern

However, despite their consanguinity as Pathans, Punjabis, Tamils, Telegus, Malayalis, Bengalis and others, they have merged significantly into a commingled culture, united by a common language, Hindustani in spoken form and Urdu in literary expression. Inter-caste or community marriage between people of different castes or creeds is arranged spontaneously without any traditional stigmas.

As regards the sex ratio, the increase in population of Andaman was very low and this again had its odd influence on the socio-economic condition of the people resulting in the increase in moral vice and corruption.

The population growth of the last ten years from 33768 in 1941 to 30062 in 1951 experienced a considerable decline of 3706 because of the mass killing of the 'locals' during the period of the Japanese occupation (1942-45) and also due to starvation and ailments. Again while the British declared the abolition of the Penal Settlement after the reoccupation of the islands in 1945, many of the local residents were allowed to leave Andaman for their own native home in the mainland. Besides, many Burmese repatriated to Burma after the Independence. Hence the net increase of the population of the islands during the last seventy years from 1881 to 1951 is only 4300 which is an abnormally slow rate of growth. The distribution of population of the islands reported in the first Census of 1901 shows the following facts:

No. of employees in government establishment	No. of convicts in the islands	No. of Free Population
1168	11947	2991

The 1951 Census figure of the population of Andaman shown in the following table brings out the facts about the fluctuation of growth. Before 1881, there had been an almost continuous growth of population through the transportation of the convicts in the islands but the decade ranging from 1941 to 1951 marked the decline for the obvious reasons mentioned above.

TABLE

Distribution of Population in Andaman

Year	*Male*	*Female*	*Total*
1881	12940	1988	14928
1891	13375	2234	15609
1901	15158	2980	18138
1911	14737	2904	17641
1921	15551	2204	17814
1931	14258	4965	19223
1941	14872	6444	21316
1951	12734	6228	18962

A large proportion of the free settlers, say descendants of convicts, known as the 'Local Borns' comprised every kind of personal character. The population of the penal settlement consisted of variegated populace such as convicts, their guards, the supervising, clerical and departmental staffs with their families and free settlers.

The population of Port Blair was distributed over an occupied area of 327 sq. miles in 29 stations where labouring convicts were kept and 34 villages where free or ticket of leave convicts resided. The population of Andaman as to the Census of 1901 numbered 18138 including 150 free persons —114 males and 36 females but in 2001, it has increased strikingly to 314084. Details of general convicts are given below:

TABLE[8]

General Convict Statistics

Particular		*1874*	*1881*	*1891*	*1901*	*1905-06*
No. of Convicts received	M	603	1102	869	1232	1507
	F	97	100	52	80	54
No. of life Convicts	M	6727	7668	8033	9204	9642
	F	836	1122	861	714	673
No. of Term Convicts	M	6	2657	2840	2037	4339
	F	–	5	4	19	42
No. of Convicts released	M	355	64	685	215	300
	F	4	3	73	32	31
Convicts admitted into hospital	M	11192	25531	22328	12319	25991
	F	842	827	1094	1290	1246
No. of Convicts died	M	107	534	435	433	529
	F	9	18	17	17	30
No. of Convicts escaped	M	24	15	14	5	13
	F	–	–	–	–	–
No. of Convicts executed	M	6	13	12	6	5
	F	–	–	–	–	–

Over the years, the marriages among the convict descendants, 'Local Borns' show that there was no notion of hypergamy and that under pressure of surrounding conditions, caste had to be set aside in marriages and could only be maintained by ignoring the caste of the mother. This casteless and egalitarian group has only religious divisions—Hindu, Muslim, Christian, etc. These divisions are stratified.

Details of population according to the religion-wise distribution in Andaman on 31 March, 1906 are shown on next page:

TABLE

Religion-wise Distribution

Category	*Christians*		*Hindus*		*Muslims*		*Buddhists*		*Others*		*Total*	
	M -	F	M -	F	M -	F	M -	F	M -	F	M -	F
Civil	58	-	38	-	10	-	1	-	-	-	107	-
Military	155	-	202	-	157	-	-	-	3	-	517	-
Marine	12	-	-	-	2	-	-	-	-	-	14	-
Police	2	-	382	-	211	-	-	-	-	-	595	-
Free Resident*	22	58	636	552	80	161	3	2	4	4	845	777
Convicts	37	-	7657	440	3676	251	2460	8	151	16	13981	715
Convicts released	-	-	8	2	3	-	-	-	-	-	11	2
Children	37	34	498	408	194	157	4	1	5	3	738	603
Total	**323**	**92**	**9421**	**1402**	**4433**	**569**	**2468**	**11**	**163**	**23**	**16808**	**2097**

* The free population included traders from India and Burma, domestic servants and voluntary settlers (Census, 1911).

Occupations

In 1921, when a decision was announced to abolish the settlement, 1168 convicts out of 11532 were self- supporters but in December, 1926 out of total convict population of 7740, there were 2105 self-supporters drawing wages from the government and 2272 living on agriculture and other activities.[9]

Again within the next ten years from 1931 to 1941, there had been a rapid growth of population because of sanctioning tickets of leave to the convicts and allowing them to send for their families from the mainland or marry the local female convicts. Thus the population rose from 17814 in 1921 to 21316 in 1941 and subsequently a sharp rise in female population from 2263 to 6444 was marked.

For the next three decades from 1930, the policy of colonization and development of the Andaman settlement continued and the number of prisoners during this period varied from 5604 to 6537.[10] Finally after reoccupation by the British from the clutches of Japan in 1945, the penal settlement was abolished and the convicts were allowed to repatriate to the Indian jails and nearly 4000 ex-convicts repatriated to the mainland at the government expense.

After the abolition of the penal settlement in 1945, the total population in Andaman was reduced to 14000 and those who stayed back in Andaman were mostly the descendants of the convicts, usually known as 'Local Borns' who knew no other home than Andaman. It was one of the main considerations which led the Government of India to continue the penal settlement even after the declaration to abolish it in 1921. Moreover, to facilitate them, in 1926, a regulation was passed under which grants of land with scope for development on a tenure which may extend to 60 years, could be offered. The occupancy rights could be given to those who tilled even small holdings.[11]

During the tenure of Colonel Ferrar as Superintendent of penal settlement, Port Blair, the Jail rules were liberalized and self- supporter tickets were issued more liberally. During the period (1923-31), comparatively large homogeneous communities of Moplas, Bhantus, Burmans, etc., were formed. Eventually the local born society became a wonderful mélange of turbulent Pathans of North West Frontier Province, orthodox Brahmins of Uttar Pradesh, sentimental Bengalis, and soft-natured Dravidians of South India.

Under the benevolent administration of Col. Ferrar, the economic framework of the convict settlers went through a lot of changes. Livelihood index of the people also changed. Though agriculture formed the main occupation, the new avenues of the government jobs diverted more than 50 per cent of these people to such jobs resulting in decline in the relative importance of agriculture.

According to the Census of 1931, the following figures state the relative importance of major occupations.

Agriculture	-	40%
Rural Crafts	-	2.9%
Fishing	-	0.7%
Trade	-	4.6%
Govt. Jobs	-	53.8%

The above figures clearly show that a great decline in the agricultural occupation gave rise to an unbalanced economy.

Interestingly enough, the 1951 Census shows a further decline in the agricultural occupation and the break-up of the total population is as follows:

Labour (Skilled and semi-skilled)	-	33%
Agriculture and Plantation	-	29%
Office works, Trade and Commerce	-	38%

Hence the liberal policy of Col. Ferrar has made the local people more conscious about their well-being and led them to the path of economic development. As a result of these developments following the policies of Col. Ferrar, he may be regarded as the architect of the Local Born society.

Local Born Association

During the Commissionership of Richard Temple (1894-1903), Colonel Douglas (1903-20) and Colonel Beadon (1920-23), the Local Born people got moral support and other facilities to enable them to be united. Consequently 'Local Born Association' was formed in 1921 at the aegis of Col. Beadon to safeguard the interest of the local people and he became the first President of the Association. Khan Sahib Nawab Ali of Port Blair, retired Veterinary Asst. Surgeon happened to be the first Indian President amongst the Local Borns.

The objectives of the Association were as follows:

1) to organize the Local Born Community.
2) to uplift the socio-economic condition of the local people.
3) to protect their interest for allotment of land.
4) to secure employment and reservation of seats for professional courses anywhere in India.
5) to develop feelings of brotherhood.
6) to eradicate social evils from the society.
7) to look after the well-being and advancement of the local born community.

During the Second World War, after the fall of Rangoon, when the Japanese invasion to the Andaman and Nicobar Islands was imminent, the defence mechanism of the region was reduced to 'no-defence'. The British realized that their existence in the mainland was synonymous with the safety of India.

On March 1, 1942, following the order of General Wavell, the Gorkha Battalion was withdrawn from the islands and sent back to the mainland leaving the whole islands without any defence. Sadder is the fact that most of the Europeans, along with prominent civilians left Andaman in a frenzy and the fate of the local people was thrown at the mercy of the Japanese occupying army. Only a few higher-ups among the local people such as,

Ramakrishna, Durga Prasad, Narayan Rao, etc., were placed on government duties to run the administration in the absence of the British officials.

The bloody orgy of the Japanese rule started with the inhuman killing of a chivalrous young man Zulfiquar Ali, alias Sunny and went on till the reoccupation by the British in 1945. During the bloody period after Japanese diabolic rule, though the peace and tranquility of the islands was ruptured and the life of the "Andaman Indians" was put in disquietude yet the local born people did not surrender to Japanese atrocities since their arrival on 23 March, 1942.

In the first week of April, 1942, a Peace Committee was formed under the chairmanship of Haji Subhan Ali. Peace and order of Andaman was maintained mostly by the Peace Committee.

When Netaji Subhash Chandra Bose paid an official visit as the Head of the Andaman and Nicobar Islands on 29 December 1942, a public meeting was arranged on Gymkhana ground at Port Blair where the local people assembled to render a standing ovation to the firebrand leader. On that occasion, Ramakrishna, the Chairman of the Andaman Branch of Indian Independence League gave a welcome address and presented a purse of Rs. 10,000/- on behalf of the local people to Netaji.[12]

Again on 31 December 1942, against the disapprobation and disincentive efforts of the Japanese authorities, a meeting was organized in honour of Netaji at the Browning club, later renamed as Netaji Club near Aberdeen bazar where all local born people assembled to listen to him. That day too Ramakrishna handed over a sum of Rs. 5000/- to Netaji on behalf of local people as a token of integrity to the Azad Hind Government. Among the local people, Master Kessar Das was honoured by Netaji for his wonderful voice to sing patriotic songs to welcome Netaji.

Even during the nightmarish days under the Japanese rule over the islands, the moribund local people, though tortured terribly, did not loose heart. Some of them started schools and other social services to boost up the morale of the islanders.

The Association continued somehow till 1951. In 1954, K.R. Ganesh, a young trade union leader of Andaman took the rein of the Local Born Association and reorganized it with renewed vigour. He renamed it as 'Andamanian Association'[13] He also published the first ever journal from Port Blair "Hamari Awaz" in order to organize the local youths and give vent to the sentiment of the Local Borns. Under his leadership, mass rallies and demonstrations were organized to protest against the settlement of refugees from East Pakistan. The wild rumour that the islands, the homeland of the Local Borns being designed to be an appendage of West Bengal, fanned up the aggressive temperament of the local born people and K.R. Ganesh could successfully exploit the situation to organize the people under the banner of 'Andamanian Association'.

To explain the then social and political condition of Andaman, the Census of 1951 comments: "An impression was painfully apparent sometime ago that these islands belong only to the 'local born' people and the settlers are interlopers. But this is gradually dying out. In fact the term 'settler' used to denote only displaced persons settled there is a misnomer as all non-tribal people in the Andamans are settlers—the difference is only the point of time of settlement".[14]

However, due to their vehement protest and ostensible reluctance, the refugee settlement in South Andaman was stopped and the movement of the 'Andamanian Association' remained defunct for a couple of years.

Again during the Presidentship of John M. Lobo from 1979-1990, the activities of the Association resumed and turned emphatic on 20 August, 1980 when a mass rally was organized on behalf of the Association for the redressal of their legitimate demands, i.e., allotment of house sites, prevention of encroachment, restriction on influx of outsiders, etc.

On 9 June, 1990, the Association sent several representations to the Prime Minister, the concerned Ministers and to the Lt. Governor, AndaNico Islands, containing a charter of demands i.e., reservation of seats for local born students in M.B.B.S., Dental and Veterinary Surgeon, Engineering and Agriculture. Significantly the thrusts were given on three cardinal points—to check the influx of outsiders, to oppose the reservation of posts for scheduled caste and to regularize the excess/encroached land recorded till 31 December, 1961. Though the Local Born Association tried hard, the influx of outsiders continued unabated. Indeed, over the years Local Borns have been outnumbered by the migrants.[15]

Long back in 1936, Raizada Hansraj addressed the members of the Local Born Association and called them as descendants of the freedom fighters of 1857. Though it was just denying the verity, the local people were inspired and instigated. Being overwhelmed, the local people demanded certain percentage of reservations in government services for them, grant of more facilities in trade and other professions and more scopes for the education of their children along with the opening of a girl's school at Port Blair. Mohammed Yamin Khan also laid stress on improving the lot of the local born people by providing them more facilities for suitable employment.[16]

The prevailing social environment in the penal settlement in early days was innocuous but peculiar as the free people embarked in these islands on various reasons, looked askance at the local born people extending no sympathy and instead, looked down upon them as if they were ostracized. Even they did not mix with them nor develop any marital relations with the descendants of convicts. But over the years, insurmountable distance from the mainland India, close contacts among themselves, compulsion of undergoing a rigorous life, absence of religious diktats forced them to defy the stigmas of caste, creed and provincialism and a unique society was in the offing.

Indeed, out of 504 districts in India and Burma, 347 districts were represented among the islands, immigrants, the convicts. The population of these immigrants as it stood in 1931, drawn from the various provinces of India was as follows:

Province	*Number of State-wise population*
Bengal	947
Bombay	495
Bihar/Orissa	619
Central Province	426
Madras	2727
Punjab	1983
United Province	2431
N.W.F.P.	397

It is interesting to note that in 1901, the people of the penal settlement belonging to the different provinces of India and Burma, spoke as many as fortyfive regional languages in their homes but in due course, relinquishing all barriers of their own, adopted simple Hindustani which has become the lingua franca in the islands. Thus this common language acted upon all diversities as cementing force and did the foundation of a unique ethereal society. In some respects, free population of Andaman was better than their counterparts on the mainland.

With the passage of time, the 'Local Borns' got eminence and eventually played a vital role in the making of a unique society in which this little community of roughly 10,000 souls, according to the Census of 1951, has cut across all barriers of social diversities free inter-marriage irrespective of caste or religion has gone on with perfect ease and without the slightest shock or violence to the general social structure contributing considerably to the growth of the population.

Indeed, religion to these people is completely a personal matter and is not allowed to interfere with the secular life of the community. This process of integration of a variety of territorial and religious groups has produced a most interesting community of people with a remarkable quickness of intellect and practical sense. This great fusion has been largely facilitated by the prevalence of Hindustani as the common language of the people. These islands are witnessing perhaps the birth of the organic essence of Indian humanity.

In the Provincial Gazetteers of India, 1908, it is stated, "...it would be an entire error to suppose that the better elements in human nature are not exhibited and many convict descendants have shown themselves upright, capable, hardworking, honest and self-respecting. On the whole considering their parentage, the 'local born' population is of a much higher type than might be expected".

Indeed the present generation is honestly proud to become the scions of convicts who had been in these islands and created a new world of their own spending every drop of their blood and sweat, forgetting their past, renouncing the barrier of caste, creed and customs and regenerating a new society based on human values. Throughout this long soul-cleansing journey, they have tried to regain solemn values of life echoing peace and prosperity. This has given birth to a truly egalitarian society.

Unfortunately that society till recent past lamented over identity crisis feeling themselves rootless or scared being outnumbered. A section of them has even raised their voice in order to desecrate their own progenitors with a view to implicating themselves to the ancestry of the freedom fighters but over the years, they have realized the reality.

The young generations of the lineage of the convicts settled for good in Andaman, feel proud of being the local borns. One among many is Dr. Rashida Iqbal who is presently the Curator of the National Memorial Cellular Jail, Port Blair where her father had been once incarcerated on being transported on the charge of murder. After securing the ticket-of-leave, he settled in Andaman. Begum Rashida feels always elated while ruminating the past memories of the sepia-tinted days and is obviously proud on showing the muniment of her father's only invaluable possessions, the holy 'Quran' wrapped in a black cotton cloth and his metallic driving licence issued from Peshawar. Her eyes glitter with delight while she utters her allegiance to the local borns, "I do not hesitate to introduce myself as the proud daughter of a convict".

What Rashida boasts of, is now-a-days verbalized by each one of her generation. This is the veracity of their relentless striving to eminence by dint of their perseverance and erudition.

In fact, the people of these islands, especially the 'local borns' are setting an example as to how people of different origins can compose their differences and live in social harmony. It is a unique community which has its own cultural identity being evolved in the islands itself.

"The evolution that is peacefully proceeding in these islands might be termed as a laboratory carrying out an experiment on an all-India basis showing how a secular state is being successfully founded".[17] It is heartening to note that the conflicting phenomena of the mainland resulting in the tensions between peoples of different ethnological origins, religions and castes are significantly absent in these islands which represent a classical example of the religious bonhomie and communal harmony.

K.R. Ganesh, the Young Turk of the territory and the first elected Member of the Parliament rightly remarked, "We have a soul in the islands".

Indeed, the Andaman society is completely free from the viruses of communal strife, caste-divide, criminalization of politics, the other social evils eating vociferously the contemporary society of the mainland India.

Over the last hundred years or more of migration to Andaman, the migrants with divergent cultural, social and linguistic backgrounds, irrespective of their homelands or races, have really evolved a society which can be precisely termed as the cultural pot-pourri of the country.

In these islands, it is possible to sample cross sections of humanity which are not available anywhere else. The "local borns" are in many ways a legacy of the penal settlement and the champion of national integration. Hence it would be wrong to think of these islands as a part of an archaic world condemning it as *Kalapani*, rather it would be wise to conceive that the complex population structure epitomizes the essence of Mini India. Of course, everyone should be conscious that the agony of losing cultural identity is an emotional brouhaha which may turn to belligerence to blight the commingleness among themselves if it is not toned down and appeased.

ENDNOTES

1. National Archives, New Delhi, Home Deptt. Public Branch., Proceedings. No. 1-12, 1 April, 1864.
2. Captain Merk, W.R.H., Head of Administration, Penal Settlement, Port Blair, 9 April, 1904.
3. N.A.I., Home Deptt. Port Blair Branch, A. Proceedings. No. 28-40, July 1906.
4. Ibid.
5. Captain Man, H., Superintendent of the Penal Settlement, Port Blair from March, 1868 to March, 1871
6. State Archives, Port Blair, Letter No. 1337. dt. 31 Oct, 1871 of Superintendent of Port Blair Settlement to the Govt. of India.
7. Census Report, 1951, Appendix A.
8. Provincial Gazetteer of India, 1908
9. N.A.I., Home Deptt. Resolution No. 20/26, Jails 27 February, 1926
10. N.A.I., Legislative Proceedings. vol. iv, 1935, p 3030 & Debate of the Council of State, 11 September, 1933
11. N.A.I., New Delhi, Home Deptt. File No. 20/26 Jails.
12. "Black Days in the Andaman & Nicobar Islands," by Rabin Roychowdhury. Pub: Manas Publications, N.D., p 151-159.
13. Source: *The Hindu*, June 12, 1967, quoted in the *Andaman Aaj Tak*, February, 2004,
14. Census Repot, 1951, Appendix A.
15. ANNUAL REPORT of Local Born Association, signed by N.A. Jagdish Narayan, General Secretary.
16. N.A.I., New Delhi, Home Deptt. File No. 119/1/36 Jails.
17. "The Andaman Story", by Iqbal Singh, p 303.
18. Administrative Report of Andaman & Nicobar Islands, 1947-48.

16

EPILOGUE

While the colonization scheme resulted into an influx of population on a large scale and that led to clearance of forest land proportionately, it was not fully realized that removing the forest cover may be damaging as it threatens to reduce the islands to waste land and to endanger the existence of the human beings who inhabit there.

During the era of colonization, the policy-makers sitting in the ivory towers ignored the ecology of the sea-girdled islands and due to their ignorance of various climatic and edaphic factors which these islands are subjected to, the islanders may become victims of their policies.

According to Sir Harry Champion, a renowned world authority on tropical forestry, the forests of these islands are unique and of highest scientific significance as they are still virgin and may be the last bastion of the precious gene resources of rare species of flora and fauna. Indeed, territory is aptly ascribed as 'a living museum of planet earth'.

In the same context, Dr. ND McVean, an IUCN (International Union of Conservation of Nature) expert, visited these islands in February-March, 1976 on a study tour specially to assess the impact of deforestation on the island ecosystem and to formulate guidelines for land use and conservation. He along with other experts advised the halt on clearance of forests to continue and to carry out a land use capability survey with the help of aerial photographs to define the various uses of land taking into consideration the climatic, edaphic and configuration factors.

Dr. McVean also suggested that certain areas of virgin forests were indicated to form 'nature reserves' or 'biosphere reserves' so that these may serve as the gene pool reserves for the threatened species of plants and animals.

In these islands, canopies of luxuriant foliages prattled with a chorus of chirping birds, humming insects and cacophony of monkeys vibrant with brilliant tropical flowers and orchids extend shades and shelters to the wild cats, iguanas, green lizards, wild pigs and deer. The creeks are infested with many varieties of snakes and crocodiles. In all, there are 250 species of birds, 46 species of mammals and more than 500 species of fish are known and need to be reserved. Along with human settlements, all these flora and fauna should be preserved.

Nature Reserves in Bay Islands

As a first step for studying the eco-system of these islands, proposals have been approved by the Government of India for the creation of biosphere reserves to study all those rare species.

Under the Central Agricultural Research Institute (CARI), a biosphere reserve has been developed at its own Sipighat centre to culture germ plasma of edible fruits like coconut. Centers for gene pool have been set up in small islands like Redskin, Jolly Buoy. The same in Wandoor and Turmugli Island have already been functioning with the financial assistance from FAO and World Bank.

The Mahatma Gandhi Marine National Park at Wandoor, 29 kms from Port Blair has been established to develop and preserve coral reefs, exotic varieties of coloured coral fish and other marine species. The Park provides a rich and varied habitat for endangered marine animals which range from the smallest zoo plankton to the large sea mammals like Dolphins. This also provides congenial atmosphere for nesting grounds of sea turtles like Green Sea, Leatherback Hawk Bill and Olive Ridley.

Ritchie's archipelago has been declared as 'Dugong Sanctuary' and it is presumed that not only Dugongs but sea turtles, dolphins, crocodiles, etc., all will be safe in the creeks and coastal waters around the archipelago. Within the sanctuary, land flora and fauna will also be saved.

The protection of wild life in these islands has engaged the attention of the Andaman and Nicobar Administration since long. In 1949 by a notification, killing of some species like Norcondum Hornbill, Oriols, etc., has been prohibited under the Wild Life Protection Act, 1972, which came into force with effect from 31 January, 1974. In due course, some more species i.e., Dugong, Giant Rubber Crab and Megapode have been declared protected. Later on, destruction or collection of corals, turbo, Trocus, etc., are banned. Thus the wild life of endemic species has been preserved and biosphere reserves are developed to protect and regenerate the endangered species. .

Jaques Cousteau, the legendary French environmentalist, recommended that national marine sanctuaries be located at Norcondum, South Sentinel and Ritchie Islands which can be a prolific breeding ground for sharks. These waters are rich in shells and corals. The Turbo and Trochus are in great demand overseas. The flesh and cholestrol-free blood of turtles are also in great demand.

Thrusts on Agriculture

Considering the growth of population and acute shortage of food due to poor production, in 1987, the integrated farming systems have been introduced in Andaman in order to boost up the production of crops as well as to ensure steady income. Side by side, the farmers have been inspired to adopt the modern technology in cultivation.

The pilot experiments conducted by the CARI in the last few years, have demonstrated that 2-3 crops can be taken from the same field in a year provided proper technology is adopted. Following the integrated farming system, agriculture, animal husbandry, fisheries, vegetables, horticulture and plantation crops are raised under a system where these enterprises not only work to mutual advantage but also provide maximum benefits. Such a system automatically serves as an insurance against crop failures due to vagaries of weather or other causes.

To cite an example, various attempts have been made at cultivating imported cash crops but the overall effort seemed unpromising in the case of rubber plantation on Katchal Islands where 10,000 acres of forest were felled and replaced with rubber seedlings. This was more than eight years old and ready for tapping but arrangements for labour and smoke drying were still unavailable so the rubber trees remained unexploited. Another 10 hectares had been planted with Nigerian red oil palm at Katchal and Little Andaman which were bearing fruits but for want of proper arrangement to recover either fruits or oil, the scheme has resulted in a total loss.

In these islands, there are about 9000 farming families, out of which about 25 per cent farm families own 2-4 hectares of lands, the other 27 per cent own 0 to 6 hectares of land, and 50 per cent of the land-holding of the farmers are valley lands and the remaining are hilly areas. The land utilization plan should be so drawn that more than one or even all the four components, viz., agriculture, animal husbandry, fisheries and horticulture form part of the farming system that a farmer follows. Unfortunately these were not conceived so farmers suffered and lost interest.

Even thorough soil survey has not been conducted so that two to three crops of paddy can be raised. Maize can also be grown successfully; barley and gram will require trials for introduction. Pulse, oilseeds, spices, vegetables and potatoes can also be grown but all in vain.

For the success of integrated farming, the farmers should have training in different aspects of such a system. For this purpose, workshops were organized earlier on from 14 August to 28 August, 1986 under the auspices of Ministry of Agriculture and Rural Development at Port Blair by CARI but no follow-ups were made.

Indeed, agriculture is the mainstay of the developmental activities of these islands. The economy of the settlers is directly and indirectly linked with the development of agriculture so the selection of land for clearance on the basis of capability, taking up adequate soil conservation measures, would be the governing principles to stabilize the economy of the settlers.

Precisely, the ultimate objectives to adopt modernization of agriculture are to achieve higher production, better standard of living and better economic stability. Above all, self-sufficiency would be the ultimate goal behind all economic exercises. In reality achievement is far nigh and improvement in farming system as well as of the financial condition of farmers is not remarkable.

Forestry and Plantation

Prime Minister Indira Gandhi expressed her concern about the ecological condition of these islands and forthwith a multidisciplinary study team was constituted to have a thorough review of the feasibility of the different projects with special reference to the effects of deforestation on the islands. Pending such a review, Indira Gandhi ordered a complete halt on clearance of land for fresh settlers or for commercial plantations.

Dr. McVean rightly observed that Andaman and Nicobar Islands were essentially forest terrain unsuitable for large scale agricultural settlement or agriculture based enterprises and the economy of the islands must be based on forestry and forest projects if severe damage to the islands' environment was to be avoided.

Moreover, he observed that immigration for land settlement as well as further allocations of land for second generation of settlers or other residents was considered inadvisable.

However, awareness is growing and deforestation has been banned on principle. A halt has also been called on further settlements. The Techno Economic survey of the Andaman and Nicobar Islands made by the National Council of Applied Economic Research revealed that Andaman is one of the most overstudied regions of India. Unfortunately the deforestation continued and thrusts on afforestation as well as on plantation were not sincerely exerted. The Rubber Board runs the rubber farms at Katchal for the Rehabilitation Ministry on scientific lines but they are not necessarily on commercial lines. The NCAER suggested creating a plantation corporation in AndaNico, but the proposal was fraught with difficulties.

Ultimately 'Andaman-Nicobar Islands Forest and Plantation Corporation' has been formed after much ado with the objective to achieve the annual harvesting of 120,000 cubic meters of timber from Little Andaman and North Andaman where infrastructural facilities have already developed adequately. Under the Corporation a prospective project has been chalked out to generate an employment potential of 71,000 man-days of skilled workers and 630,00 man-days of unskilled workers.

Moreover, Andaman with 80 per cent, though doubtful, forest cover has almost reached the saturation point so far as its carrying capacity is concerned. If more and more people are allowed to settle down, it would lead to serious strains on land, water, electricity and sewage disposal systems and the consequence would be catastrophic. So it is an immediate need to check the swarming population into these islands.

Fisheries

In AndaNico Islands, there is tremendous potential of fisheries development but want of infrastructure, dearth of fund and habitual fishermen, that sector has not been exploited properly.

For the first time and probably the last time, a private fishing corporation named Andaman Marine Development Corporation Ltd. was established in 1947 for the exploitation of the fisheries both in the littoral and deeper waters and also in creeks and estuaries but the Corporation survived only for 9 months due to lack of knowledge of local conditions and heavy expenditure in operations. In 1949, a fisheries research unit was established to gather information on the fish fauna, fishing grounds, etc. Mr. Robert of Singapore was given a licence for fishing in the waters around these islands on condition that he would give complete tidings about the catches, fish fauna, fishing grounds, etc., but this too was not fruitful.

Settlement of Fishermen

Under these circumstances, the settlement of seagoing fishermen from the mainland, especially from Andhra Pradesh was considered very essential to build up a fishermen population.

The settlement was started in 1957 and till 1976; 86 fisherman families were brought from the mainland. Also in the Fifth Plan, the scheme to develop such colonies was included. Even the migrating fishermen were encouraged to settle in these islands.

According to the settlement plan, each family would get Rs. 2000/- for house building and Rs. 2500/- to purchase fishing equipments. This amount was half as loan, half as grant. Besides, Rs. 900/- were given to buy utensils and for passage money and also to cover subsistence allowance @ Rs. 75/- per month per family for six months.

Of course, this amount was not sufficient to acquire all the essential requisites to catch fish all the year round. So instead of giving money, they should have been provided with a dingy and all fishing gear needed to catch fish from the next day of their arrival in the island. Moreover, steps should have been taken for the proper marketing of fish and to assure reasonable price for their catches so that they can be inspired to go to further fishing.

However, the settlement plan though sounds optimistic, the efforts proved futile because many of the fishermen settlers have taken to agriculture and fishing has become secondary to them. This is due to the fact that they are not able to make out a reasonable living by fishing alone because the cost of living in Andaman is too high.

The exploitation of fishery resources in and around the AndaNico Islands cannot be achieved in a piecemeal manner. Only in October, 1971 the Ministry of Agriculture and

Irrigation setup a unit of the off-shore fishing station, now called Exploratory Fishery Project at Port Blair. The development of fisheries did not get sufficient attention for want of qualified hands. The post of a Director of Fisheries was created only in October, 1975 and at least on paper, the development of fisheries in these islands has been given high priority. In reality, emphasis has been given on the elevation of posts of the officials but not on the settlement of the fishermen. Moreover, local youths are not interested to adopt the adventure fishing and deep sea-fishing. Only if they are motivated to opt for the fishing profession duly trained to operate long liners suited for tuna and tuna-like fish, available in plenty in Andaman Sea, the project of the fisheries development will be a success. Besides, vessels having bulk freezing facilities, not merely trawlers, may be provided to catch fish in the deep sea so that at times, it may serve as mother factory-ship.

However, the following features in a nutshell may be considered for the future planning in pisciculture in the islands which no other areas in India can aptly provide. The salient features are shown according to the following areas:

(a) Tuna Fisheries which is abundant in these islands.
(b) Pearl culture which can be developed successfully.
(c) Adventure fishing and deep sea fishing which can generate employment and fetch foreign currency.

Exclusive Economic Zone (EEZ)

With the development of marine culture, the strategic importance of the islands should be kept in mind. The value of these islands has to be assessed according to the significance; they command in the international arena of Indian Ocean strategy and inter-action of Big Power's manipulations.

India has an Exclusive Economic Zone (EEZ) of 2015409 sq. miles and is the largest of the Indian Ocean EEZs. About one third of India's total EEZ lies around the AndaNico

Islands. Hence, there are great potentials to develop Indian Fishing Industry in these islands.

Further the principle of 200 mile EEZ around these islands adds another 3000 sq kms. which is almost 38 times the land area of these territories and has been earmarked not only for exploring oil, gas and minerals but also for the need to ensure that smuggling, poaching, gun running and narco terrorism does not become the way of life of this part of India.

Indeed, EEZ has become a strategic force builder. Hence a new dimension is needed in defence strategy which calls for a thrust to the exploration and exploitation of the seas and sea-bed for development purposes without disturbing the fragile ecosystem and instead utilizes defence requirements to help the growth of the economy of this region.

The AndaNico should not be viewed as far-flung island territory but as an integral part of India with the added advantage of being able to accept and sustain the spectrum of nation-building activities and to act simultaneously as a geographical tripwire for sea-borne adventurism and also as a vehicle for national development.

While considering the development of these islands it must be kept in mind that one should not disturb the traditional, religious and cultural feelings of local population. It may create internal instability and that may pose a great threat. Communal or intra-tribal tensions may destabilize the integrity of the island groups and external powers may take benefit of this. Therefore, encouragement or indulgence should not be given to any disintegrating activities for political or economical gain in these islands in future.

The future well-being of the islanders linked to their social and economic integration and government's policies, should be framed to promote it by all means. At times it seems that the entry and influx of large number of mainlanders into these islands since 1949 and the accompanying social and cultural influences at work have tended to weaken the trends towards assimilation of various ethnic groups among themselves. The geographical barriers to integration of the island's inhabitants are another point that should not be ignored.

Today the territory has gone a long way from its sordid past and is shaping itself, however slowly and staggeringly into a green paradise, evolving to become a Mini-India. It has both a heritage and a future. With vision and proper planning this territory can be made to blossom into an asset to the nation's economy, besides being a much sought after destination for tourists.

The discovery of oil in the Andaman Sea is an event of great consequence and the tourist potentiality leads to great prospect. The islands have perennial sea routes, nature's gift to us at no cost and only investment we have to make is on shipping and marine services which would be relatively modest in comparison with the magnitude of development inputs that India makes through her five year plans.

The Islands Development Authority of India should plan to develop self-sufficiency in the islands at least for basic necessities. The fishing industry, industries based on marine wealth, forest and agro based industries should be given priority, and appropriate technology which will help in rapid progress of these islands, should be sorted out. Local skills and manpowers are to be utilized. While doing this, ecology and environment of the region should be left unaffected. So far the arrangements have been ushered in smoothly and the adjustments are made sensibly, but the territory is getting overburdened due to unrestricted flow of people from the mainland and presently the entry of even a few thousand outsiders may disturb the ecological balance awfully. Hence proper means and ways are to be sorted out to restrict the influx so that the unity that has been forged over the years should not be disturbed and spoiled.

Moreover, while planning for development to make the islands economically stable, socially idyllic and culturally holistic, the aphoristic comment of the former Prime Minister Indira Gandhi should be remembered that "neither resettlement nor development should be made an excuse to uproot tribal inhabitants and any disturbances may threaten their survival. They are important anthropologically and the forests are valuable economically".

In pursuance of this observation and direction of the former Prime Minister, Dr. McVean after in-depth study on the impact of deforestation on the environment of these islands, inter alia, recommended the continuance of moratorium on farther deforestation till a comprehensive land use capability survey through aerial photography is completed and suggested wide spread extension of crop husbandry and soil conservation.

Hence, deforestation for whatsoever needs and the transfer of heavily forested land to either Defence or industries should be resisted and carefully judged on the impact on each case. Even to implement the ambitious Master Plan for a Greater Port Blair that requires random felling of trees, the warning of the formar Prime Minister as well as the caution of ecologists should seriously be kept in mind or it may lead to disaster.

Considering all these factors, the AndaNico Administration should be careful while planning for development. Apparently amity and cohesion is felt among the populace, yet reluctance surfaces while there is conflict of interests. Though the settlement has been stopped, until and unless the influx of outsiders is restricted, this specious unison will make room for deterrence.

APPENDIX I

Small islands available for colonization or for other use

Name of the island	Flat land for paddy (acres)	Sloping land for paddy (acres)	Garden and grazing (acres)	Cocoanut or other plantation fodder (acres)	Total (acres)
1	2	3	4	5	6
Land Fall	200	Not explored.	... ...	...	200
Smith Island	20	...	...	400	420
Defence Island	...	100	...	700	800
Ranger	...	...	...	600	600
Interview	...	...	...	26000	26000
Anderson	...	...	...	1200	1200
Bennite	...	...	...	1000	1000
North Reef	...	...	...	400	400
Flat Island	...	...	...	100	100
Long Island	...	...	...	3200	3200

contd...

1	2	3	4	5	6
Strait Island	...	20	...	400	420
Kyd	...	40	...	200	240
Tarmugli	900	200	300	400	1800
Boat Island	...	...	600	...	600
Alexendri	100	100	200	600	1000
Redskin	50	50	100	400	600
Hobdey	300	50	200	300	850
		Total	**78,080 acres.**		

Locality (Island)	Flat land for paddy (acres)	Sloping land for terraced paddy (acres)	Grazing and garden land (acres)	Cocoanut land (acres)	Total (acres)
North Andaman	7490	13500	14290	4430	3971
Middle Andaman	25035	28600	13600	4525	73760
Barrtong	2160	7500	5600	2040	17300
South Andaman	3100	5550	4200	1300	14150
Total	**37785**	**55150**	**37690**	**12295**	**1092520**

Appendix II

Analysis of Andamans area

(MAINLY ESTIMATED)

Area of Islands 2,500 Square Miles

Description	Area Sq. Miles
Old settlements & secondary jungle	40
Jarawa Reserve (Hostile tribes)	190
Sentinel Island (Tribal area)	20
Little Andaman	290
Inland waterways (Creeks)	80
Unproductive forest	100
Unworkable islands	60
Mangrove forest	300
Accessible timber forest	1420
Total	**2500**

Appendix III

Programme for clearing for Colonisation and for regeneration area in acres

Year	South Andaman Colonization Shoal Bay		Regeneration	Middle Andaman Colonization		Regeneration	North Andaman Colonization		Regeneration	Coloniza-tion	Regeneration	Total
	East	West		Rangat Betapur	Browlington to Yoljig		Tugapur and Webi					
1949-50	1200	200	1000	1500	...	1000	...	...	...	2900	2000	4900
1950-51	1000	400	1000	1000	...	1500	...	...	...	2400	2500	4900
1951-52	800	700	1500	500	500	1500	750	250	500	3500	3500	7000
1952-53	...	1000	1500	500	1000	1500	1000	500	500	4000	3500	7500
1953-54	...	1000	1500	500	1000	1500	1250	750	1000	4500	4000	8500
1954-55	...	...	1500	100	1500	1500	1750	750	1000	5000	4000	9000

Note: The estimated total to be cleared in 1954-55 is 9000 acres. This should be increased to 12000 as soon as possible.

APPENDIX IV

Names of Administrators since the founding of the territory (1858-1981)

Name	Tenures	
	From	To
Dr. James Pettison Walker	1858	(First Superintendent of Jail, Port Blair)
Captain Haughton	1859	
R. L. Tytler	1862	
Lt. Col. Ford	1864	
Colonel H Man	1868	
Major General DM Stewart General Sir Donald Martin	1871	(First Chief Commissioner)
Stewart CGB GCSI CIE	1872	1875
Major General CA Barwell IA	1875	1879
Col. T Cadell VC IA	1879	1892
Col. N.H. Horsford IA	1892	1894
Col. Sir Richard C Temple IA	1894	1903
Mr. F.E. Tuson	1903	1904
Mr. W.R.H. Merk CSI	1904	1906
Lt. Col. H.A. Browning IA	1906	1913
Lt. Col. M.W. Douglas IA	1913	1920
Col. H.C. Beadon IA	1920	1923
Lt. Col. M.L. Ferrar KCSI CSI CIE IA	1923	1931

contd...

Mr. J.W. Smyth I C S	1931	1935
Sir W. A. Cosgrave CIE ICS	1935	1938
Sir C.E. Waterfall CIE JP ICS	1938	1942 Taken prisoner by Japanese.

Japanese Occupation 23rd March, 1942 to 6th October, 1945

Name	Tenures	
	From	To
Mr. N.K. Patterson OBE ICS	1945	1947
Shri I. Majid I.C.S.	1947	1949
Shri A. K. Ghosh I.C.S	1949	1953
Shri S. N. Maitra I.C.S.	1953	1956
Shri C. Ramachandran I.A.S.	1956	
Shri T. G. N. Ayyar I.C.S.	1956	1958
Shri M. V. Rajwade I.A.S.	1958	1961
Shri B N Maheshwari IAS	1961	1965
Shri B. L. Chak. I.A.S.	1965	1966
Shri Mahavir Singh I.A.S.	1966	1968
Shri H. S. Butalia I.A.S.	1968	1972
Shri Harmander Singh I.A.S	1972	1975
Shri S. M. Krishnatry I.A.S.	1975	1979
Shri S. L. Sharma I.A.S.	1979	onwards
Shri M. L. Kampani	1982	1985 (First Lt. Governor)
Shri T. S. Oberoi	1985	1990
Shri R. S. Dayal	1990	1993
V. Purushottaman	1993	1996
I. P. Gupta	1996	2001
N. N. Jha	2001	2005
Prof. Ram Kapse	2005	2006

APPENDIX V

D. O. No. 1-732/52

Port Blair,
The 25th October, 1952.

My dear Banerjee,

Thank you for sending me a copy of your D. O. No. 670SB dated the 6th October 1952 to Sen. My reply to the telegram from Chatterji (Joint Secretary, Ministry of Rehabilitation) was as follows:

"YOUR TELEGRAM OF 2ND OCTOBER ABOUT SETTLING FIVE HUNDERD REFUGEE FAMILIES IN ANDAMANS THIS YEAR (.) QUITE IMPOSSIBLE RECEIVE FIVEHUNDRED FAMILIES BY MIDDLE DECEMBER (.) YOUR PROPOSAL THAT REFUGEES LIVE IN TENTS AND RECLAIM LANDS FOR CULTIVAION IMPRACTICAL (.) EXPERIENCE OF SETTLING EAST PAKISTAN DISPLACED FAMILIES IN ANDAMANS SHOWS SUCH PEOPLE INCAPABLE OF CLEARING VIRGIN FORESTS AND TO PUT THEM IN JUNGLES WITHOUT COMMUNICATIONS AND WATER AND OTHER ARRANGEMENTS WILL ONLY MEAN THEIR RETURNING CALCUTTA IMMEDIATELY OR SOON AS MAINTENANCE ALLOWANCES CEASE (.) PARA (.) INDIA GOVERNMENT HAVE ALREADY SANCTIONED LARGE SCHEME SETTLING TWENTY THOUSAND PEOPLE IN ANDAMANS DURING NEXT FIVE YEARS (.) SUGGEST YOU SEND DISPLACED PERSONS ACCORDING THAT PROGRAMME WHICH NOW ABSORBING ALL OUR RESETTLEMENT EFFORTS= ANDAMANS".

As you have pointed out to Sen in your DO of the 6th October, we have been able to take refugees from Bengal only because after the war quite a number of ex-convicts returned to the mainland of India, abandoning their holdings here. These holdings are all reasonably near Port Blair; and refugees could be settled on them without any preliminary preparation. But I am afraid we have very little ready land for allotment now; and in future appreciable areas can be made available only by clearing forests, uprooting roots and stumps and making the land ready for cultivation at considerable cost. The Government of India has sanctioned a scheme under which this Administration will clear 20,000 acres of forests in five years and settle some 4,000 families on the land – not all refugees.

I am afraid Chatterji's suggestion that refugees be put in tents and set to clear their own lands is quite impractical. I have some experience of this, for I have twice tried to get refugees to clear lands for themselves, paying them monthly wages in the meanwhile. In both cases not only has the cost been prohibitive, but also the refugees have found it all but impossible to clear even secondary forests (forests from which the bigger trees have already been removed). Untrained people without the proper equipment will find it impossible to clear jungles and reclaim land for cultivation.

I am afraid the Andamans can do very little to relieve the pressure of refugees in West Bengal: you have many lacs of them on your hands; whereas even over a period of five years we can take at the most twenty thousands. Therefore, ours is really a long term plan for the colonization of the Andamans, not a plan to give immediate relief to West Bengal.

I am sorry to be so discouraging. But it is better to face facts, and not try to do the impossible. To send large numbers of cultivators to the Andamans now will only mean their returning to Calcutta as soon as their maintenance allowances stop; which, while not helping you, will mean wasting large sums of government money.

Yours sincerely,

Sd/-

(A. K. GHOSH)

Chief Commissioner,

A.&N. Islands

Sri H. Banerjee, I.C.S.,
Secretary to the Government of West Bengal,
Refugee Rehabilitation Department,
Writers Buildings,
Calcutta, 1.

Appendix VI

THE INDIAN INDEPENDENCE ACT, 1947

An Act to make provision for the setting up in India of two independent Dominions, to substitute other provisions for certain provisions of the Government of India Act, 1935, which apply outside those Dominions, and to provide for other matters consequential on or connected with the setting up of those Dominions, (18th July 1947).

Be it enacted by the King's most Excellent Majesty, by and with the advice and consent of the Lord Spiritual and Temporal, and Commons, in this present Parliament assembled and by the authority of the same, as follows:

THE NEW DOMINIONS

1. (1) As from the fifteenth day of August, nineteen hundred and forty seven, two independent Dominions shall be set up in India to be known respectively as India and Pakistan.

(2) The said Dominions are hereafter in this Act referred to as 'the new Dominions' and the said fifteenth day of August is hereafter in this Act referred to as 'the appointed day'.

TERRITORIES OF THE NEW DOMINIONS

2. (1) Subject to the provisions of subsections (3) and (4) of this section, the territories of India shall be the territories under the sovereignty of his Majesty which, immediately before the appointed day, were included in British India except the territories which, under subsection (2) of this section, are to be the territories of Pakistan.

(2) Subject to the provisions of subsection (3) and (4) of this section, the territories of Pakistan shall be-

(a) the territories which, on the appointed day, are included in the provinces of East Bengal and West Punjab, as constituted under the two following sections;

(b) the territories which, at the date of the passing of this Act, are included in the Province of Sind and the Chief Commissioner's Province of British Beluchistan: and

(c) if, whether before or after the passing of this Act but before the appointed day, the Governor-General declares that the majority of the valid votes cast in the referendum which, at the date of the passing of this Act, is being or has recently been held in that behalf under his authority in the North-West Frontier Province are in favour of representatives of that Province taking part in the Constituent Assembly of Pakistan, the territories which, at the date of the passing of this Act, are included in that Province.

(3) Nothing in this section shall prevent any area being at any time included or excluded from either of the new Dominions, so, however, that-

(a) no area not forming part of the territories specified in subsection (1) or, as the case may be, subsection (2) of this section shall be included in either Dominion without the consent of that Dominion; and

(b) no area which forms part of the territories specified in the said subsection (1) or, as the case may be, the said subsection (2), or which has after the appointed day been included in either Dominion, shall be excluded from that Dominion without the consent of that Dominion.

(4) Without prejudice to the generality of the provisions of subsection (3) of this section, nothing in this section shall be construed as preventing the accession of India States to either of the new Dominions.

BENGAL AND ASSAM

3\. (1) As from the appointed day–

(a) the Province of Bengal, as constituted under the Government of India Act, 1935, shall cease to exist; and

(b) there shall be constituted in lieu thereof two new provinces, to be known respectively as East Bengal and West Bengal.

(2) If, whether before or after the passing of this Act, but before the appointed day, the Governor-General declares that the majority of the valid votes cast in the referendum which, at

the date of the passing of this Act, is being or has recently been held on that behalf under his authority in the District of Sylhet are in favour of that District forming part of the new Province of East Bengal, then, as from that day, a part of the Province of Assam shall, in accordance with the provisions of subsection (3) of this section, form part of the new Province of East Bengal.

(3) The boundaries of the new Provinces aforesaid and, in the event mentioned in subsection (2) of this section, the boundaries after the appointed day of the Province of Assam, shall be such as may be determined, whether before or after the appointed day, by the award of a boundary commission appointed or to be appointed by the Governor-General on that behalf, but until the boundaries are so determined-

(a) the Bengal Districts specified in the First Schedule to this Act, together with, in the event mentioned in subsection (2) of this section, the Assam District of Sylhet, shall be treated as the territories which are to be comprised in the new Province of East Bengal;

(b) the remainder of the territories comprised at the date of passing of this Act in the Province of Bengal shall be treated as the territories which are to be comprised in the new Province of West Bengal; and

(c) in the event mentioned in subsection (2) of this section, the District of Sylhet shall be excluded from the Province of Assam.

(4) In this section, the expression 'award' means, in relation to a boundary commission, the decisions of the Chairman of that commission contained in this report to the Governor-General at the conclusion of the commission's proceedings.

SHORT TITLE

This Act may be cited as the Indian Independence Act. 1947.

SCHEDULES

FIRST SCHEDULE

BENGAL DISTRICTS PROVISIONALLY INCLUDED IN THE NEW PROVINCE OF EAST BENGAL

In the Chittagong Division: the districts of Chittagong, Noakhali and Tippera.

In the Dacca Division: the districts of Bakarganj, Dacca, Faridpur and Mymensingh.

In the Presidency Division: the districts of Jessore, Murshidabad and Nadia.

In the Rajshahi Division: the districts of Bogra, Dinajpur, Malda, Pabna, Rajshahi and Rangpur.

SECOND SCHEDULE

DISTRICTS PROVISIONALLY INCLUDED IN THE NEW PROVINCE OF WEST PUNJAB

In the Lahore Division: the districts of Gujranwala, Gurdaspur, Lahore, Sheikhupura and Sialkot.

In the Rawalpindi Division: the districts of Attock, Gujrat, Jhelum, Mianwali, Rawalpindi and Shahpur.

In the Multan Division: the districts of Dera Ghazi Khan, Jhang, Lyallpur, Montgomery, Multan and Muzaffargarh.

Bibliography

Unpublished Records with National Archives of India, New Delhi

1. Proceedings of the Government of India in the following branches of the Home Department:

   (a) Port Blair Branch from 1873 to 1947

   (b) Political Branch from July 1907 to 1947

Unpublished Records with Defence Ministry & Others

1. 'Andaman Interlude' – Diary of Major Danis McCarthy.
2. 'The Andaman Islands under Japanese Occupation: 1942-1945' memories of Rama Krishna, Retired Deputy Commissioner worked during the Japanese Occupation at Port Blair.
3. Recorded interviews with the elderly people of Andaman who survived the Japanese occupation.
4. 'History of Japanese Administration in the Andamans' File No. 601/76524 – dispatches by the Allied Intelligence Bureau.

Published Records of the Government of India:

1. Census Report, Andamans and Nicobars, 1901 by Richard Temple
2. Census Report, Andamans and Nicobars, 1911, Vol-ii by R. F. Lowis
3. Census Report, Andamans and Nicobars, 1921, Vol-ii by R. F. Lowis
4. Census Report, Andamans and Nicobars, 1931, Vol-ii by C. J. Bonnington
5. Census Report, Andamans and Nicobars, 1951, Vol-xvii by A. K. Ghose
6. Census Report, Andamans and Nicobars, 1961, Vol-v by S. K. Sharma
7. Appendix O to Census Report, 1921, Page 48-50, Nicobarese Folklore by E. Hart.

8. Appendix E to Census Report, 1951, On the Origin of the Andamanese by Dr. Lidio Cipriani.

9. Appendix E to Census Report, 1951, On the Shompen of Great Nicobar by B. S. Chengappa.

10. Indian Antiquary: January - December, 1819, Vol-xxviii., "Papers relating to the Settlement in the Andaman Islands in the 18th Century", by Richard Temple.

11. Journal of the Royal Geographical Society, article published, "Narrations of an Expedition to Andaman Islands in 1856-62," by F. J. Mouat. 1863, Indian edition, pub. Mittal Publications, N. Delhi -59

12. Selections from Records of Govt. of India, Vol. LXXVII:

    (a) A Short Description of Nicobar by G.B. Hamilton.

    (b) On the Islands of Nancowry and Camorta by R.H. Colebrooke.

    (c) Extract from Voyage of the Austrian Frigate Nobara. –23 February, to 26 March, 1858.

13. "Exploration and Survey of Little Andaman," by M. V. Portman, 1888 vol. 10.

14. Imperial Gazetteers of India, articles published, a) "Hell on Earth" by Col. Wedge Wood, b) "Andaman and Nicobar Islands", by W.S. Molesworth, 1909.

15. Journal of the East India Association "Andaman Penal Settlement 1914." pp. 159-181.

16. The Andaman and Nicobar Information, 1957-1990.

17. Reports on the administration of the Andamans and Nicobars and the Penal Settlement of Port Blair from 1864 to 1866.

18. Yojana, vol. xx, Number 13 & 14, pub. 15 August, 1976.

19. Report on Special Areas Development Programmes, its Schemes and Implementation, Dept. of Rehabilitation in Andaman & Nicobar Islands, March 1972, Port Blair.

20. Report of a Commission on the Organization of the Indian Army, 1959.

21. "Social Panorama of Andaman & Nicobar Islands and Prospect of Anthropological Research" - A. & N. Information, 1965, V. K. Kochar.

22. A note of Insanity, Convict, Marriage, Census 1911, vol.ii, Part I–III

23. 'Law of the Sea: Winners are Losers' pub. in *Economic & Political Weekly*, June, 12, 1982, by B.S. Chimori.

24. Displaced persons (Legal Proceeding) Act. 1949 no. XXV
25. General Administrative Report 1966-67
26. Report of the Ministers for Rehabilitation of Displaced Persons in West Bengal
27. Indian Independence (Misc. Transitional Provision Ordinance, 1947)
28. Colonization in the Andamans, its effect in Forest Management
29. Annual General Administrative Report, 1964-65
30. Ordinance No. XXIII of 1948 (Displaced Persons)
31. The Andaman and Nicobar Islands (Adm.) Regulation, 1979.
32. Influx from Pakistan (Control) Repealing Act, 1951.
33. Displaced Persons (Claims) Supplementary Act, 1954.
34. Displaced Persons (Compensation and Rehabilitation) Act, 1954.
35. The Defence of India Act, 1962
36. Note on Rehabilitation Programme in Great Nicobar, March, 1981
37. The AN Islands in the Second Five Year Plan, Port Blair.
38. The Criminal Tribes Act, 1924
39. The Displaced Persons (Institution of Suits and Legal Proceedings) Amendment Act, 1950
40. Annual General Ad... nistrative Report of A. & N. Islands, 1963-64
41. The Influx from Pakistan (Control) Ordinance XXXIV 1948.
42. The Delhi Refugees Registration (Amendment) Ordinance, 1947 (XXIV)
43. The Forests of the Nicobar Islands. Ministry of Food & Agriculture, G.O.I.
44. The Registration of Foreigners Act. No. XVI of 1939
45. The Requisitioned Land (Apportionment of Compensation) Ordinance No. XXI, 1949
46. The Prisons Act 1894, Pub. from Calcutta, 1905, G.O.I.
47. The Indian Independence (Rights, Property and Liabilities) Order, 1947
48. Report of Study Group of Estimates Committee of Parliament (1972-73) to A. & N. Islands.
49. Annual General Administrative Report of A. & N. Islands, 1964-65.

50. Land Acquisition Ordinance No. XX of 1948 for resettlement of displaced persons.
51. The Displaced Persons (Legal Proceedings) Act. 1949, No. XXV.
52. The Displaced Persons (Debts Adjustment) Act. 1951
53. Rehabilitation, A draft outline of Fourth Five Year Plan, G.O.I.
54. Report of 1960-61, Ministry of Rehabilitation, G.O.I.
55. Report of the Committee of Ministers for the Rehabilitation of Displaced Persons in West Bengal, 1954
56. Studies in Social Tensions among the Refugees from Eastern Pakistan, Memoir No.1, 1954, Department of Anthropology, G.O.I.
57. Colonization in the Andamans, a Note by I.G. of Forests, G.O.I.
58. "A Study of Port Blair Town", Pub. in the Journal of the Anthropological Survey of India, vol. 57, No.4, Dec. 2002.
59. Annual General Adm. Report of A.N.I., 1966-67.
60. Report of Estimates Committee, 1967-68, Ministry of Labour, Employment and Rehabilitation, G.O.I.
61. Report of Estimates Committee, 1961-62, 170th Report, Ministry of Rehabilitation.
62. "Refugees in W. Bengal: A Study of the Growth and Distribution of Refugee Settlements within the C.M.D.", - Pranati Choudhari, Centre for Studies in Social Sciences, Calcutta.
63. "Memorandum on the Rehabilitation of Refugees from Eastern Bengal", - Pub. Charu Chandra Roy, Amerendra Nath Banerjee.
64. "Millions on the Move. The Aftermath of Rehabilitation", G.O.I., May 1957
65. 'Rehabilitation Retrospect', Ministry of Rehabilitation, G.O.I., May 1957
66. 'Rehabilitation of Displaced Harijans', Nine Years' Report, 1948-57, G.O.I.
67. Working Report of Ministry of Rehabilitation, 1950-51, G.O.I.
68. Summary : Ministry of Rehabilitation, 1953-54
69. Estimates Committee's Report, 96th, 1959-60.
70. "Bangla Desh : Results & Prospects" - Tariq Ali, New Left Review, London, No. 68 July-Aug. 1971
71. 'Marginal Nation' - Ranabir Samaddar, Pub. Sage. 1999.

72. 'The Demographic Upheaval of Partition : Refugees and Agricultural Resettlement in India, 1947–67 in South Asia, vol : XVIII, – Gyanesh Kudaisya 1995

73. 'Relief and Rehabilitation of Displaced Persons in West Bengal', Refugee Relief and Rehabilitation Dept. Govt. of W.B., 1956.

74. Rehabilitation of Refugees, 1955 : A Statistical Survey, Calcutta

75. 'Reactive Migration : Sociological Prospectives on Refugee Movements', Pub : Journal of Refugee Studies, 1993

76. 'They live again : Millions came from East Pakistan', Govt. of W. Bengal, 1957

77. Annual Report of the Department of Rehabilitation, 1951, Deptt. of Rehabilitation, G.O.I., 1961.

78. 'Coming out of Partition: Refugee Women of Bengal', Gargi Chakraborty.

79. 'Refugees : A Study in Changing Attitude', B.N. Saxsena

80. 'Refugees in West Bengal : A Study of the growth and distribution', Pranati Chaudhari

81. 'The Bleeding Humanity, poignant story of refugees from East Bengal', Sanjib Sarkar

82. "India's Refugee problem: causes and Cures' – S.M. Gokhale, 1948.

83. 'A Pilot Plan for resettlement of Refugees', A. Chakraborty.

84. 'Refugees in West Bengal: Institutional practices and contended identities', by Pradip Kumar Bose.

85. 'The Unending Trial', Khushwant Singh, 1957

86. 'Sri Lankan Crisis and India's response', V. SuryaNarayan, 1991

87. 'Rehabilitation', P.N. Luthra, Ministry of Information and Broadcasting, 1972

88. "Rehabilitation of Camp Refugees", B.C. Ray, Oct. 1958

89. 'The East Bengal Refugees. A lesson in Survival', Nilanjan Chatterjee

Reference Books :

90. Annual Report of the Deptt. of Rehabilitation, 1951.

91. "Military logistics, the third dimension", by Brig. Parmodh. Sarin, Manas Publications, N.D.

92. 'The Land of Naked People', Madhushree Mukherjee, Pub. Houghton Mifflin Co. Boston, New York.

93. 'Sociology and Social Anthropology', Veena Das, Pub. Oxford, 2003, vol. 1411,

94. 'India's Colonial Encounter', Ed. Mushirul Hasan, Narayani Gupta, Pub. Manohar Publications, N. Delhi-2

95. 'Island Tribes of Andaman and Nicobar', by S.S. Shashi 1995, Pub. Anmol Publications Pvt. Ltd., New Delhi-2

96. "Netaji S.C. Bose and Indian War of Independence" by Dr. Satish Ch. Maikap, pub. Punashcha', Kolkata-9

97. 'Andamans and Nicobars' by Boden Kloss, 1902.

98. 'Islands of Marigold Sun', by Suresh Vaidya.

99. 'Peasant Protests and Revolts in Malabar', Ed. by K.N. Panikkar, Peoples Pub. House, New Delh-1990

100. "Land and People of the Andamans", Probhat Kr. Sen, Kolkata, 1962

101. "Andaman & Nicobar Islands", B.L. Chak, Publication Div., N.D., 1971

102. 'Pen Pictures of the Andaman and Nicobar Islands', S. Yusuf Hussain, Lucknow, 1954

103. 'The Andaman Islands', by Lidio Cipriani, Pub. Weidenfield & Nicolson, 1966.

104. 'Andaman Islands—A Social Study', by A. Brown Radcliffe, Illinois, 1922

105. 'A History of our Relation with the Andamanese', M.V. Portman

106. "The Nicobar Islands", E.H. Man, London, 1933

107. "Penal Settlement in Andamans", R.C. Majumdar. Publication Div., Govt. of India, 1975

108. 'History of the Andaman and Nicobar Islands', L.P. Mathur, Delhi, 1969

109. "The Andaman Story", Iqbal Singh, Vikas Pub., 1978

110. 'My I.N.A. Days in the Andamans', R.L. Avasthi

111. 'Andaman Ke Itihas Ka Safar', Sivram Shakuntala, Pub. Confluence International, N.D. January 2003.

112. 'Cellular Jail, Cells beyond Cells', Swapnesh Choudhuri, Priten Roy, N.D.

113. 'A Tale of Woes of East Pakistan Minorities', by Voice of New India. 1966.

114. 'Refugees and the State: Practices of Asylum and Care in India', 1947-2000, Ed. by Ranabir Samaddar, SAGE Pub. New Delhi-17

115. 'The Black Days in Andaman and Nicobar Islands', by Rabin Roychowdhury, Pub. Manas Publications, New Delhi.

116. 'The Story of Rehabilitation', U. Bhaskar Rao, Publication Div.

117. 'Marginal Men : The Refugees & Left Political Syndrome in West Bengal', Prafulla Kr. Chakraborty, Pub. Naya Udyog, Cal, 1999

118. 'Diwan Singh Kalapani'-A Profile by Iqbal Singh, Punjab.

119. 'Bhantu : Migration and social changes', Palash Chandra Coomar, A.S.I.

120. The Andamans: Land of the Primitives', B. Gupta, Pub : Jijnasa, Cal-9, 1968

121. 'The Uprooted', Kanti B. Pakrasi, Pub. S. Ghatak, Calcutta.

122. 'The East Bengal Refugees, A lesson in Survival' vol. II, Calcutta, 1990, Ed. By. Sukanta Choudhari

123. 'On Some Aspects of Family Structure of the Refugees of W. Bengal, 1947-48', Kanti B. Pakrasi, Sociological Bulletin, Mumbai, 1965

124. 'Andaman & Nicobar Islands: Challenges of Development, Strategic Significance of Andaman & Nicobar', by K.R. Singh.

125. 'The Unification and Division of India", B.B. Misra, Oxford University Press, 1990

126. "In Andamans, the Indian Bastille", Bijay Kumar Sinha, Kanpure, 1939

127. "My Life and Times: Octave Nine (1946-1953)' Mackenzie, Compton, Pub. Chatto & Windus, London, 1970

128. "All Over the Place," Compton Mackenzie, Chatto & Windus, London, 1949

129. 'Human Migration – A Social Phenomenon', Amal Dutta, Mittal Pub., N.D.-59

130. 'Socio Economic Aspects of Migration', G.S. Mehta, Deep & Deep Pub. N.D.

131. 'Principles of Demography', D.J. Bogue, Pub. A–10 Mohan Garden N.D.–59

132. 'Bengal Divided: The Unmaking of a Nation, 1900-1971', Nitish Sen Gupta, Penguin Viking

133. 'The Great Partition: The Making of India & Pakistan', Jasmeen Khan, Penguin Books.

134. 'Remembering: Violene, Nationalism & History in India', Jnanendra Pande, 2001

135. 'The other side of Silence: Voices from the Partition of India', 2000, Urvashi Butalia

136. 'A Suppressed Chapter in History: The Exoduş of Hindus from East Pakistan and Bangladesh, 1947-2006', Tathagata Roy, Pub. Bookwel, N.D.-2

137. Two decades with Dr. B.C. Roy' - S.M. Bose.

138. 'Jinnah of Pakistan' - Stanley Wolpert, Oxford University Press, 1989

139. 'Thy Hand, Great Anarch' - Stanley Wolpert

140. 'The Transfer of Power in India' - V.P. Menon, Orient Longman, 1993

141. 'Udbastu' (Displaced Persons), Hiranmay Banejee, Sahitya Samsad, Cal, 1970

142. 'The Prolonged Partition and Its Pogroms' - A.J. Kamra, Voices of India, Delhi

143. 'Crisis in South Asia - A Report',—Senator Edward Kennedy on Problem of Refugees and their settlement', Nov. 1, 1971, U.S. Govt. Press.

144. "Bengal Divided : Hindu Communalism and Partition, 1932-1947", Jaya Chatterjee, Cambridge University Press, 1995

145. 'Beyond Belief: Islamic Excursion among the converted peoples' - V.S. Naipaul, Penguin Publication, N. Delhi.

146 'India's March to Freedom' - Har-Anand Pub., N. Delhi.

147. 'The Partitions of Memory' - Suvir Kaul, 2001, Permanent Block, Delhi-92

148. 'The Liberation War' - Md. Ayoob, K. Snbrahmanyam, Pub. S. Chand & Co. 1972

149. 'The Partition in Retrospect'- Ed. Amrik Singh, Pub. : Anamika, N. Delhi 2000.

150. 'Count down to Partition' - Ajit Bhattacharjee, Pub: Harper Collins, N. Delhi -2

151. 'A Nation in Turmoil', 1937-58' - Yuras Samad, Pub: SAGE Publications, 1995

152. 'Muslim Politics in Bengal, 1937-47' - Sheela Sen.

153 'The Man who divided India: An Insight into Jinnah's Leadership and Aftermath" - Rafiq Zakaria, Pub: Popular Prakashan.

154. 'Migration & Social Changes: A Study of the Bhantus of Andaman Islands' - Palash Ch. Coomar, 1997, A.S.I. Cal-16

155. 'Prisons' - B.K. Bhattacharya, Pub. S.C. Sarkar & Sons. Cal-12, 1958

156. 'Partition of India: Legend and Reality', - H.M. Seervai, Pub. : N.M. Tripathi Pvt. Ltd., Bombay, 1994

157. 'British India', - 1772-1947', - Michael Edwards, Pub. Rupa & Co. Kolkata, 1993

158. 'The Refugee in the Post War World' - Vernant Jacques, London, 1959

159. "Mission with Mountbatten" - Campbell - Johnson, Allan, N.Y., 1951

160. 'The Refugee Problem', - Hope Simpson, London, 1939

161. 'Government and the Displaced Persons' - C.N. Vakil, P.H. Cabinetmaker, Mumbai, 1956

162. 'A Study of the Refugees' - M.N. Basu, Ranchi, 1951

163. 'A History of S.E. Asia' - D.G.E. Hall, Pub: Macmillion, 1968

164. 'The Proudest Day' - Anthony Read & David Fisher, Pub: PIMILICO, London

165. 'Disciplining Punishment' - Satadru Sen, Pub: Oxford, N.D. 2000

166. 'The State of the world's Refugees, 2000' - UNHCR, Pub: Oxford.

167. 'New Citizens of India' - Alexander Horace, 1951

168. 'Refugees and Regional Security in South Asia' - S.D. Muni & Lok Raj

169. 'India's Indian Ocean Islands' - Samhita Athawale, A.B.C. Publications

170. "The War against Japan", Vol III, by Woodburn Kirby, U.K. Military Series.

171 "Prelude to Partition" - D.J.H. Page, New Delhi, 1976,

INDEX